Advertising, Society, and Consumer Culture

Roxanne Hovland and Joyce M. Wolburg

M.E.Sharpe
Armonk, New York
London, England

To Lucia Thorne Hovland—R.H.

To George S. Machen and Thelma J. Machen—J.M.W.

Copyright © 2010 by M.E. Sharpe, Inc.

Library of Congress Cataloging-in-Publication Data

Hovland, Roxanne.
  Advertising, society, and consumer culture / by Roxanne Hovland and
Joyce M. Wolburg.
     p. cm.
  Includes bibliographical references and index.
  ISBN 978-0-7656-1546-6 (hardcover : alk. paper)—ISBN 978-0-7656-1547-3 (pbk. : alk. paper)
  1. Advertising—Social aspects—United States. 2. Consumption (Economics)—Social
aspects—United States. 3. Consumer behavior—United States. I. Wolburg, Joyce Marie.
II. Title.

  HF5813.U6H637 2010
  306.3—dc22   2009048088

Printed in the United States of America

| IBT (c) | 10 | 9 | 8 | 7 | 6 | 5 | 4 | 3 | 2 | 1 |
| CW (p) | 10 | 9 | 8 | 7 | 6 | 5 | 4 | 3 | 2 | 1 |

Contents

CONTENTS

Preface

Advertising is inherently controversial. There are as many ways to study controversies in advertising as there are controversies. Whether the focus is on a single ad, a class of ads, or advertising as an institution, there's no shortage of literature about the mixed value of advertising in our culture. So why do we need yet another book about advertising and society? Or, more importantly, why do we need this particular book?

We need this book because it provides a philosophical map of advertising issues seen through the lens of classical liberalism, which can guide us through issues we face now and in the future. Based on the work of some of the most revered scholars in communication including James W. Carey, Vincent P. Norris, David M. Potter, and Kim B. Rotzoll, our treatment offers a foundation based on enduring wisdom. We've adopted Carey's institutional view, which approaches the study of advertising from a rich historical and philosophical context. Equally significant, we've adopted Rotzoll's explanation of the classical liberal model. As Rotzoll and his coauthors argued, many of the recurring controversies in consumer culture can be traced to contradictions inherent in the model on which our society was based. To gain the historical perspective, we turned to David Potter, who called attention to the importance of wealth as a prerequisite to not only advertising but to democracy itself. When he coined the expression "the institution of abundance," he defined advertising as emblematic of consumer culture long before consumer culture had fully developed. Finally, to round out these views, we turned to Vincent Norris, whose work challenged the naïve, mechanistic view of advertising as simply information by pointing to advertisers' economic incentives. In the process, Norris also offered a simple, elegant, three-part definition of institutions that makes Carey's view operational. These authors' views form a foundation that supports every chapter in the book. Their writings and other articles about specific issues can be found in the companion book—*Readings in Advertising, Society, and Consumer Culture*, edited by Roxanne Hovland, Joyce Wolburg, and Eric Haley.

This book thus begins with an institutional view of advertising that recognizes the profound impact of the classical liberal model. Chapter 2 presents an historical examination of the simultaneous rise of advertising and consumer culture by identifying key events, persons, and trends over the last few centuries. As Chapter 2 presents this history, it also makes a point that is reinforced throughout the book—the inextricability of advertising from consumer culture. Chapter 3 then presents a sampling of some of the most enduring communication theories that are consistent with an institutional approach to advertising. Several of these theories help explain the inextricable relationship between advertising and consumer culture. However, the point is also made that studying advertising warrants consideration of multiple paradigms, methods, and data.

Throughout these three chapters certain concepts, values, and relationships arise repeatedly. For instance, individualism is a value that is deeply embedded in the classical liberal model on which our modern consumer culture is based. However, we must balance individualistic goals against the often-conflicting, collectivistic needs to consider the welfare of society. This particular trade-off arises in every topic raised in this book.

With this foundation, we explore some of the most challenging, macrolevel issues in advertising. Chapter 4 looks at relationships implicit in advertising and their potential consequences for consumers, and Chapter 5 examines some of the problems that arise when multinational companies market their goods and services to global audiences.

Based on the initial premise that advertising is a powerful institution in society, the next two chapters look at efforts at providing controls that protect society against chaos. Chapter 6 examines the types of legal restrictions that a consumer culture uses to regulate advertising, and Chapter 7 examines the ethical perspectives that provide moral order and make sense for advertising in a consumer culture. The last chapter, Chapter 8, offers reflections on advertising and consumer culture.

So much has changed about our culture that it's difficult to keep up. Perhaps even more daunting, however, is the rate of change. The half-life of a particular technology seems to decrease with every new invention. At the same time, advertisers seem to be in the thick of the social and economic changes taking place. This is why it's so tough to write a book on advertising that's not out of date as soon as it's published. This book, however, is intended to offer something more enduring. By not focusing on a litany of ads and the latest controversies involving advertising, our goal is to provide a perspective that may be applied to issues that go beyond the specifics addressed here.

Viewed through the lens of history, there are predictable patterns we can count on. So while we might not know the final destination, we at least can recognize the stops along the way. Based on this historical understanding and informed by the perspectives of some of the seminal works in advertising, we believe that the book will provide a philosophical map currently missing that helps us navigate the pressing issues in advertising and consumer culture.

Acknowledgments

We are indebted to a number of people for their help in seeing this book to its completion. We're grateful to more people than we can possibly name. Special thanks, however, go to Harry Briggs for his steadfast belief in us and our book. Professor Dwight Teeter provided much-needed communication law expertise. And Professor Ron Taylor was, as always, an invaluable source of wisdom and support.

Advertising,
Society,
and Consumer
Culture

► 1 ◄

Advertising as an Institution of Consumer Culture

Everybody Rides. So say the ads for a local used-car dealership. *Good credit? Bad credit? Slow credit? No credit?* Whatever your income, no matter who you are, everybody rides. This is the American Dream. And perhaps nothing expresses the American cultural ideology better than advertising. Although it's by no means the only institution emblematic of our consumer culture, it is certainly one of the most visible.

Institutions Defined

Advertising is simultaneously many things: a tax deduction, a business tool, a source of information, a source of both persuasion and entertainment. And it's everywhere. But the emphasis here is on advertising as an institution. So rather than looking at advertise*ments*, we'll look more broadly at advertis*ing*. The justification for this perspective is inherent in the following description of institutions: "Any simple thing we observe—a coin, a timetable, a canceled check, a baseball score, a phonograph record—has little significance in itself; the meaning it imparts comes from the ideas, values, and habits established about it. [These institutions that surround human activity] constitute standards of conformity from which an individual may depart only at his peril" (Hamilton 1932, 84).

Johan Stein spells out the powerful and dynamic nature of institutions in the following passage:

> An institution is a socially constructed belief system about the way things are and the way things should be that organizes human thought and action . . . Institutions are intersubjectively shared by a collective of individuals either consciously or unconsciously . . . [They are] principles that govern the creation of meaning and the pattern of actions at various social levels. In relation to other social structures, institutions are the structuration principles. As John Dewey and others have insisted, it is

3

also necessary to view institutions as evolving phenomena. This implies that institutions are both the media and the outcomes of the actions they induce. (1997, 730)

Institutions are, thus, organizing constructs that tend to induce conformity but are always changing. They bring order out of chaos but must continually evolve in order to do so effectively. Moreover, the influence of an institution may range well beyond its original nature. As Samuel Bowles points out, so-called economic institutions are likely to extend beyond simply allocating goods and services to influence the development of "values, tastes, and personalities" (1998, 75).

Institutions have several common characteristics. As advertising historian Vincent Norris asserts, at a minimum, they are *ubiquitous*—that is, they seem to be everywhere at the same time. In order to function as institutions, they must predominate within the society in which they were formed. More importantly, however, they perform two important purposes: *They order human relationships into roles;* and *they regulate the distribution of a society's essential resources to the advantage of some and the disadvantage of others.* These three characteristics—(1) ubiquity, (2) the ordering of roles, and (3) the regulation of resources—frame our discussion of institutions (Norris 1980).

Nonadvertising Institutions

Ubiquity

The institution of marriage provides a ready illustration of all three properties outlined by Norris. In twentieth-century Western society, marriage is unquestionably ubiquitous. Though the U.S. Census continues to document alternative living arrangements and family structures, legally recognized marriage between heterosexuals is still the social and numerical norm. *Merriam-Webster's* definition makes clear the other two institutional functions of marriage: "the institution whereby men and women are joined in a special kind of social and legal [i.e., economic] dependence for the purpose of founding and maintaining a family" (1998, 713).

Ordering of Roles

Roles implicit in this institutional model are easily recognized: bride, groom, wife, husband—and with the addition of children—mother, father, daughter, son, sister, brother, adoptive parent, stepparent, stepchild, heir. Socially acceptable behavior is prescribed for each member of the tableau. Fidelity and monogamy are presumed between spouses. Husbands and wives are expected to nurture and care for each other in both good times and bad. For instance, when a person becomes gravely ill, hospital visits are often restricted to the "immediate family," and perhaps no one is considered more immediate than a spouse.

Regulation of Resources

With marriage come certain legal and financial rights and obligations. This issue leads logically to the power of institutions to influence the distribution of a society's resources. Our presumptions about the rights and expectations of "immediate family" are at the root of the controversy currently surrounding the rights of nonmarried partners to receive economic benefits (such as health insurance) commonly awarded to spouses. Husbands and wives are believed to be obligated to care for each other, and our social and economic system is designed to facilitate this caring.

Although most American marriages are usually based on romantic love, the economic consequences are still readily evident in situations involving everything from federal tax status to next of kin. The concept of alimony is evidence of the enduring fiduciary responsibility presumed of spouses for each other. To paraphrase an old ad campaign, nothing says love like a prenuptial agreement. Lastly, the economic ramifications of marriage are seen in the fact that wedding-gift expenditures are second only to what Americans spend on Christmas (Otnes and Lowrey 1993). The average amount of money spent on a traditional American wedding is almost $30,000 (Sardone 2008).

The Institution of Advertising

Ubiquity

The institutional characteristics of advertising are equally compelling. The ubiquity of advertising is beyond question. The presence of advertising in our lives is pervasive and unavoidable, and the number of forms it takes continues to expand as media technology and usage evolve. With the advent of multichannel marketing (also known as integrated marketing), microtargeting (highly selective targeting of consumer groups based on tracking and research data), and direct and interactive marketing, advertising and marketing communication is with us everywhere we go and reaches us in increasingly sophisticated ways (Standard & Poor's Industry Trends 2006). One source estimates that American consumers are each exposed to approximately 3,600 commercial impressions each day (Jhally 1997).

Norris makes an interesting point, however, about the source of all this advertising. Much of the money spent on advertising comes from a relatively small group of very large companies. The top 100 marketers were responsible for over 40 percent of the measured advertising spending in 2007. Expenditures by the ten largest advertising product categories accounted for approximately one-half of all measured ad spending (TNS Media Intelligence 2007). In other words, while advertising is ubiquitous, it is hardly representative of all of the country's potential advertisers.

Ordering of Roles

Like marriage, advertising orders human behavior into roles: seller, retailer, wholesaler, consumer, target market, copywriter, art director, media planner, Internet service provider, and so forth. Certainly, it helps define behavior of people involved in the advertising process. It also teaches us how to participate in consumer culture. In fact, at a very tender age children begin to express brand preferences (Committee on Communications 2006). In theoretical terms, advertising thus sets an agenda for us as consumers by defining standards and criteria for our consumer behavior.

Advertising also reorders roles of people in the mass media. Because advertising provides the economic support in the United States for most media (Bagdikian 2000), the ability to attract advertising revenue can mean the success or failure of media vehicles including magazines, television programs, and radio stations. Furthermore, the role of magazine publisher has changed from the seller of a product to the gatherer of a target market for advertising, with the exception of publishers of magazines that do not carry advertising (e.g., *Consumer Reports*). The role of the reader has changed from "sovereign consumer to advertiser bait" (Norris 1980, 8).

Regulation of Resources

The role of advertising in the distribution of society's wealth is indisputable. Advertising grew out of the need to sell the abundance of goods that could be produced under the capitalist system in the United States. It stimulates the demand for consumer goods so that consumers will buy the goods produced and money will flow from consumers to producers (Jhally 1997). Advertising, in conjunction with branding, also developed as a means for manufacturers to set prices for their products. As Norris (1980) points out, national advertising (advertising for brands of goods rather than for the local store where the goods are sold) created a demand for a brand that allowed its manufacturer to raise the price and force more retailers to sell it. Prior to national advertising, manufacturers and wholesalers were both powerless to set prices; with national advertising, the manufacturer's role changed from price "taker" to price "maker" (Norris 1980, 8). Norris makes this point to illustrate the influence of advertising over behavior but, in fact, he shows the economic influence of advertising as well.

Some people doubt the degree to which advertising influences behavior. However, by looking at the amount of money spent on advertising in the United States, we can dispel doubts concerning advertising's ability to influence the distribution of wealth. Between 1989 and 2005, U.S. advertising and marketing expenditures averaged 2.2 percent of GDP (Standard & Poor 2006). The sheer volume of advertising underscores its power to redirect wealth, not only from one brand to another or from one class of products to another but from one political candidate or cause to another.

Three Worldviews

The reasons for the growth of advertising as an institution can be found in the principles underlying classical liberalism—a political and economic system that rose to prominence in the eighteenth century and forms the foundation for the current political and economic system. Classical liberalism is a worldview that values a self-regulating market system in which all entrants in the market operate freely, harmoniously, and without restriction.

Classical liberalism is not the only political and economic system but one that provided the most "fertile seedbed" in which advertising could emerge and flourish (Rotzoll, Haefner, and Sandage 1986). Two other worldviews that offer sharp contrasts are tradition and authority.

Tradition

Each person in a traditional system has a fixed place in the social hierarchy. The best-known example is medieval society, in which economic tasks were handed down from father to son and mother to daughter. The blacksmith's son was destined to become a blacksmith himself, and these roles were virtually set at birth. Any separation from the social roles assigned by God, society, and family was unthinkable (Baumeister 1987).

When pondering the traditional society, Rotzoll et al. (1986) conclude that the fixed nature of the hierarchy provides only a minimal use for advertising because no opportunities arise for people to change their destiny or to act upon their own desires. Since people locked in a fixed role are unlikely candidates for most advertising messages, especially ones that promote individualism and self-indulgence, there is little basis for creating desires or encouraging choices in a traditional society.

Authority

While tradition provided structure by way of the past, authoritarian societies offer structure through a political hierarchy. According to Rotzoll et al. (1986), more civilizations have used this system than any other, and variations range from the iron rule of the dictator to the more compassionate leadership of popular revolutionary leaders.

At first glance, authoritarian societies would seem to have little use for advertising; however, it has been used to reinforce action and create change on behalf of the government. For example, when supplies were scarce, the former Soviet Union used advertising to encourage members of society to buy margarine instead of butter in the pursuit of national goals.

Although Rotzoll et al. (1986) conclude that authoritarianism is not the optimal worldview because it limits the degree of individual decisionmaking, they believe that authority provides a firmer foundation than tradition for the utilization of advertising. However, they believe that classical liberalism offers greater utility for advertising and offers four fundamental assumptions about people, government, and competition on which classical liberalism is based.

Classical Liberalism and Its Underlying Principles

The classical liberal worldview presumes that people are *egoistic* and will naturally pursue their own best interests. All human behavior is presumably based on the benefit foreseen from such behavior. However, rather than a character flaw, this is perceived positively in that the collective self-striving of members of a society will hypothetically elevate the quality of life for the society as a whole (Rotzoll et al. 1986, 16).

People are also presumed to possess the trait of *intellectualism*. We assume that, given adequate and accurate information, people will make rational decisions. The "economic man" (as he is sometimes called) behaves in a deliberate and calculating manner (1986, 17).

However self-interested and calculating people may be, they are also presumed to be somewhat apathetic. *Quietism*, according to Rotzoll et al., implies that people need an incentive before they will expend energy. Without some obvious benefit to themselves, people will not take action (1986, 17).

When all members of a society behave rationally and in their own best interest based on perceived incentives, the society functions as a balanced system in which all members are equal. This *atomistic* nature suggests a society that is self-righting and, consequently, needs no other means of regulation such as by government. In other words, competition among equals acts as an "invisible hand" that keeps the system in check. This last notion, as Rotzoll et al. point out, is clearly based on a physical model in which all matter is made up of atoms (1986, 18). Viewed in this way, classical liberalism provides an inviting context in which advertising can thrive. Advertising, which promotes self-gratification ("You deserve a break today"), provides incentives for purchase (often in the form of "reason-why" copy) and information (prices, product availability, terms of sale) necessary for making consumer decisions.

Neoliberalism and Other Views

The four tenets of classical liberalism point to fundamental beliefs about people and competition and to a deep-seated distrust of government intervention. But as the world has evolved from the relatively simplistic eighteenth-century model on which classical liberalism is based, we've grown increasingly uncomfortable with these notions. In what Rotzoll et al. (1986) refer to as "neoliberalism," we're now uncertain about individuals' abilities to behave rationally and the market's ability to be self-righting. As a result, we've become considerably more accepting of government intervention. With these concerns comes a concomitant ambivalence about advertising.

One author argues that the problem lies in the fact that many of our institutions were developed under a set of circumstances that no longer exists. Like most of the institutions that govern our present consumer culture, advertising began as a response to the industrial era and has not fully evolved to reflect the characteristics of postindustrial society (Nordberg 1997).

Communications scholar and historian James Carey provides insight into this problem when he describes advertising as "an institution primarily designed to provide information on economic goods and services, but which now, under the impact of modern conditions, finds broader, noneconomic applications" (1960, 4). Further, he states: "It is hoped that the institutional function of advertising will become more clearly discernible when it is recognized how advertising is the inexorable result of certain fundamental assumptions on the nature of social life, which leads to the organization of economic activity around a system of free markets (Carey 1960, 4).

Historian David Potter (1954) calls advertising the "institution of abundance" in his book, *People of Plenty*. Like Norris, he saw the advent of advertising as a means for creating demand for the surplus of mass-produced goods. Consequently, the "abundance" Potter refers to is not indicative of the consumer's lifestyle but of the abundance of goods for which demand must be generated.

Historian Daniel Boorstin claims that mass merchandising and the department store served to "democratize luxury" by displaying high-priced products to anyone who wanted to look at them (1974). Advertising historian Michael Schudson argues, however, that this new access to expensive goods merely "democratized envy" by encouraging everyone to desire the same products—even among those for whom they would be hopelessly out of reach (Schudson 1986, 151). Schudson, based on the work of Stuart Ewen (1976) and others, points out that in contrast to the general growth of affluence early in the twentieth century, "the working class did not share much in the prosperity" (1986, 176).

Potter (1954) further contends that unlike other institutions that exert social control, advertising lacks a fundamental sense of social responsibility. Advertising, according to Potter, wields social control without the social conscience that is evident in other institutions like the church. Rotzoll, Haefner and Hall observe, however, that the classical liberal model also lacked any "explicit expectation of responsibility beyond individual self-interest" (1996, 71). Advertising (without social responsibility) is thus entirely consistent with the egoistic perspective that begot it.

As Schudson so eloquently put it, "Advertising is capitalism's way of saying 'I love you' to itself" (1986, 231). Like long-married spouses restating their love for each other, advertising is a refrain that provides constant affirmation of the consumer culture that inspired it. Our feelings about advertising are inextricably tied to our feelings about ourselves and the ideology on which our society is based. The love-hate relationship we have with advertising is indicative of the mixed feelings we have toward classical liberalism in general. All four tenets of the classical liberal model can be called into question; yet as a culture, we remain devoted to the idea of the laissez-faire society. This is perfectly illustrated by the financial crisis that culminated in the bailout of 2008, as we will see in the next section.

Criticism of the Four Tenets: Trouble in Paradise

Egoism

The pursuit of self-betterment implicit in the idea of egoism is a profoundly American ideal and is still valued in many ways. This notion is the foundation for the American Dream and is illustrated perfectly in the novels of Horatio Alger. In an introduction to *Ragged Dick and Mark, the Match Boy,* Rychard Fink wrote, "[Alger's] novels brought heroes to sudden success, thus reinforcing the myth that the good life could be had by all . . ." (1962, 17). Further, Fink wrote, "Alger was a major pump station on the pipe line that carried the American dream" (30). As quaint as Alger's stories may seem now, we still cling to the ideal on which they're based. We applaud someone for pursuing an education or a better job.

But the hedonistic pursuit of pleasure, which seemed so characteristic of the 1980s, is criticized for being selfish and shallow. The idea that society benefits collectively from the simultaneous pursuit of self-betterment by individuals seems tragically naïve when egoism runs amok.

A good example of this is the recent consumer debt crisis. Throughout the preceding decade, lenders relaxed lending standards and loaned money even to high-risk borrowers. However, after lending standards became more stringent, consumers dependent upon borrowing had to find other ways of going further into debt. According to the *Wall Street Journal,* they've continued to wrack up credit-card debt and draw on home-equity lines of credit. "The rise in borrowing shows just how addicted the U.S. consumer has become to credit. Even as borrowers are cut off in one area, they promptly look for new sources" (Kim 2008). The pursuit of gratification by both borrowers and lenders ultimately resulted in the biggest financial bailout in history, inspiring many bloggers to ask Congress and the President not to use tax dollars to rescue lenders and borrowers from their own greed (Herbst 2008).

Intellectualism

The belief that human decisionmaking is rational also has been seriously tested. The assumption that people are rational becomes almost indefensible in the face of consumer behavior that is seemingly more often driven by emotion than reason. Few, if any, of us can claim to use logic at all times. Carey defines our changing opinion of man by saying, "Economic man, buying and selling, and equating cost and utility at the margin, has been replaced by psychological or symbolic man who makes economic decisions on the basis of economic and also non-economic but equally potent psychological need-want stimuli" (1960, 16).

In some instances, consumer behavior can appear to be downright pathological. Americans' debt epidemic is again a perfect counterpoint to the classical liberal principle of intellectualism. Low introductory interest rates for consumer credit cards, which climb to 18 percent or more annually after the initial period, can offer very strong incentives. However, some consumers quickly amass such high debts that by the time the purchases are paid in full, the actual price is more than double the initial price. Car buying can be an extreme example: If consumers were to finance new cars from the time they were in their twenties every five years for the rest of their lives, they would end up paying more than a half-million dollars in interest and payments (de Graaf, Wann, and Naylor 2001).

On another level, however, we accept responsibility for high interest in exchange for the convenience and pleasure of immediate gratification. Schudson explains that behavior that makes sense in a fast-paced society would appear irrational in a less time-intensive culture: "In 'time-famine' cultures, rational behavior may appear irrational. For instance, when time is short, 'impulse buying' may be the most rational shopping strategy. In a time-scarce society, efforts to conserve time may take the form of an increasingly extravagant use of consumer goods" (1986, 200–201).

At the same time, even when we're willing to take the time to make an informed decision, many of our purchase decisions involve products and services that are too complex for us to ever fully understand. When the consumer lacks the specialized knowledge required of a truly informed shopper, he or she may simply try to minimize the risk by buying the more expensive brand based on the heuristic presumption that price is indicative of quality. Consumers may, in fact, be willing to pay more for the "psychic value of lifestyles" associated with a more expensive brand (Abela and Farris 2001). For someone to choose the higher-priced product based on no other indicator of quality would be anathema to an economist. Again, however, such a strategy is much more convenient for the shopper than any alternative approach.

Quietism

The value of convenience notwithstanding, the notion that an individual will not expend the energy to consume without adequate incentive (quietism) is questionable. When a truly new type of product is introduced, consumers may indeed need to be told why the product is worth expending the effort required to purchase it. However, consumption is less an effort than it is a way of life for Americans. When consumers go deeper into debt in order to continue acquiring the trappings of the "good life," it looks as though they've fully internalized the incentive to consume.

This is most certainly the case with addictive products like tobacco and alcohol. Do heavy users of beer (who constitute a particularly desirable target audience for brewers) really need more incentive to consume? Alcoholic-beverage advertisers would argue that the advertising is merely trying to promote one brand over another (Guis 1996; Lee and Tremblay 1992). But the end result is the same: The advertising justifies consumption.

Based on the work of William Leiss, Schudson argues that it isn't necessarily that "new needs are manufactured and foisted upon" us but that "needs become ambiguous as individual choices multiply" (1986, 155). In other words, in high-intensity consumption cultures, we internalize the incentives to consume irrespective of our innate needs.

Again, current patterns of consumption and debt confirm the notion that Americans lack incentives to save. According to Dickerson (2008, 140),

"Debt has risen much faster than income for middle-income families in the United States and the ratio of debt to disposable income is now approximately 125 percent. Some of this debt level is no doubt attributable to the seemingly insatiable desire of U.S. consumers to have the latest gadgets, trinkets, and toys."

Atomism

Of the four principles of classical liberalism, atomism is perhaps the most problematic. In theory, a classical liberal system is supposed to be self-righting, therefore making governmental intervention unnecessary. Competition among equals acts as an "invisible hand" to keep the system in balance. Monopolies can't develop because new competitors can always enter a market. At the same time, an economic Darwinism exists wherein only the most efficient firms that cater to consumer desires succeed.

Carey provides insight into this development. With the rapid industrialization and the increasing centralization of production in the late nineteenth century, market power became more concentrated, branded merchandise developed, and mass communications displaced the old interpersonal relationships in the marketplace. When "the function of supplying market information was placed more and more in the hands of fewer and fewer participants," information was supplied by "the firms in the market rather than the market itself." Thus, there was no longer any guarantee of a self-righting process, and control was increasingly sought "in human and corporate conscience" (1960, 15). The principle of caveat emptor (buyer beware) was displaced by caveat venditor (seller beware) because the individual could no longer receive all the information necessary to make rational decisions.

The annals of American business are rife with examples that contradict atomism, and media companies such as the Disney Corporation, provide an example of how the "invisible hand" has failed. Disney shows that a single company can become so widely diversified that it is powerful in many product categories. As both Carl Hiaasen (1998) and Ben Bagdikian (2000) have noted, Disney's interests are so diversified that the company touches almost every American consumer in one way or another—from hockey teams to television networks and publishing houses.

Bagdikian makes clear the degree to which our economy has strayed from the atomistic ideal. In 1984 he identified 50 corporations with power over American media. In 1987, his list shrank to 26. Three years later in 1990, it dropped to 23 and then to less than 20 in 1993. By 1996, the number of corporations decreased to 10, and by 2003 Bagdikian counted only 5 companies dominating all American media (2004, 27).

Historically, the U.S. government has stepped in where atomism failed. In particular, the Federal Trade Commission, the Federal Communications Commission, and the courts strove to battle corporate giantism through antitrust activity. However, as McChesney and Nichols (2002, 50) point out, the concentration and conglomeration fueled by technology and a changing marketplace have been further accelerated by the government's "collapsing commitment to serious antitrust prosecution" and reduced efforts toward regulation of media. A key example of this is the relaxing of media ownership regulations that prevented the same company from owning multiple media outlets in the same market. The authors point to the 1996 Telecommunications Act and the courts' support of former FCC chair Michael Powell's reduction of ownership regulations in 2002 as key "turning points" in government control of media concentration (McChesney and Nichols 2002, 50–51).

Equally evident is the trend toward corporate ownership by global conglomerates. According to Bagdikian, two of the largest book publishers dominating the U.S. market are foreign owned—Bertelsmann in Germany and News Corporation based in Australia (2004, 3). In essence, the consolidation that's been occurring in American media is also taking place on an international level. Consequently, the structure of the communication industries defies atomism in three ways—vertically, horizontally, and globally.

Few people would argue that the pure classical liberal model ever existed, much less exists today. Rotzoll et al.(1986) call our present circumstances "neoliberalism"—a modified version of the original model that takes into account such things as man's rational and symbolic nature and the need for some amount of government regulation. However, our ambivalence toward advertising suggests that we haven't resolved how to evaluate advertising in a consumer culture that looks very little like the one in which advertising first appeared.

Our love-hate relationship with government intervention in the marketplace was played out throughout the economic crisis of the current decade. When major financial institutions hovered on the brink of extinction, with horrid consequences for corporate America as well as consumers, people clamored for the federal government to step in. When a bailout bill was first introduced in Congress, however, it failed partly because to some it smacked of socialism (Maich 2008). One expert wrote, "Don't be surprised if [taxpayers] lose faith in the supposed miracle of free markets, and in the financial system . . ." (Sloan 2008, 47). A blogger wrote, "Bailouts that keep mismanaged organizations afloat delay natural corrections to unsound business practices. Enough is enough. No more bailouts. Not with my tax dollars" (Herbst 2008). And yet, the history of capitalism is rife with similar forms of government intervention (Easton et al. 2008, 96). Sometimes the intervention even works the other way as when the U.S. government, prior to the creation of the Treasury Department, was forced to ask for help from J.P. Morgan during the gold panic of 1894 (Easton et al. 2008, 102).

As a society, we are extremely reluctant to jettison the classical liberal ideal and instead maintain an abiding faith in its principles. About the perceived sanctity of the self-righting power of the market, Frank and Weiland state, "The market is natural, normal, and irresistible. Efforts to control its vagaries, however, are artificial, dictatorial, arrogant—and undemocratic . . . Government cannot help and must stop trying; if we're poor, it's our own fault" (1997, 261).

However, Americans have come to expect government protection when the marketplace doesn't treat them equitably. Although classical liberalism is based fundamentally on individualism—a cultural value that favors people looking after themselves and their immediate family rather than people belonging to ingroups that offer certain privileges and obligations—Americans demand intervention when competition fails to perform as it should (Cho et al. 1999; Hofstede 1980). Americans like the freedom and independence that come with individualism and cling to it in the abstract. In reality, however, collectivism is a necessity when the marketplace fails to meet their needs.

Understanding this undying devotion to the principles of classical liberalism is critical to understanding our love-hate relationship with advertising. The pages that follow attempt to put contemporary advertising in context, based on a theoretical and historical perspective, so that the reader will have a richer understanding of where we are and where we're going. As both an institutional mirror and shaper of society, advertising is one of the consummate artifacts of our consumer culture at this point in history.

➤ 2 ◀

Evolution of American Society

For anyone born after World War II, it's probably difficult to imagine the United States as anything other than a consumer culture. In fact, it might even be difficult for people born earlier to remember a time when military confrontations were not given catchy brand names (e.g., "Desert Storm"), life was unlivable without a cell phone, and Twitter allowed us to monitor what Ashton Kutcher eats for breatfast.

However, the United States didn't start out as a consumer culture and didn't fully evolve into one until relatively recently. While the seeds were sown in the country's founding values of classical liberalism and individualism, consumer culture has become pervasive only since World War II. So how did we get from Adam Smith to Hannah Montana? Moreover, what role did advertising play in this evolution?

Before addressing these questions, both consumer culture and advertising must be defined. The expression "consumer culture" has become more common in the academic literature over the last decade. It is often used to describe the modern global economy. Arnould and Thompson (2005) use the term to refer to "an interconnected system of commercially produced images, texts, and objects that groups use—through the construction of overlapping and even conflicting practices, identities, and meanings—to make collective sense of their environments and to orient their members' experiences and lives" (869). Douglas Holt, on the other hand, defined consumer culture as the "dominant mode of consumption that is structured by the collective actions of firms in their marketing activities" (2002, 71).

Out of this perspective Consumer Culture Theory evolved which, in turn, "explores how consumers actively rework and transform symbolic meanings decoded in advertisements, brands, retail settings, or material goods to manifest their particular personal and social circumstances and further their identity and lifestyle goals" (Arnould and Thompson 2005, 871). There are four research streams within Consumer Culture Theory overall: Consumer Identity Projects, Marketplace Cultures, The Sociohistoric Patterning of Consumption and Mass-Mediated Marketplace Ideologies, and Consumers' Interpretive Strategies

(Arnould and Thompson 2005, 871–874). However, while we share the interests inherent in consumer culture theory, our focus here is not on consumer culture as a research paradigm but as a set of economic and social conditions.

For our purposes, consumer culture refers more broadly to the postindustrial global economy that is prevalent among nations (like the United States) that subscribe to a model of advanced capitalism. As such, consumer culture is characterized by three conditions:

1. There's a potential surplus of goods typical of postindustrial economies.
2. Continuous consumption is critical to society and the individual; commerce and culture are inseparable.
3. Objects take on significance beyond their original purpose, and all things are commodified.

Advertising, on the other hand, is characterized as having the following traits:

1. It is paid for.
2. The sponsor is identified.
3. It appears in a nonpersonal medium of some kind.
4. It is intended for a particular audience.
5. The advertiser attempts to control the content, placement, and timing of the message.
6. The purpose of the message may be to inform, persuade, or cultivate a relationship with an audience.

In this chapter, the development of the conditions that characterize consumer culture will be explored as a way of understanding the evolution of the United States from an agrarian economy to one based on consumption. Moreover, this chapter also explores the conditions that created a place for advertising in a consumer culture.

To completely chronicle the history of twentieth-century America is well beyond the scope of this book. However, it's important to acknowledge certain events that were instrumental in shaping our current culture. The events discussed in Table 2.1 are not an exhaustive list, but they at least provide a good starting point for understanding the evolution of our culture.

From Then to Now

The evolution of the American economy into its present form, while not seamless, has been a continuous process over several centuries. Certainly some of the events that shaped this progression have been unprecedented and served to mark our transition toward a consumer culture in very visible ways (see Table 2.1). By and large, however, the process has been continuous and therefore not necessarily immediately obvious to people while it was occurring. While the changes Americans have experienced sometimes may have felt revolutionary, the progression has been one of evolution rather than revolution.

The process brings to mind the old saying about putting a frog in boiling water. If you do so, the frog will jump out. But if you put him in cold water and slowly raise the temperature, he will be cooked without realizing it. This is not to say that the evolution of consumer culture is ultimately fatal. Rather, the metaphor reflects the gradual nature of the transition and illustrates the difficulty of objectively observing changes in the environment in which we are immersed.

The best way to understand this evolution is by starting with the nature of today's consumer culture. This chapter reviews the history of American consumer culture in light of the traits that characterize its present form. Beyond that, there are discernable patterns and recurring themes in the country's transition toward today's culture. This, in turn, leads to an examination of the role of advertising in the development of consumer culture.

1. The Importance of Production: There's Typically a Potential Surplus of Goods in Postindustrial Economies

Prior to the Industrial Revolution, American society was based on householding wherein most goods were produced and consumed by the same household. This system is also characterized by reciprocity (in which the exchange of goods is based on predetermined relationships and tasks) and redistribution, which is based on the will of a central authority (Norris 1980). Naturally, certain things had to be produced by skilled craftsmen, and these items would be purchased by neighbors and friends. But most of these things were made specifically for the people who intended to use them or buy or trade for them. In other words, the consumers (later to be called the market) for these goods determined which and how many goods would be produced. This is the opposite of how advanced consumer culture works, wherein which and how many goods are produced are based on production capacity and efficiency—followed by the identification of a market for them. In a society based on householding, neither the blacksmith nor the tailor was likely to have advertised an "inventory reduction" sale. As Norris points out, there was simply no need for advertising (Norris 1980).

In preindustrial America, craftsmen were limited to selling goods to people

Table 2.1

Timetable of Events that Shaped Consumer Culture

Year	Event
1750 B.C.	Earliest references to credit (in the Code of Hammurabi).[33]
Post-1400s	After the Reformation, material success viewed as God's approval of one's efforts, but thrift considered the ultimate goal of economic activity.[25]
1704	The first American newspaper ad appeared in the *Boston News Letter* and contained two notices of rewards offered for the return of merchandise stolen from a wharf and an apparel shop.[1]
1750–1875	The Industrial Revolution began in England in about 1750 and gradually spread to the United States, with its greatest impact on American life after the end of the Civil War in 1865. The Industrial Revolution created a means for mass-producing a supply of goods that required the stimulation of demand. This was to be accomplished through advertising.[30]
1776	The United States officially founded.
1794	Provident Loan Society of NY started giving loans to consumers.[33]
1830–1860	The population of the United States increased from 12.8 million to 31.4 million, and the number of cities with more than 20,000 inhabitants grew. Increases in the size of cities are historically related to the growth of advertising.[30]
1839	Photography introduced.[1]
1841	Volney Palmer became the first "media broker" in advertising by contracting for extensive space in newspapers and then reselling the space to advertisers. "Dailies" (newspapers) had a circulation of 1 million by 1850.[1]
1844	First magazine ad ran.[1]
1861–1865	The American Civil War fought. Slavery abolished in 1865 with the Thirteenth Amendment.[40]
1869	The first advertising agency, N.W. Ayer & Sons, founded by Francis Ayer in Philadelphia and was the first agency to charge a commission based on the cost of space. It was also the first agency to operate as a full-service agency with the planning, creating, and execution of complete ad campaigns with media-paid commissions.[1] The Central Pacific and Union Pacific lines connected to form the first transcontinental railroad.[37]

(continued)

Year	Event
1870–1890	During the 1870s, patent medicines became the largest category of advertising.[36]
	The creation of national brands allowed manufacturers to gain power in the marketplace by forcing wholesalers and retailers to sell specific brands rather than generic merchandise. Well-known brands that emerged at that time were Levi's (1873), Maxwell House (1873), Budweiser (1876), and Coca-Cola (1886).[35]
	Ad agencies shift from serving media to serving advertisers when George Rowell develops the open-contract system in 1875.[5]
1875–1918	During this time, which overlaps with the Progressive Era, the United States was well on its way to being an urban, industrialized nation with reliable railroad transportation. Advertising became a vital part of the American way of life. Influential leaders and visionaries played principal roles in establishing advertising agencies and the business of advertising. Advertising offered solutions to life's problems, which were many during this period of rapid urbanization, massive immigration, labor unrest, and suffrage. This was the dawn of early consumer culture.[30]
1879	The United States restored the gold standard, equating the dollar to a set amount of gold bullion.[2]
1880–1910	Corporate organization and distribution systems developed among makers of consumer nondurable products (like cereal and oats) enabling these products to be branded and advertised nationally. The predominantly agrarian way of life begins to be replaced by a more industrial economy.[26]
	The U.S. Supreme Court gave corporations the rights of individuals but without personal accountability. The Court then extended corporate property rights when it redefined property to include intangibles.[26]
1890–1910	The U.S. government introduced rural free delivery of mail. Although magazines had existed before, new innovations in photography, low postage rates for publications, and high-speed rotary presses allowed magazines to become more popular as a means of communication. For the first time in history, advertisers had a mass medium since newspapers were essentially a local medium. In the 1890s this new breed of magazines focused on entertainment, fiction, and advice including *Cosmopolitan*, *Ladies' Home Journal*, *Harper's*, *Reader's Digest*, and *Better Homes & Gardens*. By 1902, *Ladies' Home Journal* had 1 million readers and carried 100 pages of advertising.
	The federal Sherman Antitrust Act was passed in 1890 to prevent firms from forming alliances to restrict competition.[29]
	The national literacy rate reached 90 percent as a result of public education.[1]
1900	Northwestern University offered courses in advertising.[1]
1905	Gillette Safety Razor launched the first national advertising plan.[1]

1906	The Pure Food and Drug Act was the first attempt to regulate advertising by requiring manufacturers to use product labels with a list the active ingredients. Its immediate effect on advertising was considered minimal since advertisers could still say anything about products. Thus, many unrealistic claims were made, particularly for patent medicines. Still, it paved the way for future regulations that did effectively restrict outlandish claims.[26]
1910	Fidelity Savings & Trust Co. became first commercial business devoted solely to personal lending.[33]
1913	The Federal Reserve Act created a decentralized federal bank.[3]
1914	The Federal Trade Commission act created the FTC, which is charged with protecting the public against misleading and deceptive advertising.[5] The Clayton Antitrust Act banned preferential pricing by manufacturers to retailers.[29]
1917–1919	U.S. involvement in WWI. The advertising industry contributed significantly to the war effort, and because of the success of its war effort and in selling automobiles, "advertising came of age."[38]
1920s	Radio introduced. Radio was initially a noncommercial medium, and advertisers were initially reluctant to air what was perceived as crass commercial content. Program sponsorship was popular at first with shows named after their sponsors. By the end of the decade, the line between programming and advertising blurred. The attempt to restrict advertisers to sponsorship disappeared, ad agencies developed radio-advertising departments, and the medium received a big boost from the Depression.[31] Affluence grew in the United States but excluded the working class. Consumers "engulfed" in credit. Marshall Fields almost doubled its number of charge customers during the decade.[7] Advertising budgets were "massive," and ad executives were very well paid compared to others.[38]
1922	In *FTC v. Winsted Hosiery Company*, the Supreme Court defined advertising as an unfair trade practice.[29]
1928	National City Bank became first commercial bank to enter consumer loan business.[33]
1929	The crash of the stock market and the beginning of the Great Depression. Just as the early 1920s were exceedingly prosperous times, the end of the decade and the early 1930s were crushing, hard times. Many went hungry, unemployment was high, and the public blamed advertising. The public saw advertising as something that had seduced them into the lavish excesses that caused the Great Depression. Advertisers responded with no-frills ads with themes that traded on the anxieties of the day. Many agencies cut salaries and staff. Advertising industry focused on research into audiences and messages to justify is existence. During this period Daniel Starch, A.C. Nielsen, and George Gallup founded companies devoted to advertising research.[1]
1933–1938	The Wheeler-Lea Act and the Federal Food, Drug, and Cosmetic Act passed in 1938. The Wheeler-Lea Act gave the FTC more direct power over false advertising; and the Federal Food, Drug, and Cosmetic Act gave the FDA control over the labeling and packaging of products.[5]

(continued)

Year	Event
1941–1945	The beginning of the official American involvement in World War II marked the end of the Depression for many Americans. In 1942 the War Advertising Council was founded to sell war bonds, promote conservation, and encourage women to join the workforce. Since most manufactured goods were needed in the war effort, corporations were not selling consumer goods. Though the companies were out of merchandise, they were not out of business. Corporate advertising served to promote good will so that consumers would buy from those companies once the war ended.[5]
	The Supreme Court denies First Amendment protection to advertising in 1942.[39]
1945–1960	After WWII ended in 1945, a baby boom and a consumer boom occurred. "Pent-up economic demand in the form of personal savings, coupled with low-interest government loans and mushrooming private credit, led to a consumer boom unparalleled in history. The G.I. Bill spawned massive construction of new housing at the edge of American cities . . ."[41]
1947	The Lanham Trademark Act enacted to protect brand names and slogans.[1]
1948–1960	The introduction of television was so successful that by 1960, televisions were owned by 90 percent of households. Early advertising was through sponsorship of entire programs, but the selling of "spots" was soon implemented because it was more profitable for the television networks.[30]
1950–1953	First third-party universal card (Diners' Club) issued.[24,22]
	U.S. involvement in the Korean War.
	Dwight Eisenhower ran the first presidential television commercial in his bid for the Presidency in 1952.[20]
1954	Author David Potter dubbed Americans the "People of Plenty" and advertising the "institution of abundance."[68]
1958	American Express and Carte Blanche introduced universal credit cards but without revolving credit.
	Bank of America and Chase Manhattan Bank launched credit card operations after 1958 and provided an enormous boost to the revolving credit market.[33]
	John Kenneth Galbraith dubbed the United States *The Affluent Society*.[33]
	Inspired by the Soviet's launching of Sputnik, United States formed the Advanced Research Projects Agency (ARPA) within the Department of Defense (DoD) to boost the country's technology and military development.[42]

1960–1970	The creative revolution in advertising. While the decade of the 1960s experienced social upheaval with the Vietnam War, civil rights era, and sexual revolution, advertising portrayals lagged behind the times and continued to place women and minorities in subservient roles. Advertising concentrated instead on new creative strategies that changed the look of ads. Advertising industry professionals became aware of their roles in consumer culture and realized for the first time that advertising had become "an icon of a culture."[30]
1961–1975	U.S. involvement in Vietnam.
1964	Lyndon Johnson's famous "Daisy" campaign commercial airs on TV.[20]
1966	Operation of several bankcard departments were combined into two national credit card companies: BankAmericard and Interbank Card Association (Master Charge).[33]
Late 1960s–1970s	Individualism, one of the quintessential American cultural values, took on new meaning as Americans become increasingly less likely to participate in communal activities. Attributed to growing pressures on consumers' time and money, the effects of mobility, and relentless proliferation of technology and mass media, Americans (particularly younger Americans) have moved away from communal pursuits in favor of solitary activities.[4]
	In 1969, ARPAnet (the forerunner of the Internet) was commissioned by the Department of Defense and linked four hubs at universities.[42]
1970–1980	The "Me" Decade. The 1970s brought an end to the social upheavals of the 1960s and with it the disillusionment following the Kennedy assassinations, the Vietnam War, and the Watergate scandals. Cynicism and distrust of tradition gave rise to a justification of self-indulgence. Society communicated the message that self-indulgence was not only OK but also necessary for personal growth. At the same time, consumer activists became more influential, and the voice of the consumer became more powerful. Also, the introduction of the VCR, video rental, and cable TV gave consumers additional media choices.[30]
1971	The United States abandoned the gold standard.[2]
1975	Bill Gates formed Microsoft with Paul Allen.[43]
	The Supreme Court granted limited First Amendment protection to advertising.[29]
1976	Steve Jobs and Stephen Wozniak introduced the first Apple computer.[43]
	The Supreme Court more fully conferred First Amendment protection on purely commercial speech.[29]
	BankAmericard became Visa.[33]
1980s	U.S. advertising expenditures were $53 billion, while $49 billion was spent on sales promotion to consumers and retailers. Advertising expenditures outside the United States were about $55 billion.[21]

(continued)

Year	Event
1980	Federal Reserve's anti-inflation policy allowed interest rates on debt to soar, while deregulation of banks allowed banks to target consumers with high interest on deposits and pass along high rates to borrowers.[23]
	The Supreme Court established the four-part *Hudson* Test to ascertain when commercial speech is protected by the First Amendment in 1980.[29]
	Deregulation of many industries including those affecting advertising. The Federal Trade Commission relaxed its rules on broadcast media ownership and deceptive advertising.[39,51]
	The decade of media fragmentation. Media choices proliferated with new technology. The growth of sales promotion, the success of direct marketing, and home-shopping techniques changed the practice of advertising. The traditional media choices were no longer adequate, and advertisers had to become competent with a much wider range of strategies and media choices. At the same time, audiences became more fragmented, resulting in a decline in the audience size of any one media vehicle.[50]
1981	Number of banks carrying MasterCard and Visa increased around 300 percent since 1969.
	IBM released its first PC (personal computer) with Bill Gates' Microsoft MS-DOS operating system.[43]
1982	Influenced by the trend toward deregulation, The Federal Trade Commission dismissed a 1976 antitrust case against the top three cereal companies who had been charged with, among other things, using intensive advertising to maintain an oligopoly.[48]
1983	Microsoft introduced Microsoft Windows, a graphical user interface (GUI) for personal computers.[43]
1984	Bankcard operations were outperforming all other bank debt after banks started issuing cards to poor-risk customers and upping credit limits.[33]
	The Internet turned over to the private sector.[1]
	Apple airs the famous "1984" commercial for the new Macintosh computer.[44]
1990	The Interactive Era began. The 1990s saw the introduction of the World Wide Web and the growth of interactive media, which changed the role of the consumer to a more active searcher of information and entertainment. Consumers interacted with digital media by helping create and shape content. Advertisers still challenged to use these technological advances to their best advantage. "Hybrid" forms of advertising emerged such as infomercials and product placements in movies. Advertisers were compelled to experiment with more nontraditional media.[52]
	In 1991, English computer scientist Timothy Berners-Lee developed the World Wide Web for the European Organization for Nuclear Research (CERN).[42]
	This is the decade of the economy's "dot.com" bubble during which Internet pioneers like Steve Jobs and Bill Gates achieved unprecedented wealth.[55]

1993	The savings rate in the United States in 1993 was about 6 percent.[64]
1994	Consumers owed $74 billion in credit card debt, compared to $2.7 billion in 1969 (all in 1969 dollars).[33]
1996	The Telecommunications Act of 1996 was passed which further relaxed restrictions on ownership of broadcast media.[51]
1997	Total credit card debt doubled between 1990 and 1996 and was at $455 billion by October 1997.[63] By late 1997, total household debt (including mortgages, car loans, credit cards, and other debts) reached $5.5 trillion.[65]
1999	Between 1972 and 1999 and adjusting for inflation ad expenditures in America increased 203 percent, whereas credit card advertising increased 1,400 percent.
2000	The "dot.com" bubble bursts.[55]
2001	The age of convergence began wherein technology diverged while content and function converged.[53] Terrorists attacked the United States on 9/11. "Generation G" established with the birth of the third of a three-generation population group who are committed to philanthropy and social responsibility.[8]
2002	Almost $240 billion was spent on local and national advertising, while more than $250 billion was spent on sales promotion to consumers and retailers. Almost $214 billion was spent on advertising outside the United States.[21]
2005	The U.S. savings rate was negative. The last time the savings rate was negative for an entire year was in 1933.[66]
2006	By late in the year, the housing market declined leading to record numbers of foreclosures.[9] Both the percentage and the number of people without health insurance increased in 2006. The percentage without health insurance increased from 15.3 percent in 2005 to 15.8 percent in 2006, and the number of uninsured increased from 44.8 million to 47.0 million.[61] Among full-time, year-round workers, women earned approximately 19 percent of what men earned in 1960. In 2006, women earned about 77 percent of what men earned.[62]
2007	From 2006 to 2016, the economy was expected to grow more slowly as baby boomers retire.[28] The Washington Post identified the beginning of the economic crisis in June.[12,13,14] Expenditures on cell phones exceeded what's spent on residential telephone service.[27] Thirty-eight percent of Americans watched TV online.[56]

(continued)

Year	Event
2008	U.S. industrial production showed the biggest decline since 1974.[15]
	U.S. employers cut the largest number of jobs in November since 1974.[16] The country lost 2.6 million jobs in 2008.[17]
	Americans owed $2.5 trillion in unsecured debt; 61 percent of Americans describe their financial situation as fair or poor.[18]
	The U.S. government authorized a $700 billion financial bailout plan to buttress the failing economy called the Troubled Asset Relief Program (TARP).[46]
	The United States elected its first president of African-American heritage.[60]
	Barack Obama used both digital and social media along with viral marketing as part of his successful Presidential campaign. He won almost 70 percent of the vote among voters under age 25.[45]
	Almost 20 percent of all adults and nearly 70 percent of online adults visited social networks online.[49]
	MySpace Music launched.[54]
	Apple's iTunes became the number 1 music seller in the United States.[34]
	The personal savings rate increased to almost 3 percent after being below zero for almost four years.[67]
	Home prices fell in 24 out of 25 metropolitan markets.[11]
2009	High-risk, high-interest subprime mortgages to borrowers with bad credit and a lot of debt became the mortgage industry's fastest growing loans.[9] Homeownership peaked at 67.3 percent.[10]
	The federal government planned to extend bailout funds to the foundering U.S. auto industry.[19]
	Barack Obama inaugurated in one of the most heavily watched ceremonies in history.[59]
	Digital sources account for around 20 percent of recorded music sales. Album sales dropped 45 percent from their peak in 2000.[47]
	The transition from analog to digital TV scheduled to occur when either a converter box for an analog TV or a new digital TV will be required to receive standard TV signals.[58]
	The consumer confidence index in January dropped to 38.6 from 87.3 in January 2007.[57]

Notes:

[1] Arens, William. 2004. *Contemporary Advertising*. New York: McGraw-Hill.

[2] Grant, James. 1994. *Money of the Mind: Borrowing and Lending in America from the Civil War to Michael Milken*. New York: Macmillan.

[3] http://www.federalreserveeducation.org/fed101/History/index.cfm (accessed January 22, 2009).

[4] Putnam, Robert D. 2000. *Bowling Alone*. New York: Simon and Schuster.

[5] Krugman, Dean M., Leonard N. Reid, S. Watson Dunn, and Arnold M. Barban. 1994. *Advertising: Its Role in Modern Marketing*. Fort Worth: Dryden Press.

[6] Goodwin, Doris Kearns. 1994. *No Ordinary Time*. New York: Simon & Schuster.

[7] Leach, William. 1993. *Land of Desire: Merchants, Power, and the Rise of a New American Culture*. New York: Vintage Books.

[8] http://www.cultureoffuture.com/Generation_G_Breakdown_final.pdf.

[9] Pinciak-Madden, Monica R. and Katya Jestin. 2009. "Subprime Crisis: The Unraveling Promises to Increase the Number of Civil Suits and Criminal Investigations." *New York Law Journal* 241 (2): 54.

[10] Pierce, Emmet. 2009. "Homeownership Goals Created House of Cards: Lender Guidelines Were 'Obliterated in Buying Frenzy." *The San Diego Union-Tribune*, January 5: (A1).

[11] "Home Prices Fall in 24 out of 25 Metro Areas-Radar Logic." *Reuters News*, January 6, 2009.

[12] www.globalresearch.ca/PrintArticle.php?articleID=5964. (accessed January 17, 2009).

[13] Samuelson, Robert J. 2007. "The End of Cheap Credit?" *The Washington Post*, June 13: (A21).

[14] Pearlstein, Steven. 2005. "The Takeover Boom, About to Go Bust." *The Washington Post*, June 13: (D1).

[15] http://www.reuters.com/article/gc04/idUSTRE49F56B20081016 (accessed January 17, 2009).

[16] Bull, Allister. 2008. "U.S. Job Losses Worst Since 1974 as Downturn Deepens." *eWeek*, December 5. Available at http://www.eweek.com/c/a/IT-Infrastructure/US-Job-Losses-Worst-Since-1974-as-Downturn-Deepens/1/ (accessed January 17, 2009).

[17] Denning, Liam. 2009. "Gloom of Joblessness Deepens." Dow Jones Newswires, January 9, (accessed January 17, 2009).

[18] http://www.businesswire.com/news/home/20090113005918/en (accessed January 17, 2009).

[19] Cho, David and Kendra Marr. 2009. "U.S. Expands Aid to Auto Industry: Chrysler Financial Gets $1.5 Billion from Treasure; Ford Credit in Talks." Washingtonpost.com, January 17, D02, (accessed January 19, 2009).

[20] http://www.livingroomcandidate.org/.

[21] Belch, George E. and Michael A. Belch. 2004. *Advertising and Promotion: An Integrated Marketing Communications Perspective*, 5. New York: McGraw Hill/Irwin.

[22] Kammen, Michael. 1999. *American Culture, American Tastes*, 179. New York: Alfred A. Knopf.

[23] Medoff, James L. and Andrew Harless. 1996. "Unsettling Trends." In *The Indebted Society*, 3–21. Boston: Little, Brown.

[24] Ritzer, George. 1995. "Socio-History of the Credit Card." In *Expressing America: A Critique of the Global Credit Card Society*, 31–57. Thousand Oaks: Pine Forge Press.

(continued)

[25]Carey, James. 1960. "Advertising: An Institutional Approach." In *The Role of Advertising: A Book of Readings*, ed. Charles H. Sandage and Vernon Fryburger, 3–34. Homewood, IL: Richard D. Irwin.

[26]Strasser, Susan. 1989. *Satisfaction Guaranteed: The Making of the American Mass Market*. New York: Pantheon Books.

[27]http://www.bls.gov/cex/cellphones2007.htm (accessed January 25, 2009).

[28]http://www.bls.gov/opub/mlr/2007/11/art2full.pdf (accessed January 25, 2009).

[29]Lane, W. Ronald and J. Thomas Russell. 2001. *Advertising: A Framework*, 339–435. Upper Saddle River, NJ: Prentice Hall.

[30]O'Guinn, Thomas C., Chris T. Allen, and Richard J. Semenik. 2006. *Advertising and Integrated Brand Promotion*, 82–96. Mason, OH: Thomson.

[31]Marchand, Roland. 1985. *Advertising the American Dream*, 88–110. Berkeley: University of California Press.

[32]Medoff, James and Andrew Harless. 1996. *The Indebted Society: Anatomy of an Ongoing Disaster*, 166. Boston: Little, Brown.

[33]Medoff, James and Andrew Harless. 1996. *The Indebted Society: Anatomy of an Ongoing Disaster*, 6–12. Boston: Little, Brown.

[34]http://www.usatoday.com/money/media/2008-04-03-apple-itunes-sales-tops-wal-mart_N.html (accessed January 22, 2009.)

[35]Lane, W. Ronald and J. Thomas Russell. 2001. *Advertising: A Framework*, 33. Upper Saddle River, NJ: Prentice Hall.

[36]Russell, J. Thomas and W. Ronald Lane. 2002. Kleppner's Advertising Procedure, 9–12. Upper Saddle River, NJ: Prentice Hall.

[37]Norris, James D. 1990. *Advertising and the Transformation of American Society; 1865–1920*, 1. New York: Greenwood Press.

[38]Norris, James D. 1990. *Advertising and the Transformation of American Society; 1865–1920*, 166–167. New York: Greenwood Press.

[39]Teeter, Dwight L. Jr., and Bill Loving. 2001. *Law of Mass Communications: Freedom and Control of Print and Broadcast Media*, 776–791. New York: Foundation Press.

[40]http://www.americanheritage.com/events/articles/web/20060131-slavery-thirteenth-amendment-abraham-lincoln-frederick-douglass-confederacy-civil-war.shtml (accessed January 31, 2009).

[41]De Graaf, John, David Wann, and Thomas H. Naylor. 2001. *Affluenza: The All-Consuming Epidemic*, 142. San Francisco: Berrett-Koehler Publishers.

[42]http://www.pbs.org/opb/nerds2.0.1/timeline/ (accessed January 31, 2009).

[43]http://www.thocp.net/companies/microsoft/microsoft_company.htm (accessed January 31, 2009).

[44]O'Guinn, Thomas C., Chris T. Allen, and Richard J. Semenik. 2006. Advertising and Integrated Brand Promotion, 362, Mason, OH: Thomson.

[45]http://www.mediapost.com/publications/?fa=Articles.showArticleHomePage&art_aid=94861 (accessed January 31, 2009).

[46]http://www.washingtonpost.com/wpdyn/content/article/2009/01/16/AR2009011602874.html?hpid=topnews (accessed January 31, 2009).

[47]http://www.livemint.com/Articles/PrintArticle.aspx?artid=6FFB3C82-E3A4-11DD-A4F0-000B5DABF636 (accessed January 31, 2009).

[48]Editors. 1981. "The FTC's Cereal Fiasco: 'Congress Won't Let Us Bust 'Em Up,'" *Antitrust Law & Economics Review*, 13 (2).

[49]http://www.marketingcharts.com/direct/nearly-70-of-online-adults-use-social-media-often-research-products-6101/ (accessed January 31, 2009).

[50]Russell, J. Thomas and W. Ronald Lane. 2002. *Kleppner's Advertising Procedure*, 19–20. Upper Saddle River, NJ: Prentice Hall.

[51]Teeter, Dwight L. Jr., and Bill Loving. 2001. *Law of Mass Communications: Freedom and Control of Print and Broadcast Media*, 899–901. New York: Foundation Press.

[52]O'Guinn, Thomas C., Chris T. Allen, and Richard J. Semenik. 2006. *Advertising and Integrated Brand Promotion*, 49–50. Mason (OH): Thomson.

[53]Jenkins, Henry. 2006. *Convergence Culture: Where Old and New Media Collide*, 15. New York: New York University Press.

[54]http://news.cnet.com/8301–17939_109–10050206–2.html (accessed January 31, 2009).

[55]http://www.nethistory.info/History%200f%20the%20Internet/dotcom.html (accessed January 31, 2009).

[56]http://www.warc.com/News/PrintNewsItem.asp?NID=22726 (accessed January 19, 2009).

[57]http://www.warc.com/News/PrintNewsItem.asp?NID=24611 (accessed January 29, 2009).

[58]Tessler, Joelle. 2009. "House Defeats Bill to Delay Digital TV Transition." The Associated Press (January 29). Available at http://www.google.com/hostednews/ap/article/ALeqM5hyGXXrrCMCMoD-f9t5TPPFSH0CeQD960F5M00 (accessed February 1, 2009).

[59]Serjeant, Jill. 2009. "Obama Draws 37.8 Million U.S. TV Viewers." Reuters (January 21). Available at http://www.reuters.com/article/televisionNews/idUSTRE50J15820090122 (accessed February 1, 2009).

[60]Johnson, Alex. 2008. "Barack Obama Elected 44th President. MSNBC. (November 5). Available at http://www.msnbc.msn.com/id/27531033/ (accessed February 1, 2009).

[61]National Center for Health Statistics. 2007. "New CDC Report Documents Percentage of People Without Health Insurance." Centers for Disease Control and Prevention. Department of Health and Human Services. (June 25). Available at http://www.cdc.gov/nchs/PRESSROOM/07newsreleases/insurance.htm (accessed February 1, 2009).

[62]Weinberg, Daniel. 2007. "Earnings by Gender: Evidence from Census 2000." *Monthly Labor Review*. Available at http://www.bls.gov/opub/mlr/2007/07/art3full.pdf (Accessed February 1, 2009).

[63]Consumer Federation of America. 1997. "Credit Card Debts Escalate in 1997, Burdening Many XMAS Shoppers-Aggressive Marketing and Credit Extension a Key Reason." Available at http://www.consumerfed.org/pdfs/ccdebtpr.pdf (accessed February 3, 2009).

[64]Personal Savings Rate. 2009. U.S. Department of Commerce: Bureau of Economic Analysis. Available at http://research.stlouisfed.org/fred2/data/PSAVERT.txt (accessed Feb. 3, 2009).

[65]Strasser, Susan. 1989. *Satisfaction Guaranteed: The Making of the American Mass Market*, 72. New York: Pantheon Books.

[66]http://www.cbsnews.com/stories/2006/02/07/business/printable1293943.shtml (accessed Feb. 4, 2009).

[67]http://money.cnn.com/2008/10/15/news/rainy.day.fortune/index.htm?postversion=2008101614 (accessed Feb. 2, 2009).

[68]Potter, David M. 1954. *People of Plenty: Economic Abundance and the American Character*, Chicago: University of Chicago Press.

in their immediate geographic region. Moreover, they were limited to producing a small number of items by hand. So even if they could sell to people in other regions, they probably couldn't produce large amounts of merchandise quickly enough to satisfy customers in distant places. On top of that, transporting products in large quantities to distant regions would have been extremely difficult prior to the creation of the transcontinental railroad.

During the late nineteenth century and early twentieth century, the U.S. population almost doubled. At the same time, American industry produced as much as fourteen times the amount of raw materials required to manufacture goods (Strasser 1989, 6). Simultaneously, factories were being developed based on the model of continuous-process or flow production that allowed enormous amounts of raw materials to be processed automatically in a never-ending stream (Strasser 1989, 6).

No longer were people hand-producing necessary staples and trading with other households for what they couldn't create themselves. As society shifted from a predominantly agrarian economy to a more industrial economy, fewer households had the land and the resources to produce necessary goods. The simultaneous rise of mass production, transportation, distribution, branding, advertising, and urbanization resulted in all types of Americans purchasing manufactured products (Strasser 1989, 3–38).

In the process, manufacturers found ways to sell larger and larger quantities of branded goods. However, as Strasser points out, manufacturers weren't content to simply fulfill existing customer needs. They had to make people want things in order to find buyers for large quantities of mass-produced goods (Strasser 1989, 27). Ewen (1999) describes the cultural transition as follows:

> Much of late nineteenth- and twentieth-century social thought is premised on the coming of what historian Warren Susman termed "a newly emerging culture of abundance." To some extent, socialist thought has been fertilized by this expectation. For Karl Marx, writing at mid-nineteenth century, "the rapid improvement of all instruments of production" under capitalism was creating the material conditions which, ultimately, made communism possible. For the capitalist market, this enormous productive capacity would lead to a crisis of "over-production," a crisis, which Marx observed, in all earlier epochs would have seemed an absurdity." (238)

In addition to government intervention, production is spurred on by the concept of planned obsolescence. Even in the best of times, American business nurtures the idea that whatever product or service was purchased yesterday is inferior in comparison to what's available today. In 1930, advertising practitioner Elmo Calkins described continuing modification as a strategy: "The purpose is to make the customer discontented with his old type of fountain pen, kitchen utensil, bathroom, or motorcar because it is old fashioned, out-of-date. The technical term for this idea is obsoletism. We no longer wait for things to wear out. We displaced them with others that are not more effective but more attractive" (Ewen 1996, 243, citing Calkins).

Ultimately, obsoletism was supposed to be good for both the economy and the consumer. As Ewen points out, the practice of replacing products before they'd worn out, in combination with higher incomes and the availability of consumer credit, during the period between 1945 and 1960 led to the perception of American society as one of pronounced abundance (Ewen, 1996, 243–245). Marchand (1985) describes the importance of advertising to production:

> By selling ideas and stimulating the demand for goods, they [advertising writers] revealed themselves as the geniuses behind a newly discovered economic perpetual-motion machine. By stimulating desires for a higher standard of living, they inspired people to work harder. Hard work then contributed to new levels of production, for which advertising agents would find buyers by stimulating a new pitch of consumer desire. (31)

But the preoccupation with increasing production and the impetus it provided for consumer culture weren't truly cemented until Americans were forced to deal with first, the Great Depression, and then World War II. The devastation caused by the Depression led Franklin D. Roosevelt to develop the New Deal, and he thus initiated the idea of government-stimulated production. In addition to the obvious humanitarian benefits of putting people to work, the program illustrated the power of the government to jumpstart the economy by forcing increased productivity. In the face of human suffering and economic disaster, the laissez faire attitudes toward minimal government interference seemed impractical at the very least.

Additional support for the importance of stimulating production through all necessary means came from British economist John Maynard Keynes. In fact, it wasn't until FDR fully endorsed Keynes's policies a few years before the country entered the war that the new philosophy truly gained credibility: "In 1938 the Depression deepened. Reluctantly, F.D.R. embraced the only new idea he hadn't yet tried, that of the bewildering British 'mathematician.' As the President explained in a fireside chat, 'We suffer primarily from a failure of consumer demand because of a lack of buying power.' It was therefore up to the government to 'create an economic upturn' by making 'additions to the purchasing power of the nation'" (Reich 1999, 102).

Implicit in this philosophy was the idea that economic uncertainty is both fiscally and psychologically damaging to the nation. In contrast to the classical liberal assumptions about the self-righting nature of the market, however, Keynes believed that market economies were inherently unstable. Government intervention into the economy was then viewed as a simple, justifiable way of reducing the uncertainty that had wreaked so much havoc on the United States throughout the 1930s and 1940s.

According to Reich, "In order to keep people fully employed, Keynes theorized that governments have to run deficits when the economy is slowing" (1999). Thus deficit spending was embraced as a cure for uncertainty. Production levels have to be maintained at all costs.

The financial crisis beginning in 2007 that led to the appropriation of $700 billion in bailout funds for American business is an illustration of Keynesian thinking. Perhaps understandably, Keynesian economics is enjoying newfound popularity (Skidelsky 2008a). Rather than clinging to the 1980s faith in deregulation, American industry is looking to the government to stabilize the economy. Even Alan Greenspan, former chairman of the Federal Reserve during the height of deregulation during the 1980s, now admits he overestimated the ability of the market to regulate itself (Skidelsky 2008b).

When American society changed from a "producer's culture into a consumer's culture," the focus shifted from simply producing the minimum amount of goods needed to a society that "must be adjusted to a new set of drives and values in which consumption is paramount" (Potter 1954, 173). This leads to the second class of characteristics of consumer culture.

2. The Importance of Continuous Consumption: Consumption Is Critical to Society and the Individual; Commerce and Culture Are Inseparable

The importance of continuous consumption arises as a direct result of the importance of sustaining production levels in a capitalist economy that, in turn, leads to an abundance of mass-produced goods. In order for the society to fully flourish, there must be continuous production and consumption. Both are essential to the development and maintenance of consumer culture. The role of marketing and advertising, therefore, is clear: Demand must be stimulated to absorb production. Unlike a society based on householding, where consumers dictated the type and amount of goods made, a capitalist system depends upon the creation of demand for goods among consumers. In a capitalist economy, consumer spending is absolutely essential to the health of the society.

During slow economic times, consumer spending is far more important than saving. Support for this is found in the work of John Maynard Keynes. In stark contrast to the austere work ethic on which the United States was founded, Keynes argued that consumer spending was more beneficial to the economy than saving. Accordingly, "Keynesian-oriented economists warn that too much saving does terrible damage. When consumers don't spend enough, businesses stop investing because demand for their products has fallen. This in turn leads to recession and unemployment" (Schor 1998, 171).

The importance of spending was perfectly articulated by Phillip H. Geier, Jr., chairman emeritus of Interpublic Group and chairman of the Geier Group, in a full-page advertisement in the *New York Times* in January 2009. According to Geier, " . . . the best way to stimulate the overall economy is to boost consumer spending . . ." because, said Geier, "if the consumer doesn't spend, the economy will not improve" (*World Advertising Research Center* 2009).

Relentless consumption obviates the need for infinite discretionary income. Most Americans, except for the very wealthy, cannot afford to continually purchase goods without steadily increasing their income or borrowing money. In the absence of expanding personal fortunes, the significance of the availability of consumer credit is thus critical to the development and perpetuation of a consumer culture.

Steadily improving salaries and quality of life seemed possible for parents of baby boomers after World War II. People who came of age during World War II could reasonably expect to achieve a standard of living markedly better than that of their Depression-era parents. For Baby Boomers and their children, however, a steadily improving quality of life can't be presumed (Medoff and Harless 1996, 6). Homeownership went from 44 percent to 63 percent between 1940 and 1970 and remained at that level until increasing to 67.3 percent in 2006 (Pierce 2009). However, the increase in homeownership occurred only as a result of the epidemic of subprime mortgages that ultimately led to the financial crisis that began in 2007.

As the certainty of an increasingly prosperous future declined, the availability of consumer credit grew. In this sense, contemporary consumer culture can be traced partly to the advent of consumer credit at the beginning of the twentieth century. Marshall Field's (one of the first department stores), for instance, practically doubled its number of credit accounts during the 1920s (Leach 1993, 299).

Buying on credit isn't the only way consumers make purchases in a consumer culture, but it certainly enables a wider range of consumers to keep consuming. This point was clearly reinforced when in the 1980s banks started offering credit cards to consumers who had been previously classified as high risk. As cards were issued, credit limits were raised and interest rates were increased, and consumers continued to charge more while paying only minimum amounts each month. It's no surprise that credit cards outperform all other forms of bank debt (Medoff and Harless 1996, 12). This scenario was repeated recently when lenders started giving mortgages to high-risk borrowers.

Americans seem to have taken to credit like fish take to water. Schor argues that the "see-want-borrow-buy" syndrome is so deeply ingrained it's become almost a Pavlovian response (Schor 1998, 73–74). Pavlovian or not, consumer use of credit cards has driven overall credit card debt up exponentially. According to Schor (1998, 72), total credit card debt doubled between 1990 and 1996, and household indebtedness (including mortgages, auto loans, etc.) was close to $6 trillion by the end of 1997.

In part, this trend can be traced to the steady stream of solicitations consumers receive from credit card companies and by the number of cards held by Americans. "Almost half the adult population (48 percent) holds three or more cards" (Schor 1998, 232). Moreover, according to the Direct Market Association's 1999 *Statistical Fact Book*, "adults with the most credit cards tend to receive the most third-class mail." Consumer response to third-class solicitations for credit cards is second only to solicitations for securities. From 1972 to 1999, annual dollars spent on credit card advertising increased from just under $16 million to $876 million (LNA Media Watch Service 1999).

One factor to which debt *can't* be attributed is lack of education. Surprisingly, savings decrease with higher levels of education while shopping tends to increase, particularly for women. Schor concludes, "the highly educated are more immersed in the culture of upscale acquisition" (1998, 76).

Maintaining credit card debt is remarkably common as almost half of all Americans report this kind of debt (Schor 1998, 232). Moreover, as credit card companies target younger and/or high-risk consumers, the trend seems likely to continue. What's fueling this seemingly self-destructive behavior? Medoff and Harless point to the power of habit in the escalation of personal indebtedness. Determined to maintain a standard of living they were raised to expect, consumers borrow without regard to interest rates or economic conditions. Americans exhibit a powerful resistance to downward mobility (1996, 14–16).

Evidence of this is plentiful. Even though real wages fell or were stagnant during the 1970s and 1980s and the Consumer Price Index (CPI) never regained its 1969 high, consumers continued to incur more debt. In fact, the 1994 CPI was only 68 percent of the 1969 level indicating a profound tendency to borrow money without confidence in the economy (Medoff and Harless 1996, 14–16).

Under such conditions, consumer values seem suspect. Citing William Leiss (*The Limits to Satisfaction*, 1976), Schudson emphasizes consumers' apparent confusion of needs and wants:

> . . . a society of high-intensity consumption is not so much one in which new needs are manufactured and foisted upon consumers as one in which citizens lose a secure understanding of what their needs are and to what extent commodities can satisfy them. Needs become 'ambiguous' as individual choices multiply. (Schudson 1984, 155)

One interesting effect of purchasing via credit cards is the potentially different psychology that surrounds these purchases. William Leach, writing about the phenomenal growth of credit in the 1920s and 1930s, points out that the rate of payment default and the amount of goods returned skyrocketed. Credit purchases accounted for a disproportionate amount of returned goods. In fact, according to studies conducted at the time, the defaults and returns were directly attributable to the expansion of credit. As consumers acquired goods more easily by charging them, they felt less responsibility for paying for them and placed less value on owning them (Leach 1993, 300–301). Accordingly, "credit card tips tend to be higher than with cash, and people report feeling looser with their money when they use plastic. The painlessness of spending with plastic makes it a hard for many people to control" (Schor 1998, 73).

Given the importance of consumption to our economic and social wellbeing and the lengths to which we're willing to go to keep consuming, it's clear that our culture revolves around consumption. One could argue that consumption is an underlying theme that permeates virtually every aspect of our society.

It's not surprising then, that American culture is thoroughly imbued with commerce. Product placements and sponsorships of cultural events cut across every demographic group and lifestyle. Whether it's the strategic placement of a box of Wheaties in a Hollywood film or Rolex sponsoring horse trials events, consumer goods are everywhere. Along with them is the constant affirmation of the high-consumption lifestyle. A.J. Frutkin (2007, SR4–SR6) describes this method of integrating commerce with culture by saying: "The line between commercial pods and editorial content is beginning to blur. Digital and mobile extensions play key roles in almost every negotiation. In some cases, advertisers are bypassing networks altogether to create their own forms of branded entertainment."

Pompper and Choo (2008, 49) support this idea by saying that product placement has become a specialization independent of advertising and public relations firms. The authors also point out that as consumers increasingly exercise their ability to avoid commercials with technologies like TiVo, the integration of products and services into media content is an even more effective way of getting through to target audiences:

First, marketers anticipate even greater prominence of product placement as a tool that uniquely links brands with entertainment because viewer-consumers are highly involved with film and television stories and are relaxed and unprepared to detect ads as they do when clearly defined commercial breaks interrupt television programs. Hence, product placement conditions through "product integration," as put by one respondent, and reinforces a brand's role in "everyday culture," according to another. (Pompper and Choo 2008, 66).

In addition to product placement, event marketing, sports marketing, and product sponsorship are other ways marketers are integrating their brands into culture. According to Close et al. (2006), event marketing typically involves staging an event. It may or may not involve payment. Sponsorship occurs when a marketer pays for the right to be affiliated with an event or an organization. Sports marketing is one form of event marketing and the most common. Overall, most (96 percent) of U.S. marketers engage in event marketing (Close et al. 2006, 420–422).

Like product placement, the purpose behind these techniques is obvious: to create a positive association in the consumer's mind between the brand and a popular context that eliminates the consumer's ability to avoid the marketer's message. The venues for these kinds of promotions are not always inherently commercial. Struggling municipalities and nonprofit organizations have turned to corporate sponsorship to make up for what's lacking in public funding. Corporate promotions now permeate zoos, hospitals, and schools (Schor 2004, 85). Perhaps most controversial are the ways in which exhortations to consumer have infiltrated public schools. As Schor points out, schools have been selling space on buses, gymnasium floors, on interior walls, and in classrooms (2004, 88–89).

The pervasiveness of proconsumption messages has been accelerated by the advent of social media and viral marketing. Largely evident in computer-mediated media environments, the two techniques combine a mixture of advertiser-supplied messages with user-generated content in an attempt to inspire word-of-mouth (or "word of mouse"—consumer communication about the advertiser's message that is passed along via the computer) communication called "viral advertising." Barack Obama was highly successful using this approach in his presidential campaign, but it was also already being used by some of the world's largest advertisers (Golan and Zaidner 2008); The objective is to fly beneath the consumer's "radar" and, in the process, impart consumer-to-consumer endorsements of products (Golan and Zaidner 2008).

3. Objects Take on Significance Beyond Their Original Purpose, and All Things Become Commodified

As a consequence of the importance of production and consumption, along with the integration of commerce and culture, there has been a concomitant tendency for objects to take on significance beyond their initial function and for intangible things to become commodified. In addition to production and consumption of tangible goods, selling products or services to fulfill other desires and as proxies for intangibles like time or beauty was good for the economy.

As Leiss, Kline, Jhally, and Botterill explain, there are three trends that account for the ability of consumer culture to transform life from the literal to the symbolic:

> 1) the recognition of consumption as a legitimate sphere for individual self-realization; 2) the discovery by marketer and advertisers that the personal or psychological and interpersonal (or social) domains of the consumer, rather than the characteristics of the goods, were the vital core of merchandising; 3) the revolutions in communications and mass media technologies that made possible the rapid evolution of advertising formats, including the special significance of visual or iconic imagery. (2005, 225)

The commodification of intangibles is presented so expertly through advertising that as a culture we no longer question or criticize it. For example, holidays—even those that are religiously based—have been converted into cultural spending opportunities in ways that cut across individual conceptions of the meaning of the holidays. Easter, with its profound roots in Christian doctrine, has been repackaged as a secular holiday replete with adorable bunnies and lots of chocolate. Moreover, no holiday is too insignificant for marketers to encourage its celebration through spending. Groundhog Day, President's Day, St. Patrick's Day, and every other day warrant celebration through shopping. Furthermore, consumers are coached to begin their holiday spending well in advance of the actual date of the holiday. Christmas promotions appear immediately after Halloween. St. Patrick's Day displays sprout before the Valentine's Day decorations have been put away.

All cultures find ways to mark the passage of time by celebrating meaningful holidays and observing personal rituals such as birthdays, graduations, weddings, and anniversaries; however, the commodification of holidays and rituals requires product use as well as advertising. In a consumer culture, advertising not only teaches consumers which products are needed as ritual artifacts but how to enact the rituals. For example, the diamond engagement ring is so much a part of wedding ritual that few brides-to-be feel properly engaged without it. Acquiring a diamond engagement ring not only allows women to join the "consumption community" of all women who have owned such rings (Boorstin 1974), but also avoids the potential feelings of alienation from not receiving one (Otnes and Scott 1996). Over time, the DeBeers diamond company's advertising campaigns have been so successful in convincing consumers of the need for the engagement ring as a ritual artifact—to the extent that it is now taken for granted—that the advertising messages have shifted to educating consumers on how to enact the ritual by dictating the price one should expect to pay (e.g., two months' salary). Once the ritual for giving engagement rings was firmly established, DeBeers introduced new ritual artifacts with the "10th Diamond Anniversary Band" and the "25th Anniversary Diamond Necklace" (Otnes and Scott 1996, 37–38).

When holidays and rituals are commodified, celebrations without the necessary artifacts can bring about feelings of rejection for the recipient and guilt or humiliation for the giver. The mother who does not receive a Mother's Day card or gift may feel unloved by her children, regardless of how many spontaneous, noncommercial expressions of love are expressed. Furthermore, consumer cultures not only commodify rituals and holidays with products but with the *right* products. A YouTube video for the retailer JCPenney plays upon the fear of giving the wrong gift with the message, "Stay out of The Doghouse this holiday" (YouTube 2009). The video tells the story of a husband who gives his wife the "best vacuum cleaner she'll ever receive" as an anniversary gift but ends up in The Doghouse—a place where "a lot of guys end up for the holidays because they give thoughtless gifts." The way out of The Doghouse is a gift of jewelry—naturally from JCPenney's.

As commodities go, perhaps no other is as intangible as time. The anthropologist Edward Hall (1959) refers to the way Americans view time as monochronic—the idea that time is a limited commodity that can be saved, spent, wasted, or squandered. "Time is money" is the mantra of monochronic cultures, and it follows that products are often advertised for their ability to save time for consumers. For instance, product claims can include everything from microwaveable meals that cook fast and require no clean-up to medicines that relieve pain in a hurry because there is no time to be sick. A related time concept is that what's new and improved is better than what's old. The new and improved claim is so highly valued among consumers that advertisers can easily rely on its persuasive ability, especially with consumers who have been taught to believe in all that technology brings (Wolburg 2001). In fact, the perceived superiority of new products is why the idea of obsolescence discussed earlier in the chapter resonates so well with consumers.

The evolution of cosmetic surgery also illustrates the commodification of intangibles perfectly. Inspired by the need for reconstructive surgical procedures on veterans of World War I, cosmetic surgery began as a humanitarian effort to help disfigured soldiers resume normal lives. By the early 1930s, however, cosmetic surgery began to be viewed as a means of achieving more "social and economic security" after the confidence-shattering experience of the Depression (Haiken 1997, 106).

Another factor in the development of surgery for purely cosmetic reasons was the burgeoning field of psychiatry and, in particular, recognition of the "inferiority complex." Feelings of inferiority were believed to be epidemic in post-Depression America, and advertisers addressed these feelings as motives for purchasing products (Haiken 1997, 112).

As Haiken points out, the inferiority complex became a common indication for cosmetic surgery in the medical literature (Haiken 1997, 114). As surgeons became convinced of the importance of personal appearance, they endorsed "the gospel of self-improvement through plastic surgery" (Haiken 1997, 105–106). According to Haiken, Marchand, Lears, and others, a person's character and background were no longer sufficient for success while first impressions (and having the attractive face on which they were based) became paramount. But, now, a winning appearance could be purchased for the price of plastic surgery (Haiken 1997, 106).

Surgeons' ability to alleviate the suffering of soldiers maimed in World War II fueled public interest in cosmetic medicine. At the same time, other economic and social trends further added to growing popularity of the medical specialty. After WWII, " . . . the social and psychological limbo brought about by aging began to seem just as hellish as the purgatory to which halitosis had sentenced sufferers in the 1920s and 1930s, and the pervasive anxiety that had then driven Americans to the drugstore counter now drove them to the surgeon's office" (Haiken 1997, 155).

Growth in the number of cosmetic surgeries performed and in the number of cosmetic surgeons—especially in the United States—was dramatic in the 1940s, 1950s, and 1960s. Most plastic surgery was performed on women, and cosmetic surgeons aggressively sought female patients through the use of promotion and public relations (Haiken 1997, 137). Their efforts were very successful in part, according to Haiken, because these procedures were marketed to the middle class as simple yet scientific ways to acquire or restore beauty.

The evolution of the rise of cosmetic surgery reverberates with a refrain heard constantly in our consumer culture: Rather than accept and draw strength from your uniqueness, you should buy whatever is available to achieve beauty and the culturally defined standard of beauty along with it;

especially if trying to be something other than what you are pumps more money into the economy.

To illustrate the three conditions implicit in consumer culture, one need only to look at MasterCard's quintessential and long-running "Priceless" ad campaign. It included the tagline, "There are some things that money can't buy. For everything else there is MasterCard." One magazine ad in the series focuses on the love between an adult woman and her mother, and it illustrates the two women enjoying a moment of closeness at a pub. The initial lines of copy are:

> Plane tickets to the town where she was born: $1,200.
> Train to the house where she grew up: $63.
> Pints at the pub where she met your dad: $8.
> Finally understanding where your mother was coming from: priceless.

The ad acknowledges that there are some things that money can't buy; however, it is clearly possible to buy the means for achieving those intangibles (the plane ticket, the train, the pints). As members of the culture we accept the idea that the understanding of a parent is a priceless (and intangible) item, but we also see that it can be bought for a total of $1,271. The point here is that advertising teaches us that the things we hold sacred—the things we believe money can't buy—can in fact be bought. Once we believe that even intangibles can be bought, there is no doubt that we live in a consumer culture.

Recurring Trends

This chapter describes a progressive shift in society from a simpler way of living to a highly complex one in which consumption is a way of life and a means to self-identity. Examining the evolution of consumer culture naturally begs the question of the role of advertising in this transformation. Before addressing this, however, it's important to reiterate the underlying values and precipitating events evident in the transformation of America into a consumer culture.

To begin with, it's highly unlikely that American society would have evolved as it has were it not based on the principles of classical liberalism. These four principles (egoism, intellectualism, quietism, and atomism) laid the foundation for both advertising and consumer culture as a whole. The philosophical and economic ideals inherent in classical liberalism provided the underpinnings for common notions of man and the market that form the basis for deeply held beliefs about individual rights.

Turning to the events that have transpired over the last several centuries, it's impossible to say precisely to what degree specific events contributed to the formation of current American society. In fact, all the events of our history contributed to some degree. Moreover, the direction of causation is not clear. For instance, one could argue that advertising promoted branding, but the opposite is equally true. Advertising would not have come about had branding not been introduced. The reality is that all these events and trends are inherently potentiating of one another and consumer culture.

There are innumerable developments that had a profound impact on the evolution of the American economy and society. However, they can be classified by the overall trends they reflect. These trends are presented below as categories of events that serve as recurring agents of change throughout the country's transition from a society based on householding to one based on consumption. The categories are not mutually exclusive, just as the events within in them are not succinct and separate from all other events. For instance, the Internet is listed under science and technology, but it just as easily falls under the heading of sociodemographic issues, among others. Suffice it to say that the Internet, like so many other developments, represents more than one type of trend and is interrelated to every other event.

Science and Technology

As a category of developments that contributed to the rise of consumer culture, perhaps no other has been as instrumental as scientific and technological innovation. Without the introductions of electrical, mechanical, medical, and agricultural inventions along with the concomitant introductions of new ways of producing goods and new modes of transportation and media, our present world simply could not exist.

The list of scientific and technological discoveries since the Middle Ages is prohibitively long. However, the foundations of this list are found in the ideas that took place after the Reformation in the 1500s. As Carey explains, the ideas of Copernicus, Galileo, and Kepler as well as Newton and Locke, gave us the scientific understanding of both the universe and man. Without the fundamental shift in thinking that took place as a result of the Scientific Revolution, we wouldn't have had scientific discoveries and the faith in man's ability to operationalize them (Carey 1960). Newton's and Locke's ideas ultimately validated our modern philosophy that values science and technology and the rights of individuals to profit from them.

In general, inventions unfold in an evolutionary process that can take decades or longer. They are introduced and evolve, not in a vacuum, but integrally as part of prevailing technological and social conditions. They also tend to converge with other inventions as their applications multiply. Innovations also bring about profound social changes that will unfold throughout history.

Moreover, the consequences induced by technology radiate exponentially and indefinitely throughout every aspect of society.

As described above, the invention of the means to produce goods in bulk completely changed the relationships among manufacturers, wholesalers, retailers, and consumers. Moreover, innovations in both transportation and media led to profound changes in the cultural conceptions of space and time. As a result, the concept of community has been dramatically altered. Americans no longer define themselves within relatively narrow geographic parameters as the limits to our mobility have been overcome. Consequently, markets have been similarly redefined. Target audiences no longer must be limited by proximity and can be characterized by more significant attitudinal and behavioral traits.

Many things govern the rate of adoption of any particular new technology. Writing primarily about communication, Everett Rogers theorizes that the diffusion of innovations is determined by five things:

1. The perceived relative advantages of the innovation;
2. The compatibility of the invention with existing beliefs and behaviors;
3. The complexity of the innovation;
4. The reliability of the new technology; and
5. The ability of potential adopters to observe other people using the invention. (Fidler 1997, 12–15; Littlejohn and Foss 2008, 321–322)

Rogers also argues that the adoption curve is S-shaped where the rate of adoption is steepest after the earliest adopters have already embraced the technology (Fidler 1997, 12–15; based on Rogers 1986). Although Rogers's theory was put forth in the context of communication, the theory easily applies more broadly to innovations of other kinds.

Over time, the nature and rate of integration of new technologies has changed as the technologies themselves have changed. According to Putnam the rate of diffusion of technologies into the general population has accelerated dramatically. The time required for 75 percent of American households to adopt an invention decreased from 67 years for the automobile to just seven years for television. The change in the diffusion rate was not perfectly linear. In other words, it took twice as long for air conditioning (invented in 1952) to appear in 75 percent of homes compared to radio (introduced in 1923; Putnam 2000, 217). But the overall trend is clear: Inventions "that provided electronic entertainment—radio, the videorecorder, and, above all, television—spread into homes at all levels in American society five to ten times more quickly than other devices that are now nearly as ubiquitous" (Putnam 2000, 217).

Chronicles of the history of new media cite a bifurcation when the nature of media changed. The first media age was based on a centralized system of one-way communication typical of broadcast media. With the advent of the second media age in the 1980s, media became decentralized and more individually focused and interactive (Littlejohn and Foss 2008, 291–292). The proliferation of home-based, individualized electronic entertainment increased sharply after 1980 as more homes added additional TV sets, VCRs, computers, and Internet access at an increasing rate (Putnam 2000, 223). These trends have also contributed to the continuing breakdown in the boundaries of time and space and have ultimately led to further redefinitions in communities and markets. More than ever, we have become a nation of individuals dependent upon highly individualized media.

Mass Production, Distribution, Merchandising, Marketing, and Advertising

As a direct result of technological innovations in transportation, production, and communication and the cultural changes they wrought, the American economy shifted from one based on geographically based markets comprised of known buyers and sellers to one based on abstract markets. As Norris (1980) points out, manufacturers starting branding their products as a way of gaining leverage over retailers. But they also did so as a means of establishing trust with buyers in the absence of face-to-face interaction.

The introduction of branding and packaging came into play as the printing press made labeling possible, and the first trademark act passed by Congress in 1870 gave manufacturers legal ownership of their brands (Strasser 1989, 41–45). Manufacturers solved the logistics of selling and distributing large quantities of merchandise in different ways. By the beginning of the twentieth century, some manufacturers awarded retailers exclusive rights to stock and sell their goods while others relied on middlemen to handle sales and distribution of their products (Strasser 1989, 58–88). As Strasser points out, the federal government became a "functional middleman" when parcel post was introduced in 1912 (Strasser 1989, 81).

The advent of mail-order businesses, department stores, and the growth of retail in the nineteenth and twentieth centuries added another dimension to growing consumer culture. Mail-order catalogs, thanks to the creation of Rural Free Delivery, introduced even the most rural households to machine-made goods. As Norris (1990, 15) observed, "Mail order houses slanted the appeal of their ads to a rural consumer, and for many an isolated farm wife, the large, lavishly illustrated catalogue became an important cultural document." The first department stores—Wanamaker's, Lord & Taylor, Macy's, and Marshall Field's—

bought merchandise directly from manufacturers and organized their stores around separate departments. Department-store advertising enticed customers (particularly middle-class women) into the stores where they would be dazzled by both the merchandise and how it was displayed (Norris 1990, 16–17).

At the same time, customer service became an indispensable means of boosting consumption. The more modern forms of customer service introduced in the first few decades of the twentieth century included everything from free delivery to nurseries for shopping mothers to attentive waiters. According to Leach, "Its pervasiveness was beginning to make many people feel that America was, indeed, a wonderful place where everyone might get the same treatment, the same first-class service" (Leach 1993, 146).

All of the innovations described above, along with the availability of advertiser-supported media, provided an ideal impetus for advertising. And advertising expenditures grew accordingly: Between 1880 and 1920, advertising expenditures relative to GNP doubled (Norris 1990, 28). Obviously, for consumers to completely comprehend advertisements, they needed to be able to read. Thanks to compulsory education, the literacy rate reached a whopping 90 percent by the dawn of the twentieth century. Billboards (the "oldest of advertising media" according to Strasser [1989]), newspapers, magazines, streetcar ads, and store displays contributed a vital element to burgeoning consumer culture.

In addition to giving manufacturers greater control over their products, advertising served to shape consumers' knowledge, behavior, and desires. A good example of the role advertising played is the 1910 Gillette advertisement for safety razors. By showing men who were unable to go to barbers, these ads "taught readers how to shave" (Strasser 1989, 99). Thus the advertising not only directed consumers to particular brands, but also showed them a more modern way of life. In the process, Americans became consumers instead of producers (Potter 1954, 171). Much later, consumers made another shift—from being mere recipients of media messages to content providers as a result of digital, personal, and Internet-based media.

The shift from producer to consumer could not have happened if Americans hadn't placed some level of trust in both advertisers and their products (Strasser 1989, 88). In many ways, it's amazing that consumers responded at all to advertising during the nineteenth century. Patent medicines (also known as proprietary medicines) accounted for the vast majority of advertising in *Harper's Magazine*, for example. It wasn't until 1892 that the *Ladies' Home Journal* refused to accept medical advertising, thus leading to the eventual demise of patent medicine advertising (Norris 1990, 48–49). Consumer trust may have been fostered by implementation of government regulations passed to protect them such as the Pure Food and Drug Act of 1906 (Strasser 1989).

Cultural Economics

The issue of trust leads naturally into the cultural economics of consumer culture. This, in turn, leads to the importance of debt in a consumer culture. Borrowing money is done at many levels and, quite often, for good reason. The U.S. government has a long relationship with debt in the form of the federal deficit. From its first fiscal year in 1789 through the present, the U.S. government has almost always operated at a deficit (TreasuryDirect.gov). There have been fleeting attempts to balance the budget (e.g., FDR in 1938), but the government always seems to revert to deficit spending (Medoff and Harless 1996, 183). So this pattern is as old as the nation itself, and it was further intensified by the abandoning of the gold standard (that was ultimately concluded in 1971). Because this ended the ability to literally convert dollars into gold, money has taken on an entirely abstract value.

According to Grant, the abolition of the gold standard in 1971 led to high inflation in the 1970s that led, in turn, to the high interest rates enjoyed by junk-bond salesmen in the 1980s (Grant 1994, 5). When more lending occurs, it increases the national economy. Throughout history, however, periods of expansion are eventually followed by retrenchment. At that point the federal government steps in to shore up the economy, just as it did in 2008–2009.

As Grant points out, debt is based on trust (Grant 1994, 5). Whether referring to the nation, the investment and banking community, or consumers, borrowing hinges on the faith of both the loaner and the borrower that it will be repaid. When circumstances make that impossible (e.g., when loans are given to parties incapable of paying them back, or interest rates on variable-rate loans rise to ruinous levels, or the value of collateral drops significantly) the entire system breaks down, as it did in the years 2008, 2009, and 2010.

So, in many ways, one could argue that indebtedness is an American way of life. Just as the dollar has become an abstraction, so too has consumer debt. In the name of growing the economy by boosting production and consumption, government, business, and consumers have come to condone debt absolutely. As individuals, the ends (keeping up with technology, acquiring newer, better material things that enhance one's self-image) justify the means (debt). Until the economy takes the eventual downturn, Americans base their lives on the complete faith that things will only improve.

Whereas in business, it may be necessary to spend money in order to make money, thus often requiring going into debt, the situation is not the same for consumers. Aside from the few purchases for which consumers borrow that actually appreciate over time (e.g., real estate) or that retain their usefulness long after the debt is repaid (cars), buying most goods with borrowed money is unwise. Naturally when people borrow hopelessly beyond their means, lenders take on high-risk borrowers, or national or international calamity occurs, people turn to the government for help. This was clearly the case in the 1980s. As Medoff and Harless (1996, 7) point out, government debt began to grow at a faster rate than the economy during the 1980s when heavily indebted Americans demanded tax relief that drove the government deeply into debt.

Government Intervention

The U.S. government played a prominent role in managing the economy, in spite of our seminal faith that the classical liberal market will regulate itself. Government has also stepped in on behalf of consumers and competitors through policies like consumer protection and antitrust. In the process, it's also been a prime catalyst for the development of consumer culture.

It's impossible to catalog all the federal organizations and programs that have been put in place over the history of the country. However, in ways great and small, the government has fostered consumer culture by the creation of everything from Rural Free Delivery to a tax structure that rewards people and things that promote economic growth, to underwriting of banks through federal deposit insurance. Obviously, the same is true at the state and local levels as well. Without compulsory education and public schools, the literacy required for a consumer culture wouldn't have been achieved. College loan and mortgage programs at various levels support the pursuit of the American Dream.

The role played by the government at all levels is highly controversial as advocates and opponents of government intervention battle constantly. Regardless of what the prevailing attitudes toward government may be, its programs and policies reveal a long history of promoting consumer culture.

Sociodemographic Issues and Trends

Again, the sheer scope of social and cultural shifts that contributed to consumer culture defies a complete accounting here. Nevertheless, fundamental trends such as population growth through improved health care and longer life expectancy, along with increased immigration, were absolutely essential to the development of consumer culture. Quite simply, consumer culture can't exist without consumers. Beyond that, the trend toward urbanization that began as Americans left agrarian life fueled cultural change as factories took on needed labor. American society of the 1920s and 1930s is described as follows: "Cities were mushrooming in size, mass production spewed forth a new profusion of goods, and the Depression revealed how disturbances in the complex network of social and economic relationships could reverberate in every corner of the society, calling traditional assumptions and values into question. During both prosperity and depression, a society of more people (now more densely clustered) and more things (now available in bewildering varieties) require participation in a new intricacy of economic transactions and social interactions" (Marchand 1985, 335).

The ensuing decades were equally fraught with significant changes. Although birth rates in the United States during the Depression and throughout the war declined, the Baby Boom that occurred between 1946 and 1964 resulted in the largest population in U.S. history. At the same time, growing affluence resulted from international trade and a growing national economy. According to Fidler, "Rising incomes and government assistance programs made it possible for vast numbers of people to buy new homes, appliances, and cars, to get a college education and to have children" (Fidler 1997, 110).

In addition to acknowledging the impact of the United States as a world superpower and the enormous population growth due to the Baby Boom, Fidler also recognizes "the rapid diffusion of television and other electronic media throughout all social and economic strata of society" (Fidler 1997, 109). For baby boomers, television was a powerful mainstream leveler that cut across social and economic groups. As Fidler states, "the TV set became their paci-fier, their baby-sitter, their teacher, and their companion . . . TV brought the homogenizing images that defined this generations' sense of reality and itself (Fidler 1997, 110). For subsequent generations, however, newer media allowed them to ignore mainstream media and connect and interact with mixed media environments to create their own reality (Fidler 1997, 112).

Instrumental in all this are the changes that took place in the American family over the last several decades. As economic growth slowed, the number of two-income households rose dramatically. The traditional American model in which the husband works outside the home to support his wife and children had become the exception instead of the rule: Forty-one percent of families fit this description in 1969 compared to only 20 percent in 1993 (Medoff and Harless, 1996, 122). The percentage of women working outside the home doubled between the 1950s and the 1990s (Putnam 2000, 194). According to Putnam, "The movement of women out of the home into the paid labor force is the most portentous social change of the last half century" (Putnam 2000, 194).

The impetus for this shift is economic. It's become increasingly difficult to support a family on one income, particularly in a consumer culture where goods once considered luxuries are now considered necessities, and ads pro-moting these goods permeate all forms of society. Along with financial stress comes emotional stress leading to an increase in the divorce rate (Medoff and Harless 1996, 122). The overall trend toward increasing numbers of single parents raising kids contributed to a concomitant change in the way children experience childhood. Children from single-parent families inevitably take on more adult responsibilities and "wield more power in family decision making" (Schor 2004, 15–16). At the same time, kids' exposure to adult media through technology and marketers' efforts to sell directly to children not only contribute to their growing up faster but to their becoming consumers at a much younger age (Schor 2004, 16).

Until the last few decades, marketers targeted kids through their parents—a strategy called the "gatekeeper model." Today marketers not only target kids directly, they attempt to get them to "join forces to convince adults to spend money" (Schor 2004, 15–16). Perhaps as a result, children's expenditures have risen from $6.1 billion for kids aged four to twelve in 1989 to $30 billion in 2002 (Schor 2004, 23). Kids also begin shopping at an earlier age. Twenty-five percent of kids enter stores alone before they even begin elementary school (Schor 2004, 23). Overall, American consumer culture is training children to consume through more focused marketing and advertising techniques aimed at them at a younger age. And it is clearly succeeding.

At the same time, the number of both single-parent and single-person households has increased for several reasons—higher divorce rates, larger numbers of children born to two-income households, the decline in the number of people who are married, and the increased number of widows who live alone (Putnam 2000, 277). The net result of this is that the number of persons per household has decreased.

Technological innovation and social trends potentiated the development of consumer culture. The profoundly American value placed on individualism, in conjunction with the proliferation of increasingly specialized telecommunication media capable of delivering highly sophisticated forms of advertising, have become hallmarks of modern consumer culture. As Putnam points out, increasingly individualized media content and the increasing ability to consume it privately have changed our social behaviors dramatically (Putnam 2000, 217). Americans have achieved the seemingly contradictory states of isolation and interconnectedness simultaneously. Many authors argue that this has been accomplished at the great expense of necessary social interaction (Putnam 2000) or the social wellbeing of American children (Schor 2004). The consequences of modern consumer culture are open to debate, but the foundation for consumer culture and the trends and events that nurtured it are evident over several centuries. It's clear that a confluence of technological, economic, marketing, and social trends have led to a consumer culture of world renown.

➤ 3 ◀

Perspectives for Understanding
Advertising

Thus far we have concluded that the United States is grounded in such powerful ideas as classical liberalism and individualism, which laid the foundation for the evolution from an agrarian economy to a consumer culture. In this chapter, we ponder the role of advertising in this transformation. How does advertising teach individuals to consume? How does the institution of advertising transform citizens into consumers?

Studies of the effects of advertising fill thousands of pages of books and scholarly journals. Many of these are intended to determine the impact of advertisements on consumer attitudes and behavior. Still others focus more broadly on the effects of advertising on society in a variety of ways. Though studies of all kinds involving advertising are relevant in a book about advertising and consumer culture, the focus here will be on the interaction of advertising and consumer culture. To this end, we'll focus on models and theories for understanding the relationship between advertising and consumer culture.

Compared to many other institutions and academic disciplines, advertising is quite young. Perhaps as a result of its relative youth, one would be hardpressed to identify a "unified field theory" of advertising that cogently explains either how it functions as an institution or the science of how it works. Given advertising's youth and highly interdisciplinary nature, positing a single theory seems both unlikely and unwise. Moreover, advertising is only one aspect of consumer culture (albeit a very visible one), so the prospects for identifying a unifying theory or set of theories to explain advertising and consumer culture seem especially dim.

This is not to say, however, that there aren't enough theories being bandied about. In fact, there are so many potentially relevant theories, and from so many related (and seemingly unrelated) disciplines, that it is difficult to consider them all. There is a lot to be learned about advertising from cognitive psychology, cultural anthropology, economics, social psychology, and many other fields of study. Advertising is an inherently interdisciplinary field after all.

Some of the theories specifically involving advertising and/or consumer culture aren't germane here and, consequently, won't be addressed. For instance, within the marketing and advertising literature, numerous theories have been posited about the effectiveness of particular message, media, and research strategies. Theories about effective message frequency that are intended to guide media schedules are extremely important to strategic advertising planning but don't necessarily explain the institutional effects of advertising. Similarly, within the study of economics and marketing, theories exist about the cultural dynamics of consumer spending and saving. These, too, however, focus too narrowly on specific components of consumer culture.

The focus here, instead, is on an institutional view of advertising within consumer culture. As mentioned in Chapter 1, advertise*ments* are of less interest here than advertis*ing*. So theories purported to explain how advertising works for a certain product or in a particular medium are less relevant to this discussion than macro-level theories.

Even after drawing this distinction, however, the number and variety of theories one can apply to the study of advertising and consumer culture defies thorough inventory. Part of the problem is that advertising theories tend to be subsumed by communication and media theories and those, in turn, can't always be distinguished from social theories. As McQuail (2000, 5) points out, "It is hard to draw any clear line between theory of media and theory of society." Certainly, theories about human information-processing, risk behavior, and social interaction could be used to explain certain advertising phenomena. Likewise, economic theories about market structure and pricing might also be relevant.

Within the confines of mass communication theory, a whole host of theories might usefully be applied to the relationship between advertising and society. These range from the rather narrow mechanistic models that often deal with technology to the very broad culturalist approaches that focus on social phenomena (McQuail 2000, 7). At the same time, the methods typically employed with one approach or another also vary. The most common distinction is made between the scientific or positivist and the humanistic paradigms. A third class of approaches, called social-scientific has, according to Littlejohn and Foss, elements of the other two but is also different. Different paradigms lead to the application of different kinds of data and methods of analysis, ranging from quantitative data that are evaluated empirically to qualitative data that are explained through interpretation (Littlejohn and Foss 2008, 8).

The point is that no one paradigm, theory, method, or kind of data is appropriate in every instance. Whether through induction or deduction, the research phenomenon to be studied should ideally dictate which approach is best. Moreover, studying a phenomenon from multiple perspectives is usually the best way to derive the richest understanding. In other words, if something is worth studying, it's worth studying from more than one perspective.

All theories are based on concepts that have been consensually defined (Reynolds 1971). Given the highly abstract nature of social-science theory, it seems especially important to start by defining terms. We begin with a definition of consumer culture. A definition of advertising is then proposed. Finally, several theories are proposed that offer insight into how advertising as an institution has contributed to the development of postmodern consumer culture.

Consumer Culture

As defined in Chapter 2, consumer culture is characterized by three distinguishing characteristics. While not exhaustive, this list at least captures the more obvious hallmarks of consumer culture:

1. There is typically a potential surplus of goods in post-industrial economies.
2. Continuous consumption is critical to society and the individual; commerce and culture are inseparable.
3. Objects take on significance beyond their original purpose, and all things are commodified.

The ephemeral nature of "consumer culture" brings to mind Supreme Court Justice Potter Stewart's comment about obscenity—though he couldn't define it, he knew it when he saw it (Nelson, Teeter, and Le Duc 1989, 329). The expression "consumer society" is also commonly used and, for now, it will be used interchangeably with consumer culture. Technically, however, culture (e.g., learned behavior, or the collective programming of the mind; Hofstede 1984, 21) could be assumed to be a part of society that would include a broader range of characteristics of a given group of people.

As mentioned in the preceding chapter, a surplus of goods is a prerequisite for consumer culture. So before a consumption-intensive society can develop, mass production and distribution will have resulted in an amount of goods that exceeds demand. Unlike preindustrial societies where consumers produce the goods they need for themselves as they are needed, demand for postindustrial goods is stimulated because of the surplus of goods produced.

Michael Kammen (1999) argues that the transition to consumer culture was not immediate, direct, or seamless. He refers to consumer culture as the point at which "commerce and culture could no longer be tidily compartmentalized," and most scholars agree that "the flowering of consumer culture dates from the 1920s" (Kammen 1999, 53).

Consumer society, according to Sut Jhally (1990, 196), exists when "consumption is the mode of living of modern culture." Based on the relationship between people and things, it constitutes the third stage and follows traditional preindustrial and industrial society. According to Jhally,

> Consumer society resolves the tensions and contradictions of industrial society: the marketplace and consumption take over the functions of traditional culture. Into the void left by the transition from traditional to industrial society come the "discourse through and about objects" and the reconstitution of the population not into social classes as the primary mode of identification but into consumption classes. (1990, 196)

Describing the work of Baudrillard (1981) and others in analyzing "advanced capitalism," Jhally explains how objects change in a consumer culture. "Objects," states Jhally, "lose any real connection with the basis of their practical utility and instead come to be the material correlate (the signifier) of an increasing number of constantly changing, abstract qualities" (1990, 11).

The expression "conspicuous consumption" is often invoked to describe the nature of consumer culture. Coined by Thorstein Veblen in 1899, Veblen's prophetic description of life among the leisure class offers an accurate (if quaint) characterization of modern consumer culture: "Conspicuous consumption of valuable goods is a means of reputability to the gentleman of leisure" (Veblen 1932, 75). As goods take on complex meanings that are often independent of their purpose, the importance of acquiring them increases dramatically. Within consumer culture, one might say, "I consume, therefore I live." Vanderbilt argues the point by saying:

> The consumption of goods is now so closely linked to identity that a new form of social analysis has emerged in which classes are defined not by property or profession or even income but by what products they purchase. (1997, 141).

At the same time, consuming is considered part of our civic duty. Calvin Coolidge said, "The business of America is business." So if you want to strike a blow for America, buy things. More specifically, buy American things. John Dewey further commented in 1930 that "the need to buy had become as much an American 'duty' as saving had once been." Moreover, Kammen observes, the Depression underscored the importance of American consumption of U.S. goods for restoring the country's "productive capacity" (Kammen 1999, 55).

In consumer culture, consumption is thus critical to our physical and psychological comfort and to the success of our economy. Given this combined personal and civic incentive for consuming, there is strong pressure for us to consume everything. One way this is expressed is in a tendency to commodify things—even nonmaterial things. Whether it's drinking water, the state of Tennessee, or feminine beauty, everything can be objectified and consumed. The history of cosmetic surgery is a classic illustration of how female beauty was objectified and made available for sale (Haiken 1997). Taken to an extreme, this trend toward commodification can be manifest in the objectification of the self wherein we see ourselves as exchange commodities (Pollay 1986, 25).

Advertising

In comparison to defining consumer culture, defining advertising might seem simple. However, given its complexity, constant state of evolution, and significance to our culture and economy, a simple yet exhaustive definition of advertising is difficult to find. Nevertheless, the glossary of any introductory advertising text is likely to include something like: paid, nonpersonal communication through various media from business firms, nonprofit organizations, and individuals who are in some way identified in the advertising message and who hope to inform or persuade members of a particular audience (Krugman et al. 1994, 599).

This is based on the American Marketing Association's 1948 definition, and it is the one most often used. It has been useful because it distinguishes similar forms of communication from advertising. In other words, it makes clear what advertising isn't. That it is paid for distinguishes it from publicity such as a press release, which is believed to be newsworthy. Similarly, an advertiser is identified in an ad whereas that usually isn't the case in publicity.

Nonpersonal communication rules out personal selling. The emphasis on placement in media distinguishes advertising from sales promotion and personal selling. A particular audience is identified for an ad which specifically is targeted to that audience.This is not always the case with other forms of communication.

In essence, advertisers control the placement and timing of their messages. In most media, the advertiser can decide (as long as he or she is willing to pay for it) whether the ad will appear on a back cover, in the sports section, during the nightly news broadcast, or above a busy intersection. Regardless of whether the information or persuasion used is implied or explicit, the advertiser controls what is said and shown in his ad. Though mistakes can happen, advertisers don't have to wonder how the ad will look or sound—it won't be printed or aired until they're satisfied with it.

However, the degree of control exercised by an advertiser over the timing and context for the ad is one way in which advertising is changing dramatically. Starting with the television remote control which allowed viewers to avoid or mute commercials, followed by the VCR which made it possible for viewers to view programming independently of when it was broadcast, and finally ending with digital recording devices which allow viewers to bypass ads altogether, audience members continue to gain greater control over advertising. This shifting locus of control is most fully manifested on the Internet. Here advertisers can certainly choose what to put up on their own Web sites and on whose sites to place banner ads, but the consumer chooses whether to look at them at all and the time and location for doing so. As our media continue to converge, so that we tend to use multiple media through a single format (e.g., listening to the radio on the Web), viewers' control will extend to other media as well. Not surprisingly, traditionally heavy expenditures on traditional media like TV and magazine have shrunk as advertisers strive to reach consumers through a wide variety of media via multichannel marketing strategies (Standard & Poor's 2007).

Changes in the advertising industry are also evident in how advertising agencies service their clients. According to Standard & Poor's (2007) summary of advertising industry trends, "marketing services, excluding traditional advertising and media planning and buying, accounted for 54% of revenues in 2006." Instead of providing traditional advertising services, ad agencies are focusing on "higher-growth, nonadvertising businesses, such as market research, media planning, interactive media, and customer relationship management."

At the same time, the other distinctions between advertising and other forms of communication have become less pronounced. As advertisers strive to move seamlessly between the various elements of integrated marketing communication (IMC), it becomes more difficult to distinguish between advertising and event marketing or public relations.

When advertising slogans become part of our language (e.g., "Where's the beef," "Just do it") they appear to stop being advertising and start becoming a part of the culture. One way to look at advertising is as part of the culture. After all, if we're looking at advertising in a consumer society then, by definition, it can't be separated from culture (Kammen 1999, 53). According to Vanderbilt, the inextricability of advertising and everything else will only grow more pronounced as current trends in marketing continue: "As life becomes a 'perpetual marketing event' we will no longer be able to discern where advertising begins and where it ends" (1997, 142).

Traditionally, the purpose of advertising was different from the intent behind other promotional methods and from the purpose of editorial or program material. Jhally describes the goal of advertising as follows: "Advertisements have to move us in some way, make us think or react; they have to pull at our emotions, desires and dreams; they have to engage the audience actively in some thought process that will, advertisers hope, lead to the purchase of their product in the marketplace" (Jhally 1990, 106).

However, this, too, is changing. According to Vanderbilt, "'Aftermarketing' will attempt to make the purchase the first step in the advertised life, rather than the last, and other novelties, such as 'relationship billing,' will hit consumers with ads based on the kinds of purchases recorded on their credit card statements . . . In the new media, the goal of the marketing message is not the 'purchase,' but 'further interaction'" (Vanderbilt 1997, 142).

Rather than simply trying to generate sales, advertising is now also used to build a long-term relationship with a consumer, based on the integration of the advertised brand into the consumer's lifestyle. The purpose of the ad is to perpetuate this relationship. This is clearly evident in the shift by some advertising agencies to focusing on "customer relationship management" (CRM) which, according to Standard & Poor's Industry Trends (2007), has become industry giant Omnicom's fastest growing source of business and "entails event marketing; brand design; and direct, field, and promotional marketing."

One of the catalysts of the development of consumer culture at the beginning of the twentieth century, says Kammen, was the increase in "sophistication and impact" of advertising (1999, 51). Oddly, the same statement is likely to be made now at the beginning of the twenty-first century, though the dynamics have certainly changed. Of the multitudinous developments over the last 100 years, perhaps none has had greater impact on advertising than the introduction and spread of digital technology. Besides spawning the various digital media, digital collection and storage of information have allowed advertisers to know their audiences with a profound degree of intimacy.

As a result of these developments, the fundamental nature of advertising has changed. Based on the accumulation and analysis of consumer data, advertisers can now target consumers with a great deal more precision than was ever imaginable at the beginning of the twentieth century. It is this capability that enables advertisers to develop relationships with consumers. Frank and Weiland (1997) call the use of data to segment audiences the "new Leviathan." According to Vanderbilt:

> The new consumer society will no longer need the general advertisements broadcast from without at the entire populace; it will, rather, speak to consumers directly from within . . . novelties, such as 'relationship billing' will hit consumer with ads based on the kinds of purchases recorded on their credit card statements. As *American Demographics* put it, new media

consumers will 'be more tolerant of advertising because it will be more appropriate and customized.' In other words, advertising would cease to be perceived as an exogenous intrusion endured because it is believed to subsidize the cost of media. Instead it will be something sought out by consumers because of its relevance. (1997, 142)

According to Standard & Poor's Industry Trends, "The increasing availability of accurate consumer data via tracking and marketing research firms has enabled advertisers to better target their audiences. It is now possible to microtarget select segments of the population in the development of marketing campaigns, thus improving the effectiveness of those campaigns" (2007).

Given how advertising has changed and its increasing similarity to other communication forms, it's easy to see why advertising is regularly confused with other aspects of marketing and communication. However, what distinguishes advertising from other promotional tools may be a question of degree. To a much greater degree than other marketing elements, advertising has the following characteristics:

1. It is paid for.
2. The sponsor is identified.
3. It appears in a nonpersonal medium of some kind.
4. It is intended for a particular audience.
5. The advertiser attempts to control the content, placement, and timing of the message.
6. The purpose of the message may not only be to inform and persuade but also to cultivate a relationship with an audience.

This still leaves a lot of potential overlap between what we've defined as advertising and other elements of marketing and promotion. To a large degree, this is unavoidable. A caveat must therefore be added: Whenever advertising is alleged to be having an impact on consumers and/or culture, it must be determined (if possible) that advertising is truly responsible. Very often, overly broad generalizations are made about the effects of advertising that lump advertising and other aspects of marketing together. Just as it's easy to confuse advertising with the principles of classical liberalism that inspired it, it's easy to confuse advertising with other elements of marketing and promotion.

The line between advertising and content that is editorial or entertainment is no longer as clear as it once was. With the continuing evolution of promotional material from the infomercial through the advent of social media, it's increasingly difficult to discern the difference between what's intended to sell and what's not. Ad agency CEO Moses Foster commented, "There used to be two major types of content: publishers' (magazines, TV shows, radio programs) and the shorter forms of content that intermediated or bookended it (i.e., advertisements). . . . But now it's all converging. We the marketers are also becoming the news publishers, the film producers, the Hollywood writers. The content is becoming longer-form and organic. And it's being consumed as much for its ability to educate, inform and entertain as it is for its ability to sell" (Foster 2008, 20).

It's also easy to confuse the values implicit in advertising with those of the culture that surround it. This problem is manifest in the theoretical and empirical work on the effects of advertising. It's not uncommon to see "advertising" used interchangeably with several other terms such as "commercialism," "materialism," and "marketing." In all fairness, it's easy to understand how advertising could be mistaken for marketing, the mass media or the broader culture of which it is a part.

Mark Harmon encountered an analogous problem when he attempted to measure the effect of TV viewing on viewers' materialistic attitudes. His study failed to show a consistently strong link in a quantitative analysis of secondary data and speculated that materialistic values may "be too subtle to be observed via quantitative survey methods"—that "other variables such as culture, message and viewer age are likely to play key roles" (Harmon 2001, 416).

From an empirical perspective, it's very difficult to measure advertising exhaustively and exclusively. As Pollay (1986) and others have noted, broadening our research tools to include methods used by anthropologists, historians, and other social scientists is advisable.

An equally vexing problem involves causation. When examining the effects of advertising on society, the inevitable chicken-and-egg issue arises. Did advertising shape our economy, values, and behaviors into what they are today, or did society dictate the nature of advertising? For example, it is widely acknowledged that companies with relatively higher advertising budgets also usually charge higher prices (Abela and Farris 2001). For years, economists have asked whether advertising allowed these firms to charge higher prices. But one might also ask whether the financial power of companies selling brands with higher margins financed higher advertising budgets. The issue then becomes a matter of whose advertising we're talking about. Some would say it's not merely the advertising by enormous global brands but the resources of huge, international corporate owners that allow them to pay top dollar for premium placement in stores, which warrants investigation (Wolburg 2003). Whether advertising contributed to the growth of these companies and their brands in the first place then brings the question of causality full circle.

All that notwithstanding, a tentative theoretical framework for understanding advertising and consumer culture is necessary. Specifically, one set of models and various theoretical points of view will be presented: the ritual versus transmission models of communication (and advertising); symbolic interaction; cultivation theory; social learning theory/frame analysis; and a postmodernist view of consumer culture. These models and theories represent intellectual and ideological traditions. They are part of the scholarly literature of communication and are used to explain communication phenomena, though some may have first been introduced in other disciplines. As McQuail (2000, 9) remarks about the study of communication generally, the study of advertising is inherently interdisciplinary due to the "wide-ranging nature of the issues that arise, including matters of economics, law, politics, [and] ethics as well as culture."

Theoretical Perspectives

The Ritual versus Transmission Models of Communication

Communication theory has largely been governed by two very different approaches: the transmission and ritual perspectives. To say that the transmission approach has been the one most commonly employed is an understatement. Consistent with the scientific mindset since the early twentieth century, the transmission model takes a clinical, mechanistic view of communication in which communication is seen as the "transmission of signals or messages over distance for the purpose of control" (Carey 1989, 3). The parsimonious, quantifiable approach used in the sciences was applied to the study of communication, and in 1949 engineers Claude Shannon and Warren Weaver proposed a mathematical model using a sender who encodes information and transmits the message through a given channel for a receiver to decode (Tan 1985). The model also addressed various sources of distortion referred to as "noise," which threaten the accuracy of the transmission and reception of the message. Thus, our cultural infatuation with science and technology that developed throughout the twentieth century has permeated our understanding of communication theory and continues to do so.

The dominant paradigm in communication, based on the transmission view, is characterized by a linear, sequential model of the effects of communication. It is also associated with quantitative research and variable analysis (McQuail 1994, 45). A numerical measure of brand recall before and after a commercial is aired is an example of the kind of research typical of this paradigm. "In the transmissional perspective," according to Baran and Davis (1995, 284), "car commercials attempt to persuade us to buy a certain make of automobile." They are messages with a given purpose that are transmitted by a sender (advertiser) to a receiver (audience member) through a channel (the media). Volumes of transmission-view research, which are grounded in transmission-view theories, have concentrated on ways to improve the persuasiveness of advertising as a form of communication, which takes forms such as identifying factors that affect the persuasive impact, ways to enhance the encoding and decoding process, techniques to minimize interference from noise, and so forth.

The ritual approach, on the other hand, isn't just about sending messages "through space but the maintenance of society in time; not the act of imparting information but the representation of shared beliefs" (Carey 1989, 7). Thus, the ritual model looks beyond the message that is transmitted from point A to point B, how efficiently it was sent, and how persuasively it affects consumers. Older than the transmission view, the roots of a ritual approach to communication can be found in literary criticism wherein scholars believed that literature was the key to answering questions about cultural evolution (Baran and Davis 1995, 285). This is best articulated by James Carey who describes the ritual model by saying, "It does not see the original or highest manifestation of communication in the transmission of intelligent information but in the construction and maintenance of an ordered, meaningful cultural world which can serve as a control and container for human action" (Carey 1989, 7). In other words, the most important role of communication is not the exchange of information but the creation of culture. The theories and research that emerge from the ritual view can explore broad, fundamental questions such as how advertising has become an institution in society, how it constructs and maintains cultural values, and how it teaches citizens to become consumers. It can also focus on more specific questions, such as how advertising creates consumption rituals for various rites of passage (e.g., graduations, weddings, and anniversaries) and through the promotion of essential artifacts (e.g., the graduation robe and mortarboard; wedding rings; flowers, candy, or cards, etc.).

Carey further concluded that neither of these models denies what the other affirms. The ritual view does not deny that information is transmitted, nor does the transmission view deny that communication is ritual. The problem is that the transmission view has dominated American thought to such an extent that we have ignored the ritual aspects, and it is not possible to fully understand the communication process if we limit our thinking only to the transmission of information.

A ritual approach to understanding advertising might focus on how advertising messages shape and reinforce cultural values. According to the ritual view, a car commercial might shape or reinforce cultural values of independence, or cultural definitions of gender roles (Baran and Davis

1995, 284). In contrast to how the commercial would be viewed from a transmission perspective, the ritual approach to the commercial presumes two-directional interaction between the advertiser and the audience. Also called the "expressive" model of communication, the ritual view emphasizes shared understanding and communication that is not purely goal-directed (e.g., persuading consumers to buy goods) but rather is "an end in itself" (McQuail 1994, 51).

For example, the viewing of the Super Bowl is not only a ritual in itself, but it provides a way to understand advertising from a ritual perspective. Advertisers are willing to pay large amounts of money to reach such a large audience (e.g., $3 million for a 30-second ad on the 2009 Super Bowl), and over the years the Super Bowl has not only become a top draw as a sporting event but also as an advertising event, complete with various sources ranking the best and worst ads (Blackshaw 2009). For many audience members, viewing the ads is as important as viewing the game. Although the ads transmit information that may be of interest to viewers, equally important is the drama of watching the ads—the ritualistic participation in the experience with others, which includes not only the original viewing of the ads but the replaying of ads on YouTube, the ranking of ads, the discussion about ads with others the following day, and so forth. Even for those who watch the game alone rather than with friends or family, the event has become an annual celebration of advertising at its best—or worst.

Although the Super Bowl is perhaps the most obvious and memorable ritual celebration of advertising, ritual communication is part of all ads. Looking at ads is what we do in a capitalistic economy, whether or not we make a purchase or change our behavior as a result of the message. Consuming is a way of life in a capitalistic society, and our engagement in the advertising process has become a ritual in itself.

Given the value that the ritual perspective adds to our understanding of advertising, why then has the transmission view been so dominant? First, as noted previously, the transmission approach is entirely consistent with a postindustrial faith in science and technology. After all, if a positivistic approach worked for biology, chemistry, physics, and other disciplines, then why wouldn't it work for communication? Second, reliance upon clinical, linear scientific method implicit in the transmission view allowed complex patterns and relationships to be analyzed with relative parsimony. Defining cause and effect along with a measurement system *a priori* resulted in useful diagnostic assessments of mass communication. Third, it answers fundamental questions that are important to the efficient operation of the capitalistic system. Measurement of changes in a target audience's awareness, recall, and attitudes, for example, provides support for advertising budgets, which in turn affects profitability and provides justification for the economics of mass communication.

Adoption of the transmission view made sense historically, philosophically, and financially and for purposes of understanding narrowly defined effects of very specific institutional aspects of advertising. However, this view can be too limiting, for it privileges the information function of advertising over its social and cultural aspects. An institutional analysis necessitates consideration of the intended and unintended consequences of advertising as well as the impact of culture on advertising. The ritual approach is usually more appropriate for macroscopic analysis of this kind (Baran and Davis 1995, 285); thus, we now turn to various theoretical approaches that align themselves well with the ritual view of communication.

Symbolic Interaction

The ritual perspective is easily apparent in symbolic interaction. One of the first social-science theories devoted to how culture is learned and used, the ritual perspective was intended as an alternative to simplistic notions of stimulus and response. Symbolic interaction is the sociologist's view of how humans develop "knowledge of reality" (DeFleur and Ball-Rokeach 1989, 248).

George Herbert Meade fleshed out the theory, emphasizing the importance of symbols in human communication. In essence, "symbolic interaction posits that our actions in response to symbols are mediated (or controlled) largely by those same symbols" (Baran and Davis 1995, 89). Meade's ideas are summarized as follows:

1. Cultural symbols are learned through interaction and then they mediate that interaction.
2. The "overlap of shared meaning" by people in a culture means that individuals who learn a culture should be able to predict the behaviors of others in that culture.
3. Self-definition is social in nature; the self is defined largely through interaction with the environment.
4. The extent to which a person is committed to a social identity will determine the power of the identity to influence his or her behavior. (Baran and Davis 1995, 290)

According to this theory, in order to function in the world, we form impressions of others and ourselves based on symbols that guide our behavior, which were learned though interaction with others. Advertising is both part of the symbolic environment we are constantly striving to understand, as well as part of the symbols we use to guide our responses to our environment. Though "long-range and indirect," the power attributed to advertising (and the media in general) is significant because it helps us construct meaning (DeFleur and Ball-Rokeach 1989, 301).

For example, if we think of consumers' early exposure to ads for iPods prior to seeing the product in use, we can assume they would have formed an initial opinion based solely on the advertised image. Most likely, many consumers found the brand upbeat and hip while others were indifferent to it. Seeing the product in use, however, added another layer of meaning because consumers were able to see firsthand who owned an iPod, how and when people used it, and what type of identity it created for the users. The iPod also became an object of conversation, and if friends and family members happened to own one, still another layer of meaning was created because their opinion of the product would carry greater weight than that of strangers—either positive or negative. Now seeing the product advertised has a different meaning due to the interactions that have been created with others. The meaning is always in flux because each new advertising exposure and each new interaction with others adds meaning. Not only does the brand become a cultural symbol as a result of social interaction but it elicits a predictable behavioral response among those who share a similar meaning. In other words, once a group of people regard a branded product as something desirable or undesirable, not only for its functional value but for its ability to say something about the owner, it is possible to predict others' attitudes and behaviors toward it.

It is not difficult to think of other examples of brands of products that take on special meaning as a result of relationships and social interaction, even when the interaction is mediated through advertising rather than personal experience. A NASCAR enthusiast buys Tide detergent because Tide has sponsored various NASCAR Winston Cup teams, and using the brand allows him to identify with all things NASCAR—the car, the drivers, the teams, and indirectly other NASCAR fans. A college student supports a local, independent coffee shop because his friends all boycott Starbucks. Buying coffee from an independent shop allows him to demonstrate that he's one of them. A college professor who fears being perceived as technologically behind the times buys an iPhone because it allows him to project an image that he is technologically savvy, which in turn allows him to maintain credibility among colleagues. A couple from the Midwest buys a Chevrolet instead of an import because, like many other Midwesterners, they believe in staying loyal to Detroit in good economic times and bad. Furthermore, buying a Chevy ties them to a tradition set by their parents and grandparents.

Advertising's dependence on symbols is beyond doubt, not only for creating symbolic meaning for the advertised product but by using other symbols to establish its meaning within a certain lifestyle. Faced with the task of communicating a message to a disinterested audience within a very limited amount of time and space, advertisers rely heavily on a symbolic short-hand. Consumers know immediately when they see a stereotypical female homemaker that the advertiser is selling a household good. Typically, an advertiser will put forth the perfect image of a particular lifestyle, using all the right symbols, hoping that the viewer will aspire to that lifestyle and see the product as a necessary component. If the advertiser is successful, consumers will project themselves into the advertiser's image of an idealized life, regardless of the kind of lifestyle they actually lead. And, because the product is part of the picture, they will also buy the product.

Although products and services exist independently of the meaning that consumers ascribe to them, it is the interaction with advertising and others that shapes the way consumers interpret and define products. This is symbolic interaction at work.

Cultivation Theory

Although George Gerbner (1998) is most often associated with the development of cultivation theory, it could rightfully be considered a class of theories, as several derivatives have been described since Gerbner began writing about it in the 1960s. In fact, other researchers can be credited with writing about very similar theories even earlier (McQuail 1994, 111). In essence, mass media (including television specifically) are believed to influence audiences by the cultivation and acculturation of repeated exposures. Viewers are likely to adopt a "common worldview, common roles, and common values" as they consume relatively more television. Gerbner's research led him to conclude that heavy television viewers are more likely than light viewers to describe the world as it is portrayed on TV (Severin and Tankard 1992, 249). Television creates a potentially inaccurate reality that viewers internalize with repeated exposure to it (Baran and Davis 1995, 303).

Based on criticism of the theory, Gerbner modified it to include concepts of "mainstreaming" and "resonance." Mainstreaming occurs when heavy viewing leads to the formation of similar views by otherwise dissimilar groups. For example, both high- and low-income viewers may develop comparable attitudes about crime as a result of heavy viewing (Severin and Tankard 1992, 250). Resonance, on the other hand, is believed to occur when a group's characteristics cause the attitudes formed to be particularly strong as a result of heavy TV viewership. The relevance of the attitude to the group's characteristics makes the attitude resonate with members of the group. Women, for instance, might agree more strongly than men that crime is a serious problem simply because more crime is committed against women (Severin and Tankard 1992, 250).

Gerbner did not address the impact of heavy consumption of TV commercials separately from the impact of consumption of television programs, but the basic idea behind cultivation theory easily extends to advertising. Just as TV viewers of news have cultivated a certain expectation of crime and viewers of dramas, reality shows, and comedies have cultivated certain expectations of affluence among middle-class Americans, consumers of media may cultivate certain expectations based on ads. The use of product placements in television and film further extends the cultivation effect of traditional advertising, for depictions of product use by characters can offer a sense of realism that shapes the audience's view of life in new and different ways.

One macrolevel expectation from advertising, which cuts across multiple media, is that the way to solve life's problems is through consumption of products, whether it is to get rid of a nagging headache by taking pain medication, find convenient options for lunch by selecting from an array of microwaveable foods, celebrate an anniversary by buying the "right" gift, or get in shape by joining an exercise club or buying exercise equipment, which in turn requires the right wardrobe. Steady exposure to advertising potentially cultivates the belief that none of these challenges could be met without product consumption, when in fact it may be possible to use relaxation techniques to get rid of a headache, pack a lunch with natural foods, celebrate an anniversary simply by spending time together, and get in shape by walking or running. In addition to persuading consumers to consider the advertised solutions to problems, advertising has the power to define the problems in the first place. For example, advertising not only convinces consumers to buy certain products to stay attractive but defines what attractiveness is. No one exposed to advertising would argue that gray hair is more attractive than blonde or brown hair; that wrinkled, age-spotted skin is more attractive than young-looking skin; that women who wear a size 16 are more attractive than women who wear a size 6; or that "average-looking" men are more attractive than those who are young, lean, and muscular. Thus, advertising not only sets the standards of beauty but sells the products that help attain that standard.

Marshall McLuhan's notion that the "medium is the message" is also related to cultivation theory. McLuhan argued that television influences viewers' thinking processes and leads to alienation and individualism. McLuhan sees this not as the result of television content, as Gerbner proposed, but rather the sensory nature of the medium itself. It is the form of the medium, according to McLuhan, and not its content that influences viewers (Severin and Tankard 1992, 251). On a broader scale, McLuhan claimed that television would "retribalize" viewers as identities are shaped by the "systematic and widely shared messages of the mass media" (McQuail 1994, 111).

Like Gerbner, McLuhan did not directly apply his work to advertising; however, the basic ideas apply. From McLuhan's perspective the influence of advertising is indirect, but its form gives it greater impact than its content. As advertising simultaneously converges within media while it takes on increasingly diverse forms (in digital media, in the home, and in many other places), its "McLuhanesque" influence seems likely to increase.

Cultivation theory and its extensions involving media predict a different process than persuasion theories, which predict changes in attitudes after exposure to a particular message. Instead, cultivation theory predicts a more subtle but potentially more powerful process because consumers are unlikely to recognize its effects or to guard against this form of persuasion. Cultivation effects do not lend themselves to the analysis of a specific ad or ad campaign but rather the totality of advertising over time.

Social Learning Theory and Frame Analysis

There are a number of other theories that dovetail very nicely with the theoretical ideas described above. Agenda Setting suggests that the media do not necessarily persuade consumers to hold a particular view of an issue (or an opinion about an advertised brand), but coverage in the media tells consumers that the issue or product is something relevant to them. Likewise, the uses and gratification perspective (covered in Chapter 4) delves into ways that consumers use the media (and advertising).

Social learning theory, which originated in psychologists' studies of how people acquire behavior and form attitudes, is essentially based on the concepts of classical conditioning and reinforcement (DeFleur and Ball-Rokeach 1989, 212; Severin and Tankard 1992, 165). Since the starting point of learning is typically an event that can be observed, the media offer many opportunities for observation and modeling beyond what most people directly observe during their daily routines. Modeled behavior that is rewarded is reinforced, whereas behavior with negative consequences is likely to be discontinued. Social learning theory assumes that the media are primary socialization agents alongside family, peers, and teachers (Tan 1985). Programming and editorial content in the media as well as ads, particularly those that depict down-to-earth, "real-life" situations, present important opportunities for modeling.

Frame analysis was developed by Goffman (1974) to explain how people make sense of events. Frames provide a context for interpretation of reality so that seemingly neutral events take on a perspective. The fundamental notion underlying framing is that the media provide a point of view or frame for how an audience perceives social phenomena (Bennett 1993; Edelman 1993; Entman 1993; Iyengar 1987, 1991; Pan and Kosicki 1993; Price, Tewksbury, and Powers 1997; Snow and Bedford 1998, 1992; Tuchman 1978).

For example, a recent frame analysis of the Italian language version of *Men's Health* magazine concluded that the main frame for masculinity is "a body at risk," which must be protected "from illness, disease, and ultimately, death" (Boni 2002, 470). Articles use irony and lighthearted humor to deal with preventing illness, minimizing stress, recovering from workout injuries, as well as giving advice on developing weight-lifting routines, maintaining satisfying relationships with women, and eating well-balanced diets. The research also points out that 41 percent of the magazine's content is advertising, which include ads for fashion products such as clothes and accessories; body and beauty care products such as cologne, shaving products, creams, and hair-restoration treatments; workout equipment; and electronic devices such as cell phones and computers. The ads reflect the message strategy of the articles and reinforce the body-at-risk frame by telling readers "how men must present themselves, how men must take care of themselves, how they must live, what they must smell like, and what their physiques must look like" (2002, 474).

Since men are now a target market for beauty and body-care products that were traditionally sold to women, advertisers had to find a way to legitimize these products for men, which resulted in the use of stereotypical images of the male body. "Cologne and underwear ads, for example, display pictures of muscular male torsos and assertive faces with penetrating eyes staring out at the reader. Far from the androgynous, somehow subordinated male models that can be seen in many women's magazines, [the male models in] *Men's Health*'s ads display a wide set of 'powerful, armored, emotionally impenetrable' (Bordo 1999, 186) male bodies" (Boni 2002, 474).

It is possible to apply frame analysis to a single ad or to advertising in general. For example, an ad for José Cuervo Golden Margarita shows five young, attractive women laughing and drinking in a casual, outdoor setting with the headline, "Let's hear it for guy's night out." Seeing the image without the headline depicts the women as having a good time but without a particular purpose for being together. The headline frames the event as a celebratory night out for girls only in response to male counterparts spending time without them. Instead of feeling left behind (as some women in past generations have felt), these women are independent spirits who can have fun with or without men. Thus, the frame in the ad is one of celebrating gender equality—by consuming alcohol, of course. If we look at other ads for the brand, we see various other party settings with both men and women together having fun. Thus, the broader frame across a series of ads tells us that the product is a social lubricant that brings enjoyment and pleasure to any social event.

The ritual model and the various theories described above—symbolic interaction, cultivation, social learning, and framing—all imply the same basic notion: Advertising, as part of our culture and through symbolic means, presents a view of the world and a value system that are then reinforced repeatedly through a wide variety of media.

And, whether viewed as a consequence or as a cause of consumer culture, advertising is one of its defining characteristics. The messages and images in advertising not only reflect the culture but have the ability to shape it. By adopting a ritualistic view of advertising and applying the related theories, one can more clearly define its role in consumer culture. The role advertising plays is one where it is both a symptom and a prerequisite of advanced consumer culture. Frustrating as it may be to consider advertising on both sides of the equation, to do otherwise is inadequate and inaccurate.

However, this doesn't mean that advertising can't be more narrowly defined in very specific circumstances. One must recognize the difference between specific advertising messages directed to particular audiences and entire classes of messages that are disseminated to both intended and unintended audiences. As McQuail (2000, 10) points out, there are "different levels of social organization at which communication takes place." For example, there's justification for examining the effects of a single political candidate's messages on key community opinion leaders just as there's good reason for monitoring the social status of minority females implicit in a large number of women's magazine ads.

At the same time, there's a concomitant difference in the kind of methods necessary for studying phenomena at different levels of social organization. Whereas a quantitative measure of a particular message transmission might make sense in one study, a more qualitative look at shared meanings derived by consumers from multiple messages would be more appropriate in another. Just as there are a variety of theories required for describing a range of issues, there are different methods required for operationalizing them.

Under certain conditions, advertising can be categorized as either a cause or a consequence. For instance, at a given point in time in markets that have long been characterized by high concentration, advertising intensity may be seen more as a consequence of combative relations between competitors than as a direct cause of industry concentration. Taking an historical view of the same market, however, might instead make advertising appear to be a factor in the development of concentration.

Advertising in Transition

In all of the approaches we have examined thus far, we have made the basic, underlying assumption that advertising is aspirational. In other words, it creates an image that consumers can aspire to, usually by showing the brand as part of the good life that they desire.

In a recent study of how consumers use fashion magazine advertising, however, Phillips and McQuarrie (2009) found evidence that the assumption doesn't always hold. In fact, "nonaspirational" ads make up about one-third of ads in the current issue of *Vogue*, a trend that has approximately doubled in the last ten years.

Phillips and McQuarrie (2009) discovered five different consumption styles for interpreting fashion advertising, only one of which is clearly aspirational. Some participants in the study used a *cataloguing* style in which the women simply viewed ads to determine which products they want to buy. This group had no preference between aspirational and nonaspirational ads because their goal was merely to determine whether or not to buy the advertised product. On the other hand, some participants used an *idealizing* style. Women in this category best fit the traditional aspirational concept of advertising because they viewed the ad images as ideals to be emulated. Consumers not only attended to the product itself but the characteristics of the models and the attractiveness of the setting in order to know how to achieve an ideal self.

Women who used an *imagining* style used fashion ad images as story cues, and the more complex the images the better because they offer greater opportunities for imagination. Nonaspirational ads suited them better because they provided more cues for telling the story. Similarly, women who used the *sensing* style focus on the aesthetic qualities of the images and generally look for "creative, innovative, and evocative pictures." They also preferred nonaspirational images because they viewed ads as a form of art. Finally, some women used a *feeling* style in order to regulate their moods. As long as ads evoked an emotional response—whether positive or negative—they could relate to either aspirational or nonaspirational ads (Phillips and McQuarrie 2009).

Dolce and Gabbana are among the fashion advertisers who often break from the traditional aspirational formula, for they often place models in ambiguous settings and have even depicted scenes that suggest rape or other forms of violence. In March 2007, for example, the company withdrew an ad based on criticism of condoning violence against women which showed a bare-chested man pinning a woman by her wrists while three other men looked on (Vranica 2007).

Nicholson (1997) also observed a nonaspirational advertising technique in the early 1990s with certain ads that targeted Generation X, a group considered "jaded" toward traditional ads. Advertising creatives used a strategy called "the wink," that acknowledged how much more savvy the target market was than consumers of previous generations (1997, 183). Ads also created enough visual ambiguity that consumers were forced to work at figuring out what brand was being sold and what the intended message was, which created an insider status among those who "got it." Finally, ads expressed a point of view in opposition to the status quo so that purchasing the product was symbolically an act of resistance. Ads still encouraged product purchase; however, they did so without using aspirational techniques.

A recent automotive ad in the German language edition of *GQ* (April 2009) is an example of nonaspirational advertising (Figure 3.1). It promotes the limited edition Fiat 500 by Diesel with the image of the auto positioned in the center. But what draws the reader's attention is a man dressed in a black suit sitting on the floor of the garage looking intently at what appears to be broken glass and spilled milk. The woman in the driver's seat also looks at the milk, which may jar the reader's memory of the expression, "Don't cry over spilled milk." Yet, the reader may not know it's relevant.

The reader may also notice two types of gasoline at the pumps, BioDiesel and Diesel, and may wonder whether Diesel is the fuel or the clothing brand. Given the word Diesel in the upper right corner and in the Web site at the bottom right corner (www.500bydiesel.de), savvy readers will conclude that it is the brand. The headline at the top says, "In Odd We Trust," which is a play on the words "In God We Trust," but it is also the title of a book, *In Odd We Trust* by Dean Koontz. Readers curious enough to visit the "500bydiesel" Web site will see the automotive details of the Fiat 500, complete with interior upholstery by Diesel and wheel covers that say "Diesel—Only the Brave." Though the advertiser likely has certain preferred meanings for consumers—ones that enhance the auto and the Diesel brand in some manner—the ambiguity of the ad is likely to draw different interpretations from consumers. In fact, one can argue that there is no single "correct" interpretation.

Next we turn to a perspective that may shed some light on nonaspirational ad campaigns such as these, which thrive on ambiguity.

Postmodernism

The characteristics of consumer culture and nonaspirational advertising look very much like those attributed to what's been called postmodern society. Popular across a variety of academic disciplines, postmodernism has been discussed for years in reference to a variety of cultural forms such as art and literature (Firat and Shultz 1997). Mike Featherstone (1991, 1) describes the term "postmodernism"

Figure 3.1 **Example of Nonaspirational Advertising**

as one that is "at once fashionable yet irritatingly elusive to define." However, as the word itself suggests, it refers to a period that comes after "modernity." At the start of the twenty-first century, this now references the shift from a capitalist-industrial society to a postindustrial age (Featherstone, 3).

On the other hand, Littlejohn and Foss (2008) identify postmodernism as a branch within critical theory. "Postmodernism is based on the idea that social realities are constantly produced, reproduced, and changed through the use of language and other symbolic forms" (2008, 337). So postmodernism can refer to both a period of time—the postindustrial age—and a perspective for understanding human communication at a particular point in time.

Also implicit in the expression is a shift of epochal proportions in which "new forms of technology and information become central to the shift from a productive to reproductive social order" and where "simulations and models increasingly constitute the world so that the distinction between the real and appearance becomes erased" (Featherstone 1991, 3). Also associated with postmodernism is "a shift of emphasis from content to form or style; a transformation of reality into images; the fragmentation of time into a series of perpetual presents" (Sarup 1993, 132). Moreover, as Sarup describes the ideas of Jean-François Lyotard who advanced the ideas of postmodernism, "we can no longer talk about a totalizing idea of reason for there is no reason, only reasons."

Although postmodernism originated in the 1960s within the New York art community, the range of disciplines in which the expression has been applied is vast: music, art, fiction, film, drama, photography, architecture, literary theory and criticism, philosophy, anthropology, sociology, and geography (Featherstone 1991, 2; Sarup 1993, 131). According to Featherstone,

> Postmodernism is of interest to a wide range of artistic practices and social science and humanities disciplines because it directs our attention to changes taking place in contemporary culture. These can be understood in terms of: 1) the artistic, intellectual, and academic fields (changes in modes of theorization, presentation, and dissemination of work which cannot be detached from changes in specific competitive struggles occurring in particular fields); 2) changes in the broader cultural sphere involving the modes of production, consumption, and circulation of symbolic goods which can be related to broader shifts in the balance of power and interdependencies between groups and class fractions on both inter-and intrasocietal levels; 3) changes in the everyday practices and experiences of different groups, who as a result of some of the processes referred to above, may be using regimes of signification in different ways and developing new means of orientation and identity structures. (Featherstone 1991, 11)

In terms of communication and consumer culture, the second and third applications described above are the most relevant. Although not explicit, communication can be considered inherent in the cultural processes described.

In fact, as McQuail observes, "postmodernism is very much the theory of or for the 'information society" (McQuail 1994, 27). Pointing to changes in communication technology as a concurrent and potentially causal element in the shift to the postindustrial age, McQuail (59) considers the concept of postmodernism the best for making sense of the cultural shift we're experiencing. Or, as Fredric Jameson said, postmodernism is "the cultural logic of late capitalism" (McQuail 59). And advertising could be called the language of postmodernism. Josephson writes, "If we want to discover what postmodern culture is really going to be like, we should look at advertising, the Design Arts, and Popular Art. Here we will find the contemporary powers of art. It is through these arts in the mass media and mass market that our contemporary reality is being shaped" (Josephson 1996, 79).

Postmodern society can be characterized by several trends. First, there is no one unifying definition of reality. As Sarup (1993, 132) describes Lyotard's argument, "there is no reason, only reasons." Rejecting totality, "Lyotard and other postmodernists stress fragmentation—of language games, of time, of the human subject, of society itself" (147). At the same time, what's real and what's simulation becomes indistinguishable. Or, as Jean Baudrillard theorized, simulacra (the reproductions of events and objects) come to "dominate social life" until we live in a world governed by coded replications (Kellner 1989, 78). As a result, or perhaps as a catalyst, nothing is ever new. We are limited to what Jameson calls "pastiche" wherein we continually imitate what's already been done (Sarup, 1993, 146).

This, in turn, leads us to a "schizophrenic" view of time made up of continually fragmented presents (Sarup 132, 146). "As a society, we have become incapable of dealing with time" (146).

In the arts, postmodernism is associated with the breakdown of several boundaries, including those between elite and popular culture and between form and content (Sarup 1993, 132). In a postmodern world, style takes precedence over substance. Communication, the media, and advertising (all enhanced by the rapid diffusion of digital technology) provide an ever-present forum in which these boundaries can be tested.

To oversimplify the work of Baudrillard, postmodern society, at its most advanced stage, is one in which consumers become so enmeshed in simulations that they can't recall what original objects or events were like. And gradually, this kind of society turns everything into a simulation. Along the same line, Boutlis (2000) argues that people do not buy certain product attributes when they choose a brand. Instead, it's the brand itself that they seek. According to Boutlis, "A brand does not signify the intrinsic 'quality' of a product: the brand itself is the quality" (2000, 17). The notion here is very similar to one raised under the discussion of symbolic interaction and the ritual view of communication: We don't simply buy products, we buy into a lifestyle that products represent.

Postmodernism can be seen as a theoretical nexus where the theories presented earlier in this chapter intersect. The emphasis on multiple realities and rejection of mechanistic, transmission-based assumptions about senders and receivers is certainly consistent with a ritual view of communication and culture. Postmodernism is based, like symbolic interaction, on the creation and consumption of symbols. Like cultivation theory, it suggests the importance of a progressive (or perhaps regressive) and highly imitative process.

The parallels between consumer culture and postmodernism are striking. Perhaps most importantly, however, both consumer culture and postmodernism are based on conditions of surplus. Consumer culture grows out of the surplus production of goods, whereas postmodernism seems to evolve with the proliferation of simulations. In essence, postmodernism could actually be considered an advanced stage of consumer culture. And advertising (and marketing) are inextricably linked to the postmodern world. Advertising's link to the postmodern world will continue to emphasize form or style over content—the lack of a single "correct" interpretation—and other hallmarks of the postmodern world, just as we have seen in the Diesel ad in Figure 3.1.

Brown (2006, 212) describes the relationships among marketing, consumer culture, and postmodernism by saying, "the fields which have most fully embraced postmodern modes of thought regard marketing as one of the distinguishing characteristics of the postmodern condition. Consumer society and postmodern society are considered synonymous."

Concluding Thoughts

The bottom line is this: Advertising is an integral part of advanced consumer culture where it can be both a cause and an effect. From an institutional perspective, advertising should be seen as both a consequence and a catalyst of postmodern consumer culture. Although this hardly constitutes a "unified field theory," the combination of models and theories mentioned here offers a nonexhaustive, broad analytical framework on which to base examination of a whole range of issues involving advertising.

Albert Einstein sought an elusive unified field theory for physics, which would tie together all physical theories into a single model of how the universe operated. Similarly, in psychology there is a wealth of theories, each offering different perspectives and techniques that have yet to be brought together into a single unified explanation. When it comes to the study of advertising, there is no shortage of theories, but no one overarching meta theory that explains everything.

What links the theories discussed here is the basic notion that consumers are inculcated with the fundamentals of consumer culture by their institutions. Among these institutions is advertising. Bowles aptly points out: "Markets and other economic institutions do more than allocate goods and services: they also influence the evolution of values, tastes, and personalities. Economists have long assumed otherwise; the axiom of exogenous preferences is as old as liberal political philosophy itself (1998, 75).

At the same time, consumers reciprocate by influencing institutions. As advertisers strive to understand consumers' preferences and tastes, they help shape the nature of advertising. With the emphasis on relationships in marketing, there is at least theoretically some give and take between parties. Institutions are thus shaped by endogenous and exogenous influences. As Norris said, "we do not use institutions, we participate in them" (1980, 6). And this characteristic is one of the distinguishing qualities of classical liberalism and consumer culture.

➤ 4 ◄

The Behind-the-Scenes
Power of Advertising

In Chapter 3, we pondered the role of advertising and its ability to transform citizens to consumers. Specifically, we examined various theories that explain how advertising works within the consumer culture. Even though we considered advertis*ing* more than individual advertise*ments*, we still envisioned advertising as something we can all readily identify: controlled, paid-for messages that identify a sponsor, appear in the mass media for a particular audience, and have a persuasive intent—whether to inform, move consumers to make a purchase, or cultivate a relationship with the audience. Although this view accurately reflects advertising as we know it, advertising has a far less visible side that we must understand as well.

To understand its power, it's important to look at the hidden relationships driven by the advertising industry and consider the competing interests of the main players within the media: consumers, advertisers, and media companies. This chapter examines those relationships and considers what they mean for the modern-day consumer within a classical liberal model.

Competing Interests

The Audience Perspective

Consumers not only learn to recognize ads at a young age but they learn to expect promotional messages to intrude upon them when using media—particularly while watching television, listening to radio, reading magazines, and so forth. In fact, finding ways to avoid the intrusiveness of advertising has changed the way consumers use media and has redefined their relationship with advertisers. Using DVRs for TV viewing or downloading podcasts onto iPods allows consumers to personalize the media they use, and much of the appeal is the decreased exposure to advertising. However, what works for consumers can be very problematic for advertisers. Advertisers have lived with the reality that digital devices make ads "just a remote-control-button push from oblivion"

(Steinberg 2007, 16). However, in the constantly shifting media environment, video on demand and TiVo are developing new ways to show ads, which are interactive and resemble online ads more than traditional, 30-second commercials. For example, TiVo users who paused *The Biggest Loser* TV show saw a banner ad for Jenny Craig, and those who paused *Iron Chef America* on the Food Network saw an ad for Sub-Zero (Yao 2009, 3D).

With changes in new technology, consumers have carved out a different relationship with advertisers, who are struggling to adapt by using new forms of promotional messages, many of which blur the lines between editorial content and advertising. When consumers decide how, when, and where to seek out advertising, they believe they are in control. And when they make a purchase as a result of exposure to an advertising message they sought out on their own, they don't feel manipulated. Even when advertisers are able to intrude upon them, consumers don't believe that commercial messages hold much power over them, whether it's a single ad or advertising as a whole. Consumers also believe that advertising has a much greater effect on others than on themselves—a phenomenon called the third-person effect (Davison 1983). Although most consumers feel savvy about advertising and its effects, they may be unsuspecting of the more invisible, behind-the-scenes influences that advertising wields as an industry.

To make advertising's influence more visible, it's necessary to understand consumers' relationship to the media including traditional outlets such as television, radio, magazines, newspapers, and nontraditional media such as Internet, cell phones, and MP3 players. When asked what the media means to them, consumers typically say that it offers them information and entertainment. This response holds across multiple types of products—for instance, sporting events, TV news, videos on YouTube, advergames, and so forth. Blogs or social media sites such as Facebook allow ways for consumers to provide interactive content as well as receive content. Research shows that 100 million blogs are currently posted on the blog search engine Technorati, more than 100 million videos are viewed on YouTube per day, and Facebook has more than 123 million users (Mayfield 2008). Furthermore, nearly 70 percent of adults online use social media, particularly those in their 20s (Market Tools Insight Report 2008).

When consumers obtain media products including most books, DVDs, or CDs, they buy them in much the same way they would buy a pair of shoes or jeans—they shop online or go to a retail outlet and pay the price without advertiser support to lower the cost. In contrast, when they listen to broadcast television and radio programs, they pay nothing or almost nothing because advertisers pay large amounts of money for the privilege of reaching them. Other products depend upon a split source of revenue, such as the majority of magazines, which receive some support from advertisers and some from consumers. Most consumers don't think about variations in the cost of the media on the basis of advertiser support. They simply know which media products are free and which ones are not.

Consumers usually take for granted that they are entitled to free access to many media vehicles, especially news programs, because they provide information that is essential to the public interest. Consumers have also come to expect a certain amount of free entertainment, even though they may be willing to pay for additional options.

Consumers utilize media in a variety of ways, and the uses and gratifications approach to communication provides some further insights into their needs. McQuail, Blumler, and Brown (1972) originally proposed that the mass media provided four gratifications: diversion—the escape from routine and the emotional release that we associate with entertainment; socialization—the function of programs and performers to become very real in the lives of audience members; personal identity—the ability to expand consumers' identity by providing programs or articles on self-help topics; and surveillance—the function of providing information to consumers about what's happening in the world around them. Newer media such as the Internet serve many of the same needs reported in the past (Parker and Plank 2000) with the expanded ability to communicate interactively while reaching the masses (Stafford and Stafford 2001).

Though the uses and gratifications model helps us understand what consumers look for in the media and indirectly why the media companies provide certain types of content, the model looks only at two of the players—consumers and the media. The influence of the third player—advertisers—remains invisible; thus, we turn to the advertising perspective to fill in the gap.

The Advertising Perspective

If advertisers are asked about the role of the media, they are likely to answer that it delivers an audience to them. Advertisers need a way of communicating with target markets for products and services, and the media provide the most efficient and cost-effective way to satisfy that need. Advertisers have many options because most consumers can be reached through many different media (magazines versus Web sites) and through many different media vehicles (*Sports Illustrated* versus *Newsweek*). Advertisers can also choose nontraditional methods as varied as imprinting messages on sandy beaches and posting an ad in video form on YouTube rather than buying time on a television program. Once viewers became more comfortable watching videos online, YouTube no longer limited its offerings to videos under the ten-minute mark. It can offer full-length TV programs, complete with advertising before, during, and after each episode, which provides Google (YouTube's owner) with a significant source of revenue (Stelter 2008).

Certain audience members are more valuable to advertisers than others. Because the target market for most products favors a young, affluent audience, media choices that deliver those audiences are usually in greater demand than those that are popular with older, less affluent audiences. Also in high demand are media vehicles that provide the least wasted coverage by reaching only the intended audience—not those outside the target market. Much of the challenge for media planners is to match the target market to specific media vehicles on the basis of cost efficiencies and demographics, but finding a supportive platform for their messages is equally important. Advertisers want to place their messages in an environment that puts consumers in the optimal buying mood.

A recent concern is that advertisers are putting greater pressure on media to gain a higher return on their investment, including increasing references to the advertised products in the editorial content. Research companies such as Halls' Reports are hired to track the number of editorial credits (references to branded products), and the company counted several hundred thousand in twenty-six fashion/beauty magazines in 2007, an increase of 33 percent over the previous year with predictions for similar increases the following year (Moses 2008). Accordingly, the expectation for editorial credits is a long-standing practice among advertisers, but publishers are now finding that advertisers are threatening to withhold advertising pages if too few credits are given to their clients. One magazine consultant commented that advertisers "know who's holding the power" and are making bolder demands than in the past because publishers are desperate for ad revenue (Moses 2008).

One of the ironies of advertising is that with increases in the amount of time and space that the media devote to advertising, it becomes more difficult for any particular advertiser to be noticed, which creates an endless cycle of advertisers trying to increase their individual efforts. McChesney (2008) notes that when overexposed consumers develop immunities, the effectiveness of each individual ad declines. To cope, advertisers have placed even more commercial messages in the media, which has increased the ratio of advertising to program content over time, with radio advertising at 19 minutes per hour and television advertising at 17 minutes per hour (up from 9.5 minutes in 1982). The length of each ad is also shorter, meaning that consumers are seeing ads for more products in each available minute of advertising time.

McChesney (2008) refers to this heavy bombardment of advertising messages as "hyper-commercialism," which leaves both consumers and advertisers frustrated. Consumers cope by trying to avoid the messages, and advertisers see their messages becoming merely a form of "wallpaper" and have little recourse but to increase the sales effort. However, many advertisers have turned to alternative ways of reaching consumers using tactics such as product placements, especially within films and reality shows on television, because they reach consumers in ways that don't annoy them—at least not yet.

Product placements in film and television have a long history, but placements in other media are beginning to be more commonplace. For example, author Fay Weldon was paid to place Bulgari jewelry prominently in her book, *The Bulgari Connection* (Kirkpatrick 2001). Furthermore, payment of special fees for the use of licensed products has made placements in children's books widespread, especially using snack foods as the protagonists including Cheerios, Skittles, Reese's Pieces, Oreo cookies, and Sun-Maid raisins. *The Oreo Cookie Counting Book* teaches children to count using Oreo cookies, and *The Cheerios Play Book* contains pages with missing pieces for children to fill in using Cheerios glasses for mice and Cheerios bubbles for fish. The book sold 1.2 million copies in two years (McChesney 2008).

Competition for consumers' attention has challenged advertisers to find new and improved ways to reach consumers, such as Harley-Davidson's promotion of the V-Rod Muscle, a motorcycle aimed at a younger demographic than Harley's traditional customer base. The company launched an ad campaign featuring supermodel Marisa Miller, which not only appeared in magazines but included access to online content available only to those who took a photo of a print ad with a cell-phone camera and sent it to the Web site. The campaign includes various online features such as downloadable photos and wallpapers and has been linked to Harley's YouTube site (Barrett 2008). Advertising agencies and corporate marketing departments are also producing their own media, which are increasingly difficult to distinguish from traditional commercial media. An example is *Lucky* magazine, created by Newhouse's Condé Nast publishing house, in which traditional articles have been replaced with editorial copy linked to specific products (Carr 2002).

Although advertisers have been roundly criticized for their role in creating a hypercommercial culture, most are seemingly unperturbed by the censure. Since advertisers are accountable only for the return on investment for their client's brand, they are not accustomed to looking at the impact of advertising at a macro level or its impact on the media. For that reason, it's important to examine the third player in the triad.

The Media Perspective

If media companies are asked about the function of the media, the answer not only differs from those of consumers and advertisers but also from the business side to the editorial side. Employees on the business side are acutely aware of the need to make a profit, whereas those on the editorial side are more likely to emphasize the need to serve the public interest by informing or entertaining audience members. Those in the editorial group who work in news tend to see media companies as watchdogs of the government and servants of the community who fulfill a civic obligation. Journalists often see their work as a mission or sacred trust and take pleasure that their work is singled out for constitutional protection (Shaw 1999).

Satisfying both sides—drawing enough advertising support while providing content that maintains editorial integrity—requires a delicate balance within a media company. Unfortunately, most media companies are not independent entities capable of making their own decisions for finding that balance because they are part of a larger corporation. Understanding that piece of the puzzle requires a look at corporate ownership.

Corporate Ownership

Although media companies in many other countries in the world are government-owned, most media companies in the United States are for-profit businesses owned by large, publicly held conglomerates. Many started out as small independent companies but became larger and more concentrated throughout the twentieth century. By 2009, six powerful companies owned the major media companies in the world (Free Press 2009). Based on 2007 revenue figures provided to the Free Press in part by *Columbia Journalism Review*, these six are: General Electric ($173 billion), Time Warner ($46.5 billion), Walt Disney ($35.5 billion), News Corp. ($28.6 billion), CBS ($14.1 billion), and Viacom ($13.4 billion). The current trend is for marketers to link with large conglomerates for massive product placement/advertising/promotional deals across the media firm's assets (McChesney 2008). An example is a 2002 MasterCard partnership with Universal Studios in an agreement worth more than $100 million that made MasterCard an integral part of Universal theme parks, movies, home videos, and music (Friedman 2002).

Two outcomes of concentration are vertical and horizontal integration. Vertical integration occurs when one large company owns assets involved in the production, distribution, exhibition, and sale of a single type of media product (Croteau and Hoynes 2006). For example, when Disney produces a film through its production companies (Walt Disney Pictures, Touchstone Pictures, or Miramax Films), it can later control the distribution of the movie through its broadcast network (ABC) and its cable channels (A&E, Lifetime, ESPN, Disney Channel, Biography Channel, History Channel).

Horizontal integration occurs when a media corporation owns many different types of media products. For example, when Hollywood studios release movies, a number of other commercial products are generated including a soundtrack, a music video, publishing ventures such as books and calendars, an Internet site, TV specials on the "making of" the movie, T-shirts, fast-food chain promotional tie-ins, and more (Croteau and Hoynes 2006). On the surface, the control of these interests by a single corporation rather than independent companies doesn't appear to be detrimental to consumers, particularly if any cost efficiencies can be passed on to them. However, such great control puts creative limits on content. The decision to produce a movie is dependent not only upon the success of that one venture but the profitability of all the related products under the corporation's umbrella. Given the choice of producing a movie that is based on a critically acclaimed story but has limited promotional tie-ins versus one that has a weak plot but is well-suited to promotional tie-ins, the latter option will almost always prevail.

A look at General Electric's media and entertainment holdings from the NBC Universal Web site (www.nbcuni.com) offers some insights into the existing degree of horizontal and vertical integration and shows the variety of media content that one conglomerate owns and controls:

- Entertainment TV and Production: NBC, Telemundo, Bravo, Global Networks, MUN2TV, Sci Fi, Sleuth, USA, Universal HD, NBC Universal Television, Universal Production Studios
- Movies: Universal Pictures, Universal Studios DVD, Focus Features, Pay Per View/VOD, Kids
- News, Sports, and Information: NBC News, NBC Olympics, NBC Sports, Local Stations, CNBC, MSNBC
- Parks and Resorts: Universal Studios Hollywood, Universal Studios Orlando plus theme parts and hotels, Universal Studios Japan
- Shopping: NBC Stores, Universal Studios DVD, Theme Park Tickets, NBC Experience Store NY, NBC Studio Tour NY, Shop NBC, Kids.

General Electric's other business interests posted on its Web site for 2009 include aviation, enterprise solutions, healthcare, transportation, energy, oil and gas, water and process technologies, commercial lending and leasing, consumer finance, energy financial services, GE capital aviation services, global banking, healthcare financial services, real estate, appliances, consumer electronics, electrical distribution, and lighting.

If concentrated holdings were unique to one corporation, the problem could be contained. However, each of the other media conglomerates also has extensive holdings. Bagdikian (2000) argues that the commercial market power of conglomerates is exceeded only by the corporation's power to socialize new generations. For example,

> The problem is not that Disney is evil, unlovable though its internal politics may be. Most Disney media images, in fact, stress cuteness, gentleness, and adventure. Nor is it because there is no place in an affluent society of toys, games, films, media entertainment, and other Disney products. The problem is a system that permits a single corporation to have such overwhelming power, not just over the media marketplace but over youth culture in the United States and globally. That power is so concentrated, ubiquitous, and artful that, to a degree unmatched in former mixtures of entertainment, it dilutes influences from family, schooling, and other sources that are grounded in real-life experience, weakening their ability to guide growing generations (Bagdikian 2000, xx).

An ongoing concern among media critics is that the Federal Communications Commission continues to favor easing the restrictions on ownership. On June 2, 2003, the FCC voted to increase the number of TV stations that one corporation can own and to lift restrictions on cross-ownership of a TV station and newspaper in the same market (Finberg 2003). Final approval was not given until December 2007, but the decision was to relax the ban on newspaper/broadcast cross-ownership, which had been in effect for more than thirty years (FCC 2007). Cross-ownership can have far-reaching effects; it provides economies of scale for media companies, which make them more profitable but limits the number of voices within a media market and often results in employee layoffs.

Advertising Support of the Media

Like any other business, media companies must first serve the needs of the corporation and those of the shareholders. Consequently, it is more important for media companies to draw advertisers than to draw audience members, unless the company has another source of revenue that makes it less dependent upon advertising. No matter how entertaining a program is or how informative a news source is for audience members, it will not endure if it is not profitable, which explains why some TV programs with relatively small audiences are renewed for additional seasons. These programs reach a desirable demographic for advertisers, while more popular shows are cancelled because they reach the "wrong" viewers.

Similar constraints exist in the print media. A dated but well-documented case of reaching the wrong demographics involved the *New Yorker* magazine.

In 1966, the magazine was so successful that it sold more advertising pages than any general circulation magazine in the history of publishing (Bagdikian 2000). However, after the *New Yorker* took an editorial stance against the Vietnam War in 1967, the magazine began to attract a different audience than the wealthy business executives who had been its core readers. Over an eight-year period, the circulation remained the same at about 450,000 per month, but the demographics of the readers changed from a median age of 49 to a median age of 34. Normally, a young readership is coveted, but these readers were not buying the expensive, luxury items that the older group could afford. The magazine lost 2,500 pages of advertising in one year, down from the 6,100 pages sold the previous year, and profits shrank from $3 million to less than $1 million (Bagdikian 2000).

The standard cure for "bad demographics" is simply to change the content with material that will attract the kind of people that advertisers want, and failure to do that means firing the editor. The *New Yorker* eventually regained its former demographics without firing the editor, but it is very doubtful that any magazine today would have the luxury of waiting years to see an improvement in demographics.

The degree of influence that advertising exerts depends upon how large a revenue source it is for a particular medium. Revenue figures show that radio and broadcast television (with the exception of public broadcasting) have received nearly 100 percent of their revenue through advertising, whereas cable television has received roughly 30 percent from advertising and 70 percent from subscriber fees to cable systems (Lane and Russell 2001). In the last 20 years or more, magazines have increased their costs to subscribers and newsstand buyers to be less dependent upon advertising; however, they have continued to receive about 30 percent of revenue from advertising, down from 50 percent in the past. Newspapers traditionally received about 75 percent of revenue from advertising with only 25 percent from subscriptions and newsstand sales (Lane and Russell 2001); however, the diminishing circulation of newspapers and the subsequent loss of advertising support over the years have put the newspaper industry in peril. Across the industry, more than 500 newspapers in 2008 reported a 4.6 percent loss of weekday circulation and a 4.8 percent drop in Sunday circulation (Pérez-Peña 2009). To an extent, the rising traffic for newspaper Web sites offset some of the decline in circulation as well as the drop in ad revenue by producing a net increase in readership; however, this has not been significant enough for many newspapers. The number of magazine advertising pages fell across the board by 11.7 percent in 2008 and by even greater percentages in certain categories such as newsweeklies (e.g., *Time, U.S. News & World Report*, and *Newsweek*; Pérez-Peña 2009).

Ms. is a prime example of a magazine that couldn't generate enough advertising support and survived only by becoming ad-free through reader support (Steinem 1990). *Ms.* couldn't draw advertising of gender-neutral products (cars, credits cards, insurance) because the advertisers didn't believe that women were the primary target market, and the magazine couldn't draw advertising of women's products because the advertisers rejected the editorial environment of the magazine. Food advertisers expected women's magazines to publish recipes and articles on entertaining; clothing advertisers expected fashion spreads; and makers of beauty products wanted positive editorial coverage to accompany the ads, all of which clashed with the editorial content. *Ms.* may also have frightened off some advertisers who didn't want to be associated with controversial issues such as pro-choice/pro-life and sexual orientation (Enrico 1990). When the choice was to succumb to advertiser pressure, go out of business, or be one of the few magazines that could find an alternate source of support, *Ms.* chose the latter. *Ms.* editor Gloria Steinem made this comment:

> If *Time* and *Newsweek* had to lavish praise on cars in general and credit General Motors in particular to get GM ads, there would be a scandal— maybe a criminal investigation. When women's magazines from *Seventeen* to *Lear's* praise beauty products in general and credit Revlon in particular to get ads, it's just business as usual. (Steinem 1990, 19)

Finding the Right Balance

In a perfect world, all interests would be balanced in the relationship shared among consumers, advertisers, and media companies. Consumers would be satisfied with the content they receive from the media including the advertising; advertisers would be satisfied with the media options available to them for their ability to draw the right audiences at a fair price; and shareholders of media companies would be satisfied with the revenue from advertisers, consumers, and other sources. However, Rotzoll et al. (1996) predicted that advertising will continue to be a controversial third party in the media–audience relationship. The satisfaction of all interests is not always attainable, and in those instances, the more powerful interests may take precedence. One factor that threatens the balance of power is censorship.

Economic Censorship by Advertisers

Because advertising is an essential source of revenue for media companies, an inherent danger exists that "advertisers might use their economic influence to act as unofficial censors of 'the press,' thereby barring media from publishing or broadcasting certain material" (Richards and Murphy 1996, 21). Advertising influence is a serious charge, especially when it concerns censorship of news, because one of the benefits of an advertising-supported media system is that it allows the media to function without the constraints of the government. If consumers are simply trading government influence for corporate influence, one must ask whether they are better served.

Advertising has long been associated with two types of economic censorship. First, companies have been known to withhold advertising or threaten to do so as leverage against unfavorable news coverage of the company or product. Second, advertisers have withdrawn support for media vehicles with controversial content. Evidence of the first type of censorship comes from many researchers including Soley and Craig (1992), who found that 90 percent of editors of daily newspapers admitted that advertisers had attempted to influence the content of stories appearing in their papers to gain more favorable coverage. Thirty-seven percent said they capitulated to advertiser pressure and that automotive, real estate, construction, and restaurant advertisers were the biggest offenders in the sample. One example that Soley and Craig cite is a car dealership that withdrew its advertising for two months and tried to convince three other dealerships to follow suit because the newspaper had run a page-one story about a mechanical problem with the make of car, even though the story contained a sidebar that noted that no local users experienced problems.

More recent studies confirm that frequent conflicts continue to arise between the business side and the journalism side of operations at U.S. daily newspapers, and advertising directors at small newspapers are more likely to compromise editorial integrity than those at large newspapers (An and Bergen 2007). Similarly, advertising directors at chain-owned newspapers are more likely to capitulate to pressure than those at independent newspapers.

Advertising pressure is not limited to newspapers. Dave Itzkoff, a former editor of *Maxim*, offers an insider's view of the production process. He notes that someone in the ad department typically reviews the editorial pages of the magazine, scans for mentions of any brand-name product, and makes the following types of recommendations: "If advertisers' products were mentioned in any disparaging way, [the ad staffer] would approach to say, 'please delete it' or make the reference more generic. And if we mentioned a product in a favorable light that was not an advertiser, the ad-side would request we 'find a competing product who is an advertiser' and change the reference to that advertiser" (Fine 2004, 65).

The second type of economic censorship—the withdrawal of advertising support in media vehicles that carried controversial content—gained much attention in 1996 due to demands placed on magazines by the Chrysler Corporation, which was the nation's fourth-largest advertiser at the time. Though the practice had been in effect for many decades, it became highly publicized when Chrysler notified fifty magazines that it would require summaries of upcoming articles and advance notice of "any and all editorial content that encompasses sexual, political, or social issues or any editorial that might be construed as provocative or offensive" (Baker 1997, 30). These summaries were to be forwarded to Chrysler's ad agency in ample time for rescheduling of ads. Understandably, the response was very negative in journalism circles, with Milton Glaser, cofounder of *New York* magazine, predicting a "devastating effect on the idea of a free press and of free inquiry" (Baker 1997, 30).

Television has battled the issue of controversial content for decades and since issues such as abortion, gay/lesbian issues, and violence draw mixed emotional responses among audience members, advertisers often hesitate to take risks and opt for more "family-friendly" content. Richards and Murphy (1996) offer several full pages of examples from the 1970s, 1980s, and 1990s to illustrate the problem for both print and television, but two recent examples show advertisers' continued aversion to controversy.

> The 2002 talk radio program, the *Opie & Anthony Show*, was cosponsored by Boston Beer Company and encouraged people to engage in sex in public places in a contest called "Sex for Sam." Although Boston Beer's chairman made a public apology, the show was still cancelled.
>
> In 2006, the American Family Association pressured advertisers to withdraw their support of NBC's controversial program *Book of Daniel*. With the loss of advertisers Sony, Viacom Paramount, Combe's Just for Men, Chattem's Icy Hot, and Gold Bond's Ultimate Healing Lotion, the show was cancelled. (Hampp 2007, 43)

Although many advertisers have capitulated to pressure by withdrawing their ads from controversial programming, others have held firm. In 2004, Lowe's home-improvement stores and Tyson Foods, Inc., withheld their ads in the first season of *Desperate Housewives*, but enough other advertisers supported the show that it survived. Further, the American Family Association pressured Ford Motor Company to drop ads targeted to gays in 2005 but without success. Ford first agreed to pull the ads but later reversed the decision to advertise Volvos in gay and lesbian publications to maintain its "commitment to diversity as an employer and corporate citizen" (Hampp 2007, 43).

Perhaps the best example of greater tolerance toward the GLBT (gay/lesbian/bisexual/transgender) market is Disney World's policy of providing benefits to partners of gay employees and holding an annual Gay Day in Orlando (Hiaasen 1998). Despite protests at Disney World from Operation

Rescue National, an antiabortion group that also combats homosexuality, attendance remained high. Writer Carl Hiaasen applauded Disney's stand against the "morality police" with the following supportive comment, "Given a choice between intolerant moralizers and unflinching ruthless profiteers, I'll have to stand with the Mouse every time" (1998, 12).

At times, there is complete convergence of interests regarding media content. Such was the case when Don Imus made derogatory remarks against the Rutgers women's basketball team on his talk-radio shows (Garofoli 2007). Immediately after the incident, advertisers, consumer-interest groups, and media employees protested, which made cancelling the show the only option. Procter & Gamble was the first advertiser to withdraw, but they were soon followed by American Express, General Motors, Geico, GlaxoSmithKline, Staples, Sprint, and 1-800-Pet-Meds. Both MSNBC and CBS cancelled the show citing "integrity" and "goodwill" as reasons, but some say "the best way to effect change in media is to go after the ad dollars" (Hampp 2007, 43). Eight months after the controversy that made him a national symbol of intolerance, however, Imus returned to the airwaves on WABC-AM to several-hundred fans who gave him a "hero's welcome" (Farhi 2007).

Consumers also exert pressure upon the media and advertisers. When they object to the content in a particular media vehicle, they can show their opposition two ways: first, by passively refusing to be part of the audience and selecting other programs, magazines, and so forth; and second, by actively retaliating against the media companies or the advertisers (Richards and Murphy 1996). If they take an active approach, they usually boycott the advertiser instead of the media company. A large number of boycotts have been led by various consumer groups that object to controversial content (homosexuality, violence, sex, etc.). They often include conservative groups but occasionally have included groups that press for political correctness. Richards and Murphy suggest that boycotters are not necessarily trying to "change the media they use, but rather to restrict what other people see and hear in the media" (1996, 29 citing Fahey 1991, 654).

A recent example of an attempt to restrict what other people see is the protest of the Oxygen network's program, *Snapped*, a true-crime series that features women who have committed murder. Some of the women featured on the program have killed abusive husbands, whereas others killed boyfriends or husbands who get in the way of their ambitions. For this reason, *Snapped* has sparked controversy among feminist groups who claim it draws attention away from the issue of domestic violence—the most likely reason that women murder spouses (Bellafante 2007). Two nonprofit organizations, Free Battered Women and the National Clearinghouse for the Defense of Battered Women, have asked consumers to protest this program—not the advertisers—by contacting Oxygen Media and cofounder Oprah Winfrey on the basis that the show perpetuates myths, exploits the experiences of real battered women, and depicts a false form of empowerment. However, as one of Oxygen's highest-rated shows, the likelihood that it will drop the program is exceedingly small. After all, the show " . . . gives us beauty queens who kill their cheating fiancés, gold diggers, and black widows who drug their rich husbands to death" (Bellafante 2007, A15, 23).

Self-Censorship

Some say that self-censorship is a more serious problem than the more open forms of pressure. Even if there are no tangible signs that the media are giving in to threats from advertisers, a chilling effect can occur. This can happen in a variety of ways, such as when publishers turn down potential advertising clients for fear that their main advertisers will cite a conflict of interest. For example, Twitchell (1996) notes that bridal magazines have refused to take ads from companies selling used bridal gowns or even mentioning their existence in editorial content for fear that their main sponsors—companies that sell new wedding gowns—would withhold advertising. Some magazines have even refused to accept ads for smoking-cessation clinics and quit-smoking aids for fear that tobacco companies would withdraw their tobacco advertising.

TV networks have also been known to refuse to sell advertising time for messages perceived as anticonsumerist. It is common for media companies to refuse an ad to avoid public outcry over matters of taste or for controversial products such as contraceptives. However, in 1997 the Media Foundation tried to purchase air time to promote "Buy Nothing Day," which is an annual event meant to call attention to excessive consumerism and its toll on the environment.

> CBS wrote that a day without shopping was "in opposition to the current economic policy of the United States." NBC noted, "We don't want to take any advertising that's inimical to our legitimate business interests." Kalle Lasn, of the Media Foundation, found the refusals ironic, noting, "I came from Estonia where you were not allowed to speak up against the government. Here I was in North America, and suddenly I realize you can't speak up against the [corporate] sponsor. There is something fundamentally undemocratic about our public airways." (Croteau and Hoynes 2006, 188)

In an even odder twist, the Court of Appeals in Vancouver, British Columbia, ruled that the Media Foundation could pursue legal action against the Canadian Broadcasting Company and Can-West Global for refusing to air the anticonsumerist message (Morrow 2009). Perhaps Lasn will eventually find some degree of fairness in the media, albeit in Canada rather than the United States.

Self-censorship also happens when reporters consciously or unconsciously avoid stories critical of advertisers or about controversial topics in anticipation of censorship, even when media owners make no such demands on them (Baker 1997; Richards and Murphy 1996). Nicholas Johnson, former FCC commissioner, explains how the process of self-censorship evolves: "A young reporter writes an exposé, but the editor says, 'I don't think we're going to run that.' The second time the reporter goes to her editor, the editor says, 'I don't think that's a good idea.' She doesn't research and write the story. The third time the reporter has an idea. But she doesn't go to her editor. The fourth time she doesn't get the idea" (Lieberman 2000, 1).

Most journalists admit that at one time or another they have held back, choosing not to pursue a story or not to include a difficult fact, or to severely soften a story's angle. One reason that journalists unwittingly soften a story to give the most favorable perspective to advertisers is that companies diligently work at building relationships. But when people share the same worldview, there is no need for explicit rules. Here is a comment from a newspaper editor who explains the process:

> The danger is not an overt threat. I haven't seen a publisher come back from a Chamber meeting and say, "Hey, Al at the [auto] dealer said we have to have a story about xxx." But there is a similar world view, a similar feeling about what is important and what isn't, a likeness of mind about what the newspaper should be covering. They don't need to be told by an advertiser that something is important or that a news story should focus in a particular direction. Editors and publishers probably don't usually think about advertisers when they make those decisions. They don't need to. They already share the same attitudes, convictions, and worldview. (Soley and Craig 1992, 8)

What Does It Mean?

In the process of examining a host of issues surrounding advertising and its relationship to the media and to consumers, we find that the three groups clearly have different interests. In the attempt to satisfy competing needs, all players have tried and at times succeeded in using their economic clout to their advantage. Because most media companies agree in principle that the news coverage should observe ethical standards and should not be subservient to advertisers' wishes, they have tried to operate news and advertising departments as separate entities (Christians, Rotzoll, and Fackler 1991; Rotfeld 1992). This division has traditionally gone by several different names including "The Wall" and the "Separation between Church and State," with the Church referring to the media and the State referring to advertising. However, many critics say that the separation is rapidly crumbling (Moses 2008).

A recent example of the crumbling wall between entertainment and advertising is a series of Pepsi "MacGruber" ads on *Saturday Night Live*, modeled after *MacGyver* with the featured actor, Will Forte, renamed "PepSuber" (YouTube 2009). Columnist Tim Cuprisin (2009, 10B) commented that "as the economic slump hits advertising, TV is selling anything and everything." However, the crumbling wall drew even more fire when it affected news and advertising. The *Los Angeles Times* was harshly criticized for two incidents on consecutive days—first, running a front-page ad for an NBC show that resembled a news story and second, for placing a four-page ad for the movie, *The Soloist*, which was laid out like a news section (Clifford 2009, B2).

McChesney (2008, 270) argues that ad clutter and new ad-skipping technology are partially to blame for the crumbling wall, "but mostly it is due to the greed of media companies desperate to attract commercial support." Since marketers will take their ad dollars elsewhere, the temptation to merge advertising and editorial content is simply too great.

Ad spending began to drop in 2007 and continued dropping in 2008 and 2009, representing the first three-year decline in ad spending since the Great Depression (*Advertising Age* 2008); however, ad spending is showing some signs of improvement as the economy recovers. With the lack of consumer spending in the top two advertising categories—retail and auto—the most significant effects upon measured advertising media expenditures have been with newspapers. As a result, promotional spending budgets have declined or shifted, so that media expenditures sometimes give way to less costly forms of promotion such as public relations. With less money to spend comes less power; thus, the three-way relationship among consumers, the media, and advertisers is likely to change, and the full impact remains to be seen.

What is even more unclear is whether the interests of the three players were ever really balanced. Or if the imbalance has increased in recent years, can it level out in the future? Ironically, some of the limits on expression that individual consumers encounter, such as bland but safe media content, originate from activist consumer groups rather than from advertisers. Thus, consumers not only have to navigate pressures from advertisers and media companies but also from consumer-activist groups.

To ponder these issues, we return to the classical liberal model. It is likely that media issues arouse the interests of all three players (quietism) and that they all put their own interests above others (egoism). However, they may not be aroused equally because more is at stake economically for advertisers and the media. Because these issues are their livelihood, they are unlikely to be apathetic, whereas individual consumers can get caught up in more immediate problems of day-to-day living.

The power of media conglomerates, advertisers, and activist consumer groups jeopardizes the level of influence that individual consumers can exert (atomism). When that power influences content through censorship, consumers' ability to think rationally (intellectualism) suffers because they are forced to make decisions on limited, biased information. Consumers are left with a system in which they are unaware of the behind-the-scenes activities of the other groups, some of which have deep pockets. Consequently, the classical liberal model gives way to the neoliberal model once again.

There is no final resolution to the problem of competing interests—only the awareness that it exists. Perhaps in time there will be new resolutions to these problems because new technology continues to change the shared relationship among consumers, advertisers, and the media. Until then, individual consumers need to recognize that they are the least influential members in this triad, and in order to preserve the democratic process they need to seek out alternative sources of information that are not advertising-driven. Audience members in the United States enjoy a media system that lacks the constraints of government ownership, but one that requires complex skills to navigate the constraints of the economic system. In the late 1990s, the *Wall Street Journal* used the advertising slogan "adventures in capitalism" when referring to the content of the newspaper; however, the economic successes of media companies are also adventures in capitalism.

➤ 5 ◀

Crossing International Borders

Thus far we've examined the role of advertising in a consumer culture that is grounded in classical liberalism and individualism—one that is distinctly American. In this chapter, we consider the role of advertising when the promotional efforts of multinational corporations cross international borders to reach new audiences, some of whom come from cultures with very different value systems. To get a better sense of the issues, the first part of this chapter examines some of the challenges that the industry faces. It cites some blunders in international advertising and considers the impact of different campaign strategies. The remaining sections address some of the broader issues including some of the ethical dilemmas in promoting products and services to citizens of other cultures, especially those who do not know what it means to be a consumer in a consumer culture.

Challenges to the Advertising Industry

Campaigns Gone Wrong

The many advertising blunders reported in various international texts speak to the difficulty of creating and implementing a campaign for the same brand in multiple countries. One of the challenges is that successful campaigns are created out of popular culture, and what's part of one culture may not be part of another. British advertising expert Simon Anholt (2000, 59) comments that "every time something happens in the press or on TV, a scandal takes place, a new personality emerges or an old one does something newsworthy, or the movie business or the music business provide us with new stimulus, then an item of popular culture has been forged, and the creative department has a new toy to play with." In this way, popular culture gives creators of domestic ads the luxury of choosing their "toys" from an exciting, constantly-changing array within the culture. But when advertisers are charged with creating a campaign to run abroad, they look for commonalities that hold up across borders, a process that limits options and leads to stale creative concepts that become clichés. "Personally, if I have to look at one more global ad where some loathsome international executive . . . is reading his child a bedtime story from a mobile phone in his Hong Kong hotel room, I may start to scream and break things" (Anholt 2000 58).

On the surface, it may seem that a simple translation of a successful campaign in one country should work well in another country, but marketers have many failed campaigns to offer as evidence to the contrary. Not only are mistakes made with fairly simple translations, but slogans such as "Just Do It" defy almost all attempts to express anything comparable in another language. Nike's famous slogan is used in English in most countries despite non-English speakers' lack of understanding of its meaning. But when government regulations require all advertising to be in the native language of the country (e.g., France), English is not an option. The closest French equivalent is "your life is your own," which loses much of the spirit of "Just Do It" (Anholt 2000, 39).

The following three examples of blunders are the result of mistranslations of original product names or slogans, which worked in the country of origin but ran into difficulties when the product traveled across borders (O'Guinn, Allen, and Semenik 2000, 266).

> The name Coca-Cola in China was first rendered as "Ke-kou-ke-la." Unfortunately, Coke did not discover until after thousands of signs had been printed that the phrase means "bite the wax tadpole" or "female horse stuffed with wax," depending on the dialect. Coke then researched 40,000 Chinese characters and found a close phonetic equivalent, "ko-kou-ko-le" which can be loosely translated as "Happiness in the mouth."

> In Taiwan, the Pepsi slogan "Come alive with the Pepsi Generation" was translated as "Pepsi will bring your ancestors back from the dead."

> Scandinavian vacuum manufacturer Electrolux used the following in an American ad campaign: "Nothing sucks like an Electrolux."

Disaster stories are so popular that some become urban legends. Perhaps the best known is Chevy Nova. As the story goes, the Chevy Nova sold poorly in Spanish-speaking countries, and General Motors executives were baffled until someone finally pointed out that the name translates to "doesn't go" in Spanish (Olper 2006). The embarrassed automobile giant is said to have changed the model name to the Caribe, after which the sales took off. The only problem with this story is that it never happened. To begin with, the story has been attributed to several different locales such as Puerto Rico and Mexico,

South America, or simply to "Spanish-speaking countries." Moreover, the car sold so well under the Nova nameplate in Spanish-speaking countries that it surpassed General Motors' expectations.

Although it is true that "no va" literally means it doesn't go, Olper (2006) notes that Spanish speakers would hardly use that expression in reference to a car. Instead they would say it "doesn't run," which translates to "no marcha," "no functiona," or "no camina"—not "no va." Furthermore, seeing "nova" as "no va" is comparable to an English speaker seeing the word "notable" as "no table."

Finally, a car by the name Caribe did sell in Mexico, but it was manufactured by Volkswagen, not General Motors!

Standardized versus Specialized Campaigns

Over time, many American companies found it increasingly difficult to find new users of their product within the United States. The market for some brands was nearly saturated with little opportunity for future growth except to seek new consumers outside the U.S. borders. Given some similarities in the way consumers use brands in different countries, more and more companies began to think of the entire world as a consumer culture. Advertisers and marketers began to think in terms of global brands and to seek ways to make the positioning, the advertising strategy, the personality, the look, and the feel of the brand similar in order to create a campaign that works around the world. Using an identical campaign throughout the world is nearly impossible—Visa changes its logo in some countries, and Heineken means something different in the Netherlands than it does outside its own country. However, keeping many elements the same across countries has significant benefits (Aaker and Joachimsthaler 1999).

Certain economies of scale benefit all aspects of international marketing, but the efficiencies in the promotion of the brand can be enormous. In particular, developing a single global advertising campaign is much less expensive and much more manageable than developing separate campaigns for multiple markets. The *standardized* approach means offering identical or nearly identical products worldwide at the same prices through the same distribution channels and supported by identical sales and promotion programs. The challenge is making it work, for creating an effective ad campaign from a central agency in one country that gives directives to local agencies on how to carry out the campaign is a very complex process that can result in some tensions. From a practical standpoint, the motivation to follow someone else's creative ideas is low. The system also sends a subtle message that the "lead agency" does the important work and that the local agencies just carry out orders. Anholt

(2000) argues that there is something fundamentally flawed with the whole notion of lead agency, for it assumes that outsiders, who can rarely navigate a foreign culture well enough to order food and drink in a restaurant, could create meaningful, relevant messages for that culture's inhabitants.

The goal of turning a local or national brand into a global brand is based on the belief in "global communities" or "global tribes"—that consumers are the same worldwide. And the goal of using a standardized ad campaign further assumes that members of these global tribes can respond to the same communication strategy and creative message. However, Marieke de Mooij, a cross-cultural communication expert from the Netherlands, questions the entire concept. "The assumptions are that an 18-year-old in Denmark has more in common with an 18-year-old in France than he has with his elders, or a young Japanese woman shopping in the Ginza has more in common with a young American woman strolling a Manhattan street than she has with her own parents" (de Mooij 2005, 21). Yet, some of these assumptions have proven to be false.

Business travelers and teenagers are the groups, according to de Mooij, regarded as the most homogeneous throughout the world. Business travelers share certain needs such as hotel accommodations, transportation within a city away from home, effective means of communication, and other products and services. Yet, not all business travelers seek the same things. A hotel that advertises quality services at affordable rates may appeal to some business travelers but alienate others who come from countries that place a high value on status.

Likewise, European youth have been reared on the same movies and global brands such as Levi's and Coca-Cola, which has supposedly encouraged the development of a "global teenager" with common values and preferences. Though others may disagree, de Mooij believes that some marketers who have searched for global tribes of consumers have yet to find them. Homogeneous markets such as "businesspeople, youth, or rich people, exist only in the minds of Western marketing managers and advertising people" (2005, 22).

When the meaning differs from group to group, marketers have little choice but to implement a *specialized* campaign that reflects the cultural differences. These campaigns not only differ from country to country in use of language but in concepts which reflect different cultural values, different uses of the product, different meanings associated with the user of the product, and so forth.

Despite the elusiveness of homogeneous markets, standardized campaigns can and do work well for some advertisers. Philip Morris uses the famous Marlboro campaign featuring the quintessential American, individualist cowboy around the world including Ukraine (Figure 5.1), even though the

Figure 5.1 **Marlboro. Ukrainian ad in *Ego Magazine***

company created its own unique, specialized ad for its Virginia Slims brand in the Ukrainian market (Venger and Wolburg 2008). Instead of depicting women using the familiar American campaign slogans such as, "You've come a long way, baby," "Find your voice," or "It's a woman thing," the Ukrainian ad features a mysterious-looking, dark haired beauty who says in Ukrainian, "So you think you know me? Come and find out" (Figure 5.2). Another ad in

the series depicts a sensuous blonde who says, "I am everything you want, even more than you can imagine." These ads appeal to Ukrainian women's desire to have an air of mystery about them in order to be regarded as attractive to men.

The reality is that some messages can resonate universally and others can't. The American image of the cowboy and its reinforcement of individualism have wide appeal, even in collectivist countries where people identify with their ingroup. But the original message of independence in the Virginia Slims

97

Figure 5.2 **Virginia Slims. Ukrainian advertising campaign: "So you think you know me? Come and find out." Virginia Slims: "More than you can imagine."**

campaign appears to be uniquely American. "You've come a long way, baby" was about women gaining parity with men with regard to various freedoms in the United States including the right to vote, and smoking Virginia Slims became a commodification of that freedom. In Ukraine, where women already had political equality with men, the Virginia Slims campaign had to appeal to a different need—women's desire to create an image of mystery and attractiveness. Although several Ukrainian ads used smoking as a commodification of freedom, it is the freedom from communism with a switch to a market economy that brought affluence, career opportunities, and material possessions—at least to some consumers (Venger and Wolburg 2008).

Broader Issues: Critics and Defenders

Problematic Message Strategies

So far, we have focused on the challenges of promoting products and services effectively across borders in order to be profitable. However, another consideration is the cultural impact of messages carried through advertising. This is an issue for both domestic and international advertising, but ads that cross borders raise unique concerns over messages that clash with the cultural values of the target country.

To analyze the underlying messages in ads, Frith (1997) first looks at the surface elements and notes the number of people in the ad, their age, their activity, the gender and racial composition of the ad, and other factors. She then looks at the advertiser's intended message, which is another way of asking how the product or service promises to enhance the consumer. Ads typically promise to meet various needs such as status, acceptance, attractiveness, efficiency, health, and security. Frith then completes the deconstruction of ads by looking at the underlying ideological messages that are often implied rather than stated.

For example, the surface elements in the Ukrainian Marlboro ad (Figure 5.1) show a lone man, readily identifiable as an American cowboy riding a horse in the open spaces. Additional elements include cactus plants in the foreground that signify the setting as the American West. The English language text says "Come to Marlboro Country" above a small image of the product with the Ukrainian health warning written below. The advertiser's intended message is not literal but symbolic—that those who smoke Marlboro enter a special place called Marlboro Country where men are rugged, masculine individualists and are free from the constraints of urban life. Ideologically, the concepts of freedom and independence are potent ideas that tap into the cultural value of individualism, which is regarded as the cornerstone of American culture; however, it clashes with the collectivistic values of many other countries, including Ukraine. When ads such as these cross borders, they promote values that are not indigenous to the culture and may have untold effects.

Other message strategies have been criticized for sending problematic ideological messages, such as American superiority. In one of the more subtle examples, a General Electric ad that ran during the 2002 winter Olympics depicted an attractive, African-American doctor in his late 20s packing for a trip. He leaves his spacious apartment in New York and flies to Tanzania, which is a seductively beautiful country but primitive by American standards. He rides a bus through untamed terrain while listening to music through headphones and watching the wild animals run gracefully. As his journey continues to an even more remote area, he waits for a Land Rover that carries him the rest of the way. Finally at his destination, he receives a hero's welcome by the African natives and the medical workers expecting him. He makes eye contact with one of the children and removes something from his backpack. What appeared to be a laptop is state-of-the-art medical equipment. All of these surface elements provide a powerful context for the advertiser's message, which is spoken through a voiceover: "Introducing the GE portable ultrasound system. An incredible breakthrough that makes diagnostic sonograms available anytime, anywhere, to anyone." The ad ends with GE's tagline, "We bring good things to life."

The ad is a powerful narrative that stirs strong, positive emotions. Not only does our hero represent the best of American technology and education, he is also a humanitarian to be respected and admired. While Africa is a land of beauty that has a richness of its own, the United States is a country of efficiency and technology. From an ideological perspective, the ad says that without American technology brought to faraway places by trained American medical doctors, the world would be left to fend for itself.

A less subtle example but more recent example of American superiority is the Whopper Virgin campaign, which reached a sizeable television audience in the United States and also reached a secondary audience via YouTube. The premise of the ad is that one must go to the remote parts of the world to find people who have never before eaten a hamburger because these "virgins" are arguably the best subjects for a taste test between Burger King's Whopper and McDonald's Big Mac. The surface elements of the ad include the inhabitants of various remote areas who live off the land and wear handmade clothes. Though all ads are open to the interpretation of the viewer, the advertiser's message is the superiority of the Whopper, evident by its position as winner of the taste test. But in the process the ads depict the "virgins" as quaint people who are so out of step with the world that they don't even know how to hold the burger without dropping it, which ideologically positions the American way of life as superior to that of the remote villager dwellers. A full-length video showing the making of the campaign provides the commentary: "The hamburger is a culinary culture and it's actually an American phenomenon. It's been very interesting to see the reaction to the hamburger because they've never seen such a foreign piece of food before, and they didn't even quite know how to pick it up. And they didn't know from what end to eat it" (YouTube 2008).

Most concerns over cultural values apply to campaigns that cross borders.

Yet, the Whopper Virgin campaign suggests that problematic cultural messages can also be delivered to consumers within the country of origin, for the message of American superiority is problematic for Americans as well as for people outside the U.S. border.

Making Sense of Ad Campaigns

Part of the difficulty in evaluating ad campaigns for advertisers such as General Electric or Burger King stems from a fundamental lack of consensus on how advertising works, both for domestic and international audiences. Some theorists have proposed that advertising encourages unnecessary desires by diverting people from an "honest" relationship with products. Williams (1980) argues that if consumers were sensible in the way they pursue materialism, most advertising would be irrelevant:

> Beer would be enough for us, without the additional promise that in drinking it, we show ourselves to be manly, young in heart, or neighbourly. A washing machine would be a useful machine to wash clothes, rather than an indication that we are forward-looking or an object of envy to our neighbours. It is clear that we have a cultural pattern in which the objects are not enough but must be validated, if only in fantasy, by association with social and personal meanings which in a different cultural pattern might be more directly available. (Williams 1980, 185)

This perspective gives great power to advertising because it holds that ad campaigns teach consumers to view products beyond the functional needs they serve and in ways that may not be beneficial to them or for society. Followers of this perspective believe that advertising must be held in check to avoid exploiting consumers.

Other theorists including structuralists Roland Barthes (1972) and Jean Baudrillard (1981) have proposed that goods have no inherent meaning of their own, and they take on meaning only within the social context of a given culture. In their minds, there is neither an honest relationship with products that occurs naturally nor a dishonest relationship created by advertising because *all* relationships with products are social constructions. This perspective can be challenged, too, but it has the advantage of moving the debate about advertising away from a moralistic preoccupation with "true" versus "false" needs (Mazzarella 2003). Furthermore, advertising is only one of many sources of influence within a culture that define consumers' relationships with products (e.g., others may include product placements in films and television programs). Taking that view to its logical conclusion, the power of advertising may be considerable, but it is not a given. The lack of closure on the role of advertising creates a tension that we will explore in the next section.

CHAPTER 5

Creating a Consumer Culture in Developing Countries

Marketers target both the developed countries and the developing countries despite significant economic differences between the two. Understandably, marketers are drawn to the developed countries (the European Union, the United States, Japan, etc.) due to a high level of affluence among consumers; however, they are also drawn to developing countries due to the rapidly expanding economy, despite the lower level of affluence among consumers.

Even the poorest countries are not without their appeal. According to the 2008 Global Monitoring Report of the World Bank, the proportion of people living in extreme poverty on less than $1 per day is expected to decrease to 10 percent in 2015, down from 29 percent in 1990. However, trends vary among regions with sub-Saharan Africa lagging behind (World Bank 2008). Aside from reducing poverty and hunger, other goals include achieving universal primary education for all children, promoting gender equality and empowering women, reducing child mortality, improving maternal health, combating disease, using resources wisely to ensure environmental sustainability, and working to develop a global partnership for development. Below we consider, based on the work of Mueller (2004), some of the more perplexing issues that arise when companies promote goods and services to developing countries.

Advertising's Influence on the Domestic Media Scene

A common charge against international advertising is that it promotes commercialism of the media (Mueller 2004). Media companies in many developing countries have been fully or partly government supported, but over time many have developed greater dependence upon advertising revenue. Critics charge that this new dependence on ad revenue puts greater emphasis on profits than public needs, in addition to creating a highly cluttered environment where a high percentage of media content is advertising.

To complicate the issue further, many countries have imported Western media content. Not only is it more compatible with advertising because the content itself promotes consumption, but it is also popular among international audiences. For example, at its peak of popularity, *Baywatch* reached 1.1 billion viewers in 142 countries, making it is the most widely viewed TV series in the world at the time (BBC News 2001). Game shows and reruns of American comedies such as *The Simpsons*, *Everybody Loves Raymond*, *Friends*, and *Seinfeld* are also shown in syndication throughout the world. As a result, the reduced opportunities for domestic programming have prompted some countries to restrict foreign programming.

Defenders of international advertising argue that advertising support is a strong source of revenue that helps make the media independent of the government. However, media that are supported by advertising are not fully independent. When the choice is between big business and government, many agree that dependency upon big business is the lesser of the two evils, but it is not without its own set of problems as we saw in Chapter 4.

A more subtle effect of advertising is the continued support of mainstream performers and mainstream media outlets. According to a *New York Times* journalist reporting on the underground Chinese Hip-Hop culture, "because corporate advertisers almost always seek out popular stars who have been given the blessing of producers representing state-run media, the underground music scene has had to live off the enthusiasm of young music aficionados without ever being able to gain backing to spread beyond nightclub walls" (Wang 2009, C6). Such is the fate of Chinese rappers who address injustices from their perspective, such as the following words from a freestyle rapper, Wong Li. His closing lines reference the tainted milk scandal, which resulted in the death of at least six children and ended in death sentences for two dairy producers and life in prison for three others (Barboza 2009).

> If you don't have a nice car or cash
> You won't get no honeys
> Don't you know China is only a heaven for rich old men
> You know this world is full of corruption
> Babies die from drinking milk. (Wang 2009, C6)

In contrast to Wong Li is Jay Chou, a pop singer turned rapper from Taiwan, who is clean-cut, handsome, and "appeals to a sense of nationalist pride." As the archetype of a mainstream performer in China, he has been featured in ads for Pepsi, Panasonic, and China Mobile (Wang 2009, C6). The business decision to support mainstream performers who receive air time on state-run media makes sense for advertisers; in fact, to do otherwise would be unthinkable. However, the support of mainstream performers is worth noting, for it not only affects the domestic media scene but aligns advertisers with the dominant ideology of the country.

Advertising and the Allocation of Precious Resources

Along a similar vein, critics argue that scarce resources are squandered for the production, promotion, and consumption of nonessential goods, a practice that often encourages "conspicuous consumption of foreign-made goods" with money that could be better spent on such things as health and welfare programs (Mueller 2004, 317). Advertising messages discourage frugality by encouraging people in developing countries to replace goods that are still usable with new ones. This can reduce resources and deplete savings, especially when local goods are replaced with foreign brands that typically cost twice as much.

In defense, marketers and advertisers argue that the decision about how to use resources and the judgment on whether expenditures are wasteful should be left to the individuals who consume the products. Others outside of marketing and advertising have also placed the responsibility upon the citizens. Mahatma Gandhi believed that Indian consumers had a collectivist responsibility to the greater good of the nation to resist buying imported goods, such as cloth from Manchester. In his words, "How can Manchester be blamed? We wore Manchester cloth, and that is why Manchester wove it" (quoted in Mazzarella 2003, 6).

Critics, on the other hand, maintain that local governments should play a significant role in these decisions because individuals may not have the necessary level of education or sophistication to make informed decisions.

Advertising's Potential to Deceive Consumers

In the United States, First Amendment protection gives certain rights to manufacturers of legal but harmful products to advertise their products as long as the claims are not deceptive. There are no outright bans of legal products—only advertising bans for certain media, such as the ban of cigarette advertising in broadcast media. Furthermore, there are other regulations in the United States that protect consumers, such as the use of warning labels on packages of cigarettes, expiration dates on products that lose quality over time such as pharmaceuticals, bans on certain flame-retardant chemicals that cause cancer, and so forth.

Other countries take different approaches to regulations and have different legal standards, which add to the complexity of implementing global advertising campaigns. Regulations vary across countries but are typically weaker in developing countries, which opens the door to deceptive claims that exaggerate product effectiveness (Mueller 2004). This is particularly worrisome for legal but harmful products such as tobacco, for which advertisers have used some aggressive marketing tactics. As a result, consumers in many countries outside the United States lack access to vital health information about the risks of smoking (Mueller 2004). They also have very high smoking rates; for example, Indonesia has the fifth largest market in the world for cigarettes, where two-thirds of adult males smoke compared to 24 percent in the United States (Wright 2007). Consumers outside the United States are also subject to highly unethical research practices. In Thailand, Philip Morris has been charged with planting a scientist in the Chulabhorn Research Institute to shift researchers' attention away from secondhand smoke and toward other forms of air pollution (Casey 2009). A second study alleges that British American Tobacco provided funding for the Beijing Liver Foundation to shift the focus away from links between smoking and liver disease. Edouard Tursan d'Espaignet of the World Health Organization's Tobacco Free Initiative concluded that "as the high-income countries put more and more obstacles in the path of the cigarette companies, they have to look for new markets" (Casey 2009, 12A).

An increasing number of outright bans on the advertising for controversial products is expected outside the United States in the years to come (Wood and Liodice 2006). In response to concerns over childhood obesity, bans on children's advertising of "junk" food exist in some European countries and in Malaysia, and new restrictions are in place in the United Kingdom as well as the United States (Yoong 2007).

Although the potential for deception appears greater for consumers in developing countries, consumers in developed countries are by no means fully protected. Preston (1994) has devoted much of his career to the opposition of the use of puffery and non-facts in the United States and has argued that by allowing these messages to be legal, advertisers are empowered to implicitly deceive people. Furthermore, developed countries differ in what they deem important to protect. French advertising regulations, for example, prohibit the use of child actors in ads for products that are not primarily used by children in the belief that the practice is exploitative of children, though American advertising carries no such restriction (Taylor and Cunningham 2007).

Advertising's Influence on Rising Frustrations

Critics say that when advertising creates a demand for products that people cannot afford to buy, they are left with a sense of frustration. The larger concern is that when individuals become dissatisfied and frustrated with their lot in life, they are capable of acting out in ways that lead to social unrest or political instability (Mueller 2004).

Frith and Frith (1990) note that many developing countries have large percentages of families living below the poverty line, who are nevertheless exposed to the advertising of products beyond their means. Some resist the temptation of buying expensive products, whereas others squander money needed for food, shelter, and basic health on tobacco, cosmetics, soft drinks, and jeans. Most advertised products are aimed at the affluent, middle-class members of society; however, mass media messages are rarely targeted enough to reach only the middle class.

The challenge is that developing countries usually have multiple markets: an affluent group of urban dwellers, who have sophisticated tastes and wants, and can afford exported goods; suburbanites, who live 10–15 miles outside the urban area and also have some disposable income, though less than the most affluent group; and a rural population with simpler tastes and meager incomes which makes up as much as 80 percent of the total population in some countries (Mueller 2004). The goal of most advertisers is to reach the small, affluent, urban and suburban consumers; however, without targeted media vehicles, messages reach all people including those who struggle for basic necessities. Once a taste for Western products and life styles exists, the demand often trickles down to the less affluent members of society. Critics further argue that advertisers benefit by this trickle-down effect because the frustration among less affluent consumers not only makes the products desirable for their exclusivity but adds to their value as status symbols.

Defenders of advertising argue that individuals should be allowed to make their own purchase decisions and that advertising may be a minor part of the persuasive mix when other sources are factored in including American TV shows and Hollywood movies, which also promote the desire for Western-style goods. Rather than discounting the role of advertising in comparison to other sources, however, defenders must consider the synergistic effects of advertising, television, and movies in reinforcing the same message of consumption.

Advertising's Influence on Consumerism

One of the most common criticisms of advertising is that it promotes consumerism by positioning products as the solution to most needs and problems as well as the source of happiness (Mueller 2004). Advertising is further charged with stimulating artificial wants and needs, though separating the *real* wants and needs from the *artificial* ones can be challenging. Critics who advance this argument support theorists such as Williams (1980), who believe that advertising distorts the natural relationship between consumers and products.

To further understand this charge, we turn to moral philosopher George Brenkert (1998a), who makes a distinction between being a *consumer* and being a *person who consumes*. A consumer is a person who actively seeks a wide range of material goods and whose identification is closely bound to what he or she owns. Belk (1988, 160) sums up this philosophy with the statement, "we are what we have." In contrast, a person who consumes uses products for the utility and pleasure they provide but doesn't necessarily allow products to become intertwined with his or her identity. Of the two, being a consumer is more desirable for advertisers but more problematic for society because identifying oneself with possessions is contrary to many cultural and religious beliefs. Hinduism, for example, seeks spiritual liberation and release from worldly limitations, which is at direct odds with consumerism. Taken to the extreme, consumers look to products to solve all of life's problems and measure their worth by such things as the size of their home, the make of their car, and the brand of their clothes (Brenkert 1998a).

Defenders of advertising argue that consumerism may benefit a society. When ads promote a higher standard of living, such as more sanitary conditions or more nutritious food sources, advertising can lead to an improvement in people's lives. Brenkert (1998a) acknowledges that marketers have brought higher standards of quality for products, reduced infant mortality rates, improved yields of crops, and contributed to more efficient distribution of crop yields. Furthermore, Mazzarella (2003) notes that public-service campaigns were an instrumental part of family-planning initiatives in India during the 1960s when limiting the size of the population was important. As a result of these initiatives, the advertising industry in India received a degree of social legitimization, which contrasted greatly with the industry's prior image of encouraging dubious desires.

There is little doubt that advertising promotes consumerism. Perhaps a better question is the extent to which advertising teaches members of the culture to be "consumers" instead of "people who consume." Moreover, when advertising campaigns cross borders to countries that are not consumer cultures (at least not yet), what responsibilities do marketers and advertisers have to that culture?

Advertising's Influence on Indigenous Culture

Perhaps the most damaging criticism is that advertising alters indigenous culture (Mueller 2004). This criticism not only overlaps significantly with the charge that advertising promotes consumerism, but it is closely aligned with charges of cultural imperialism, the process by which a weaker society is dominated by a more powerful one so that its social institutions "correspond to, or even promote, the values and structures of the dominant center of the system" (Schiller 1976, 9). Cultural imperialism is also associated with the global spread of capitalism, which has been charged with bringing cultural homogenization to other countries, often understood simply as Americanization (Mazzarella 2003).

Critics question the ethics of promoting Western consumption values, particularly when it is not possible to "achieve Western-style goods and services for humanity as a whole," nor is it possible to sustain Western-style goods and services for as many people as have enjoyed them in the past, given the resources and materials needed to provide them (Cohen 1995, 9). Brenkert (1998a) agrees that promoting a way of life that a society cannot—or should not—live up to violates the respect that must be part of all marketing efforts. Without promoting forms of economic development that are both attainable and sustainable, the promotion of consumerism undermines cultural values. Even the marketing of inexpensive goods such as disposable razors may be exploitative, disrespectful, and unethical for cultures that place a high value on reusing, refilling, and recycling.

A close examination of certain advertising campaigns supports the charge of cultural imperialism for imposing Western culture on developing countries. For example, certain cosmetic brands impose Western standards of beauty by using American or European models in worldwide advertising campaigns, which results in consumers in other cultures investing—both emotionally and financially—in an unattainable standard. Additionally, some products explicitly offer enhancements to make women more Western in appearance, such as a print ad for Ponds Institute Skin Whitening Vitamin Cream with an Asian model saying, "I can't believe my rosy white skin caught their eye" (Frith and Mueller 2003, 236). Other products offer a nonsurgical way of transforming eye shape to appear more Western for those who are not affluent enough to have cosmetic surgery.

Ironically, one counter to cultural imperialism is anti-American sentiment. At a time when criticism of American foreign policy has increased, many regional cola companies in Central America and the Middle East gained market share by advertising their products as a political and ethical alternative to the American cola brands. Many Middle Eastern consumers, who traditionally bought American products, changed to regional brands to make a different statement with their buying habits and to voice their condemnation of American foreign policy (Parmar 2004).

Defenders argue that consumers in other countries can use Western products without losing their identity and can, in fact, be fiercely nationalistic. According to British scholar Kate Fox (2008, 14), a common complaint is that "we are living in a dumbed-down homogenized McWorld, in which the rich tapestry of diverse and distinctive cultures is being obliterated by the all-consuming consumerism of Nike, Coca-Cola, McDonald's, Disney and other multinational capitalist giants." To that charge, she counters:

> . . . As a fairly typical *Guardian*-reading, left liberal product of the anti-Thatcher generation, I have no natural sympathy for corporate imperialists, but as a professional observer of sociocultural trends, I am obliged to report that their influence has been exaggerated—or rather, misinterpreted. The principal effect of globalization, as far as I can tell, has been an increase in nationalism and tribalism, a proliferation of struggles for independence, devotion and self-determination and a resurgence of concern about ethnicity and cultural identity in almost all parts of the world, including the so-called United Kingdom . . . Just because people everywhere want to wear Nike trainers and drink Coke does not necessarily mean that they are less fiercely concerned about their cultural identity—indeed, many are prepared to fight and die for their nation, religion, territory, culture or whatever aspect of "tribal" identity is perceived to be at stake. (14)

Perhaps the strongest argument used by defenders of advertising is that much of the criticism of advertising is paternalistic—that outsiders make value judgments regarding what members of another culture choose to consume. Defenders rightly ask, "To what extent should outsiders' values dictate consumer choices that potentially affect indigenous culture?" This is a question addressed in more detail below.

A Final Perspective for Evaluating Global Campaigns

The effects of international advertising campaigns on developing countries are difficult to measure, and the lack of closure with regard to these issues leaves us questioning whether global corporations such as McDonald's are a "paragon of capitalist virtue" or an "evil empire" (Watson 1997, 6). In fact, the criticism of McDonald's is so intense that a recent article on the company's economic development opens with charges such as: " 'Mal bouffe'; junk food; seducer of children; employer of burger-flippers; exploiter of low-skilled labor; symbol of cultural imperialism; symbol of corporate greed; [and] symbol of America" (Tschoegl 2007, 1).

For those who view McDonald's as an evil empire, the perception is likely to be that of a corporation that exploits individuals' desires to consume and turns them into consumers. If it is problematic to adequately protect consumers who meet the assumptions of the classical liberal model and are expected to follow the rules of the marketplace, it is even more troubling to consider the level of protection needed for citizens who do not meet the assumptions of the classical liberal model.

Brenkert (1998a) considers three factors that can bring some degree of closure to these issues: the quality of life, the role of change, and respect for cultural identity and values. First, he argues that marketers have often provided benefits that should not be denied, such as higher standards of living, improved quality in goods and services, and other benefits. People in developing countries need and want more goods than they presently have, and it is arguably paternalistic for outsiders to decide what is best for them and deny access to goods so they can continue to live in what outsiders regard as an idealized, natural world. It follows that if such goods should be available, then the use of promotional tools such as advertising should not be denied.

Second, he argues that criticizing marketing activities simply because they bring about change is unjust. Because cultures are dynamic, change is inevitable, though some changes are admittedly more desirable than others. As people adopt new styles of dress, new styles of eating, and so forth, we can make valid objections only if more is at stake than mere change.

Third, a culture is something worthy of respect as a representation of efforts "to create themselves as humans," which is passed to succeeding generations (Brenkert 1998a, 11–12). Such respect requires an understanding of basic values of the culture, noninterference with culturally significant goals, and consideration of cultural values by not seeking to degrade or undercut them. To evaluate marketing and advertising activities, we should then be most concerned with those that fail to respect cultural values.

What Brenkert finds most unacceptable are activities that undercut cultural identification, which can result in people believing that their wants and needs require Western-style products and levels of consumption. When this happens, the value of their culture wanes.

The creation of global food preferences is an often-cited example. Defenders of advertising typically argue that food is adapted to different cultures by use of different spices, different meats, and even meat substitutes. The variety of foods offered by McDonald's is a case in point. Defenders also question why it is problematic for non-Westerners to eat Western food when Westerners eat a diverse diet of foreign foods including gyros, enchiladas, falafel, sushi, hummus, among others. The counterpoint is that when Westerners develop new food preferences, their basic identity is not changed; however, when non-Westerners eat Western foods, some are not only altering eating preferences but they are changing an array of other things. "Though they may be consuming products which have been altered for their own society, they are doing so within the framework of a consumer society in which their identities are significantly affected by the corporations who produce and market the goods they consume. People no longer understand themselves in terms of their local cultural ways, but in terms of the goods they consume and the importance of the consumption of those produced goods in order to satisfy their needs" (Brenkert 1998a, 15).

By introducing the issue of identity, perhaps we have an explanation for what has been one of the most inexplicable problems of all—that the introduction of Western-style goods overwhelms some cultures but not others. Not all countries experience a negative impact on competition, the domestic media scene, and the allocation of resources, along with an erosion of indigenous culture as the result of international advertising; however, the countries that do are likely the ones in which consumers' identities have been significantly altered. It follows that marketers and advertisers should be ethically bound to evaluate the effects of their activities on host countries and to show respect for other cultures by refraining from altering cultural identities in the course of doing business.

➤ 6 ◄

Consumer Protection and Competition

In the previous chapters we examined the role of advertising in both domestic and international markets and considered the issues that arise when advertising spreads consumerist values across borders, particularly from a consumer culture such as the United States, to those grounded in other worldviews and cultural values. Throughout this process, it has been evident that some form of regulation of advertising is needed to protect consumers—more so in some countries than in others—and the type of regulation depends upon the assumptions made about individuals in a consumer culture.

In an ideal classical liberal system, regulation of advertising and competitive practices to protect consumers and promote fair competition isn't necessary. The invisible hand of perfect competition keeps the system naturally in check. In terms of the principles of classical liberalism, the inherently self-interested and intellectual nature of consumers protects them from unscrupulous marketers. Given adequate information, human beings are both self-serving and rational and are thus capable of making wise decisions. At the same time, as classical liberal theory posits, the atomistic character of the competitive system makes it self-righting. A marketer who attempts to inflate the price of his products or to make inferior goods runs the risk of losing customers to competitors with better made or more fairly priced merchandise. So neither consumer protection nor antitrust regulations should be necessary.

But few entrepreneurs or business organizations are angelic, and frequent examples of cutting corners or outright cheating of consumers make a powerful argument for some external controls. So although there's considerable disagreement about the amount and kind of government intervention needed, most people agree that our modern-day version of classical liberalism is far from ideal. Most consumers feel safer knowing that the medicines they take have been subjected to rigorous testing. Similarly, most marketers are glad their competitors may suffer legal penalties if they colluded to fix prices in an effort to drive them out of business.

In many ways, the regulation of advertising mirrors the institutional roles of advertising. The management of competition through antitrust regulation corresponds to the economic function of advertising that, like all institutions, influences the distribution of wealth throughout society. On the other hand, the social influence of advertising can be seen in the various regulations established to protect consumers. Of the two, the regulation of competition in order to protect competitors from one another has been around much longer.

Who's Who in Advertising Regulation

The list of organizations that have some regulatory control over advertising is relatively long and diverse. Depending upon the nature of the product, the advertising medium employed, and the intended audience, there may be several governmental offices at the federal and state levels as well as self-regulatory and trade agencies influencing a particular ad. At the same time, underlying all advertising regulation is the definition of advertising under the First Amendment. The existence and nature of these restrictions are directly tied to the degree of protection accorded by the courts to commercial speech under the Constitution. All of these matters are addressed below, though their treatment here is necessarily incomplete. For more detailed examinations of regulatory bodies and issues involving advertising, consult the sources named in the reference list at the end of the book.

Regulation at the Federal Level

Given the breadth and power of their influence, the list of organizations involved in advertising regulation naturally begins with federal organizations. The most influential is the Federal Trade Commission (FTC), as it is responsible for protecting both consumers and competition in general. It regulates a wide range of consumer goods and services as well as other policies and promotions such as truth in lending, warranties, contests, and so forth. The Food and Drug Administration (FDA) is also highly influential and recently gained the power to regulate tobacco products after more than a decade of struggle. The FDA cannot ban cigarettes or nicotine but will have far-reaching powers including the possibility of ordering a reduction in nicotine levels and the elimination of other harmful ingredients, such as flavorings used to lure first-time smokers (*New York Times* 2009). Table 6.1 (see pages 114–115) provides a summary of the various U.S. federal government offices or organizations that control advertising in some form.

Regulation at the State Level

Advertising regulations exist at the state level as well. In most states, these fall under the jurisdiction of the office of the state attorney general. It's common for a division of consumer protection to handle advertising issues within a state attorney general's office. Most states have what are called "little FTC acts" on which their advertising regulation is based. However, regardless of how a state's advertising regulation is organized, they all mirror FTC's policies. In general, no state law can legally conflict directly with regulation at the national level. Thus, when federal laws take precedence over state laws, the state law is said to be "preempted" by the federal law. But it depends upon the legal issues involved, as states do have jurisdiction over certain products and practices. This is a complex area of law with its own long and complicated history and is better explored by legal scholars elsewhere.

The states vary both in terms of the ways in which they regulate advertising and in terms of how aggressively they pursue legal matters involving advertising. According to the famed advertising law and regulation treatise by James Astrachan and his coresearchers, the role of state regulation has become much more significant due to cuts in the federal budget and the acknowledgement that states may be better equipped to deal with local or regional issues in advertising regulation (Astrachan et al. 2008, 13.01, 13–3). The increased influence of the states in this regard has also been due to both stronger state statutes and the heightened level of oversight by the states' attorneys general (2008, 13.01, 13–3).

The state attorneys general function collectively as the National Association of Attorneys General (NAAG). With somewhat mixed success, the NAAG attempted to establish de facto federal controls by working collectively. However, as mentioned above, state laws work in conjunction with federal regulations and may be pre-empted by federal laws. So the ability for NAAG to implement legislation on a state-by-state basis can be limited.

The NAAG was established in 1907 but didn't become actively involved in advertising regulation until 1987. Though it lacks law enforcement powers, the NAAG can adopt law-enforcement policies and standards relative to specific industries and can be involved in litigation (Astrachan et al. 2008, 13.06[1], 13–97). Since 1987, the NAAG's activities concerning advertising have been controversial at times. However, whenever the FTC exhibits a "laissez-faire" attitude toward regulation, the NAAG has the potential to become the most powerful national regulator of advertising (Astrachan et al. 2008, 13.06 [1], 13.98).

Beginning in 1987, the NAAG issued formal guidelines regarding marketing and advertising practices involving five major industries or types of promotions: (1) the airline industry; (2) the car-rental industry; (3) food advertising; (4) environmental advertising; and (5) Internet commerce. Other actions by the NAAG or subgroups therein have been directed at cable television, deceptive credit advertising, downsized packaging, tobacco marketing to

Table 6.1

U.S. Federal Government Organizations that Control Advertising

Organization	Advertised Products/Services or Legal Matters Regulated
Federal Trade Commission (FTC)	Responsible for protecting both consumers and competition, it regulates a wide range of consumer goods and services as well as other policies and promotions like truth in lending, warranties, contests, etc. It enforces guidelines and policies for industries such as: jewelry, furniture, TV sets, furs, and wool products, etc. It also regulates marketing practices, including use of common sales terms and policies (e.g., "free," disclaimers, bait-and-switch advertising). It also deals with competition issues such as antitrust that are intended to prevent monopolies and the use of unfair tactics by competitors. The Commission works with other regulators and self-regulatory organizations to prevent deception and unfairness on the Internet and to promote good nutrition for kids.
Food and Drug Administration (FDA)	Biological products, food, drugs, medical devices, cosmetics, nonalcoholic beverages.
Federal Communications Commission (FCC)	Specific aspects of advertisements aired on radio, TV, cable and related electronic media; indirectly through licensure of above stations and networks.
United States Postal Service (USPS)	Advertisements sent via U.S. mail.
Department of Treasury	Imported goods and, through its Bureau of Alcohol, Tobacco, and Firearms (BATF), alcohol, tobacco, firearms, and explosive devices.
Department of Justice	Antitrust enforcement.
Department of Commerce	Seafood, fire detection and extinguishing devices, fruits and vegetables.

Department of Transportation	Motor vehicles, boats, and tires.
Securities and Exchange Commission	Banking and investments.
Department of Agriculture	Meat, poultry, egg products, fruits, vegetables, and seeds.
Department of Housing and Urban Development	Real estate, land, and mobile homes.
Consumer Product Safety Commission	Flammable fabrics, poisons, hazardous materials, refrigerators, toys, and bicycles.
Department of Energy	Appliances, televisions, stereos, furnaces, ovens, ranges, and microwaves.
Environmental Protection Agency	Motor vehicles, engines, fuels and additives, noise-emitting devices, insecticides, and pesticides.
Library of Congress	Use and protection of copyrighted material.
Patent and Trademark Office	Use and protection of patents and trademarks.
Congress	Direct authority through law-*making* and taxation; indirect influence through budgetary control over FTC and other regulatory offices.
Courts	The Supreme Court determines First Amendment issues affecting commercial speech. Other courts may influence various issues at the state, district and federal levels.

Source: Carter, Franklin, and Wright 2005, pp. 408–427; Fueroghne 2000.

minors, sweepstakes mailings, information privacy, sports-utility vehicle ads, telemarketing, and health devices. Congress has, in fact, authorized state attorneys general in ways previously reserved for federal agencies (Astrachan et al. 2008, 13.06 [1], 13–97–111).

Industry Self-regulation

Self-regulation fulfills a number of important functions. In addition to compensating for the failure of competition to keep the market fair in all circumstances, self-regulation helps to deter violators while also educating participants about what is acceptable. As a result, self-regulation also helps to discourage violations sooner than the government might. Moreover, because self-regulators can make government action unnecessary, they can also save everyone both time and money (Astrachan et al. 2008, 40.01[1], 40–1–40–4).

In general, self-regulation in the advertising industry dates from the "muckraking" days before the start of World War I. As advertising expenditures and industrial abuses grew (like those in the meat-packing industry chronicled by Upton Sinclair in his book, *The Jungle*), some newspaper and magazine publishers became disenchanted with phony ads and promotion of bogus patent medicines. One of the first and most widely known self-regulatory measures was the *Printer's Ink Magazine* statute in 1911, which proposed that states prohibit any untrue, deceptive, or misleading advertising and treat violations as misdemeanors. Although some states adopted the statute, Preston (1996, 96) called it "a noteworthy experiment but not a success" for it imposed a criminal penalty without requiring proof of fraudulent intent, which ultimately resulted in few convictions. Modern self-regulation didn't emerge until the consumer movement of the 1960s when the advertising industry created the National Advertising Review Council in 1971 (Astrachan et al. 2008, 40.02, 40–4). Eventually, self-regulation evolved into a variety of forms, which are described in Table 6.2.

Self-regulation is thriving. One particularly successful example is the collaboration between the FTC and the Council of Better Business Bureaus (CBBB) in founding the Children's Food and Beverage Advertising Initiative (CFBAI) to address the dietary needs of children. Started in 2006, the CFBAI now has well over a dozen participants who represent the majority of children's food and beverage advertising on television. According to the CBBB Web site, "participating companies agree to devote at least 50 percent of their advertising directed to children under 12 to promote healthier or better-for-you dietary choices and/or to messages that encourage good nutrition or healthy lifestyles. Participants' nutrition criteria defining better-for-you products must be consistent with established scientific and/or government standards,

Table 6.2

Sources of Advertising Self-Regulation

Source of Self-Regulation	How It Works
Advertisers	a. Corporate internal review of advertising before and/or after submission to an ad agency. Industry trade associations that promote legal and ethical advertising practices among members; e.g., The Wine Institute.
	b. Adoption of standards of advertising associations such as the American Advertising Federation (AAF).
	c. The Direct Marketing Association (DMA) advocates and promotes standards among companies involved in direct marketing via various media.
	d. Interactive Services Association (ISA) is a group that focuses on interactive advertising in various media—Internet, telephone, TV.
Advertising Agencies	a. Ads reviewed by agency legal staff or outside legal counsel.
	b. Advertising industry trade associations may require adoption of association standards or guidelines; e.g., Association of National Advertisers (ANA), American Association of Advertising Agencies (4As), American Advertising Federation (AAF).
Media	a. Trade associations for each medium discourage illegal and unethical advertising through their guidelines; e.g., the Transit Advertising Association, Magazine Publishers Association, Association of Industrial Advertisers, etc.
	b. The broadcasting industry, through the National Association of Broadcasters (NAB) and its Code Authority, has been especially aggressive in trying to inhibit airing of illegal or unethical advertising.
	c. In-house or outside legal counsel are regularly employed to screen advertising both before and after it is disseminated.

(continued)

Table 6.2 (continued)

Source of Self-Regulation	How It Works
Council of Better Business Bureaus (CBBB)	a. Through the establishment of its National Advertising Review Council (NARC) and its Local Advertising Review Council (LARC), the CBBB investigates complaints about advertising. In addition to monitoring advertising, the Councils also take complaints from consumers and competitors.
	b. The Council is made up of the National Advertising Division (NAD), the National Advertising Review Board (NARB), and the Children's Advertising Review Unit (CARU).
Collaborative efforts and others	a. The Interactive Advertising Bureau (IAB) and the Interactive Services Association (ISA), both made up of advertisers, tech companies, and others, are committed to interactive advertising in various media.
	b. American Association of Advertising Agencies (4As) and IAB jointly approved terms and conditions for Internet advertising.
	c. 4As and the ANA organized the Coalition for Advertising Supported Information & Entertainment (CASIE).
	d. The Internet Corporation for Assigned Names and Numbers (ICANN) is an international nonprofit group that manages domain names on the Internet. It established the Uniform Domain Name Dispute Resolution Policy (UDRP) to settle disputes regarding domain names.
	e. The Children's Food & Beverage Advertising Initiative was organized by the CBBB under the direction of the FTC and the Institute of Medicine. A number of very large food and beverage marketers pledged to either stop or modify their messages targeted to children.
	f. The Network Advertising Initiative (NAI), founded by six large Internet advertising servers, was created to respond to FTC concerns about collection of personal data.

Sources: Astrachan et al. 2008, 41.02, 41–1—42.05–42–14; Astrachan et al. 2008, 56.07[2][a] 56–137; Astrachan et al. 2008, 56.03[1][b] 56–17; Astrachan et al. 2008, 56.07[1][a] 56–135.

such as USDA Dietary Guidelines and MyPyramid, and FDA standards for health claims."

Self-regulation has been the preeminent avenue for regulation of the Internet. A major reason for this is the unique nature of the Internet. It results in a "judicial paradox" because of its ephemeral ability to thrive internationally without a fixed physical location. This makes jurisdiction over it both "everywhere and nowhere" (Astrachan et al. 2008, 56.06[1][a], 56–66.5). Consequently, there are a number of government bodies in the United States (e.g., the FTC, Congress, the courts) shaping Internet law as well as comparable government authorities in other individual countries and allied nations.

Moreover, unlike other media, the Internet offers consumers and businesses a dizzying array of content, interactivity, personal data collection, and the ability for users to generate content. This leads to problems arising with long-standing media issues (pornography, privacy, trademark, deception, etc.) and some altogether new problems like cybersquatting (Internet domain names that are registered with the hope of later selling them at a profit). All of this occurs twenty-four hours a day in every language imaginable. With the consolation that Internet advertising is responsible for adhering to the same standards facing advertising in other media (such as deception), self-regulation, if done effectively, is thus an obvious means of regulation.

The FTC published a report in 2009 expressing a continuing commitment to relying on self-regulation of Internet-based advertising and the acquisition of personal data. However, the Commission also forewarned the industry that it would take legal action if self-regulation proves ineffective (Anderson 2009). As is always the case, the question is whether the self-regulatory proposals match those advocated by regulators.

Advertising and the First Amendment

As explained above, there would be no need for regulation of advertising in a perfectly functioning classical liberal society. As we all know, however, the American economy is far from perfect. Our nation was founded on the citizens' fundamental right to expression as decreed in the First Amendment to the Constitution: "Congress shall make no law respecting an establishment of religion, or prohibiting the free exercise thereof; or abridging the freedom of speech, or of the press; or the right of the people peaceably to assemble, and to petition the Government for a redress of grievances" (Teeter and Loving 2004, 28, citing the Constitution).

Although the word "Congress" leads off the First Amendment, by the 1930s the Supreme Court of the United States had broadened the meaning to include federal plus state and local governments as entities prohibited from violating fundamental rights of religion, speech, press, assembly, and petition (*Gitlow v. New York* [1925], and *Near v. Minnesota* [1931]).

The First Amendment covers all forms of speech regardless of the form, purpose, or the medium in which it is expressed. However, common sense—plus the Supreme Court of the United States and legislative enactments—dictates that not all speech deserves First Amendment protection. Speech revealing military secrets, or obscene speech, incitements to violence or overthrow of the government represent a few examples of unprotected speech. Restricting expressions that unnecessarily endanger the lives of others is not considered an infringement of free speech rights. The same can be said of fraudulent advertising that puts consumers and competitors in jeopardy.

The First Amendment acts as a safeguard for preventing restrictions of advertising (as well as other forms of speech) from going too far. This right to free speech is the most commonly invoked argument against advertising regulations. However, advertising is considered a form of "commercial speech," which has a complex history of being treated differently under the law. In fact, the first time the Supreme Court addressed the status of advertising under the First Amendment in 1942 it unequivocally dismissed the idea that advertising be given the same protection as other speech. Since then, a balancing act has been played out in the courts as advertisers' right to expression and the public's right to receive information are weighed against the need to protect consumers and competitors from unscrupulous advertisers.

Implicit in the view that commercial speech is less deserving of protection is the idea that it is less important to the democratic marketplace of ideas than either political or religious speech. Moreover, it's been suggested that the potential "chilling" effect feared to occur as a result of restricting political speech isn't as likely to occur with commercial speech. Presumably advertisers, with their commercial, political, or social goals, are not likely to be silenced as a result of government regulation (Richards 1997, 159 citing *Virginia State Board of Pharmacy v. Virginia Citizens Consumer Council, Inc., 1976*).

The degree of protection afforded advertising (and other forms of commercial speech) has evolved over more than a half century as various courts have attempted to clarify the issues related to protection. For obvious reasons, Supreme Court cases have the potential for being the most decisive where the free-speech rights of advertisers are concerned. However, even these decisions have largely dealt with individual advertisers in specific media and markets. So the First Amendment status of advertising (or lack thereof) has evolved out of precedence and inference.

As the highest court in the country, the Supreme Court gets the last word on American legal questions. It even gets the last word when it doesn't say anything, as is the case when the Court refuses to hear a case, thereby letting stand the ruling of the last court to decide the issue. Although the Supreme Court can revise its own decisions, no other judicial body can change a Supreme Court ruling. Supreme Court justices are appointed for life by sitting Presidents and confirmed by Congress. That the justices are not elected officials does not mean their decisions aren't politically motivated. Many (though not all) justices receive distinct partisan support based on the decisions made throughout their judicial careers. Some justices' voting records reflect consistent political views while others' do not. It depends upon the individual justice.

As evident in Table 6.3, the types of cases, regulations, advertisers, messages, and media have varied widely. The outcomes of the decisions follow a very general chronological pattern with protection for advertising increasing over time. The trend, however, is hardly predictable. In fact, over just the last two decades, First Amendment protection of advertising has gone from "nearly non-existent" to nearly eliminating "the gap between commercial speech and fully protected non-commercial speech" (Hoefges 2003, 268).

In the six-plus decades that the First Amendment status of commercial speech has been debated in the Supreme Court, the level of protection afforded it by the Court varied with every case decided. Overall, commercial speech enjoys more protection now than it ever has, but the pattern is far from absolute. In general terms, the limits to this protection are found in the landmark 1980 *Hudson* case, in which the Central Hudson Gas & Electric Corp. challenged a regulation banning promotional advertising that encourages the consumption of electricity. The Court overturned the regulation because it held that a total ban on ads promoting consumption of electricity violated the First Amendment (Gower 2008). The significance of the case is that the decision ultimately proposed the following test for determining the legality of a restriction on commercial speech:

> For commercial speech to come within the First Amendment, 1) it at least must concern lawful activity and not be misleading; 2) next, it must be determined whether the asserted governmental interest to be served by the restriction on commercial speech is substantial; 3) if both inquiries yield positive answers, it must then be decided whether the regulation directly advances the governmental interest asserted, and; 4) whether it is not more extensive than is necessary to serve that interest. (*Central Hudson Gas & Electric v. Public Service Commission of New York* [1980], 447 U.S. 557)

Despite having the *Hudson* test to determine the legality of restrictions on commercial speech, debates over the validity of specific restrictions continue to arise. Across these myriad debates, four trends emerge: first, the status of

Table 6.3

Cases Involving Advertising and the First Amendment

Year	Case	Court Making Final Decision	Issue	Message	Media	Outcome & Significance/Degree of Protection
1942	Valentine v. Chrestensen	Supreme Court	NY City Police Commissioner Valentine forbids Chrestensen from distributing handbills in the street.	Chrestensen promoted tours of a WWI submarine.	Handbills	Purely commercial advertising receives no protection.
1964	New York Times v. Sullivan	Supreme Court	Montgomery, AL, Police Commissioner L.B. Sullivan sues NY Times for libel in its editorial ad.	Chronicle of African-American students' struggle for civil rights at AL State College.	Newspaper editorial ad	Protection granted to advertising for political or social issues.
1975	Bigelow v. Virginia	Supreme Court	Virginia Weekly managing editor/director originally convicted of violating VA code prohibiting promotion of abortions.	New York abortion service and announces availability.	Newspaper	Advertising that contains "factual material of clear 'public interest'" is worthy of protection.
1975	Goldfarb v. Virginia State Bar	Supreme Court	Homebuyers objected to a state Bar Association fee schedule for lawyers doing real estate title searches.	No advertising messages involved but case revolved around price fixing.	Implications for any	Court overturned the learned professions' exemption that exempted professionals from antitrust laws, thereby laying the foundation for subsequent cases involving advertising.

122

Year	Case	Court			Outcome
1976	*Virginia Board of Pharmacy v. Virginia Citizens Consumer Council*[1]	Supreme Court	Consumer groups challenged VA statute banning price advertising for prescription drugs.	Rx drug prices.	Any	Court overturned ban on basis of consumers' need for information.
1977	*Bates v. State Bar of Arizona*	Supreme Court	State Bar Association banned lawyer advertising of prices.	Price advertising by lawyers.	Any	Consumers' need for information deemed more important than controlling potential unprofessionalism. Court acknowledged right to restrict time, place, and manner of advertising.
1978	*First National Bank of Boston v. Bellotti*	Supreme Court	The Court struck down a Massachusetts statute forbidding corporations from making donations to influence ballot issues in an election.	Corporate expenditures for purposes of influencing an election.	Any	Justice Powell declared that any political argument a bank wished to make is central to the purpose of the First Amendment.[2]
1980	*Central Hudson Gas & Electric v. Public Service Commission of New York*[3]	Supreme Court	NY Public Service Commission ordered utility to stop promoting consumption of electricity.	Public utility promoted purchasing of appliances.	Any	Restriction struck down. Court offered a 4-part test for defining when commercial speech can be restricted. As applied later it had mixed results protecting advertising in some cases and upholding restrictions of commercial speech in others.

(continued)

123

Table 6.3 (continued)

Year	Case	Court Making Final Decision	Issue	Message	Media	Outcome & Significance/ Degree of Protection
1981	*Metromedia, Inc. v. City of San Diego*	Supreme Court	City ordinance limiting most outdoor advertising within San Diego upheld.	With some exceptions (political advertising), almost any message would be restricted.	Billboards in city	Though it used the *Hudson* Test, the Court allows the restriction to stand by reverting to the distinction between commercial and noncommercial speech.
1986	*Posadas de Puerto Rico v. Tourism Company*	Supreme Court	Law prohibited promotion of casino gambling to Puerto Rican citizens.	Gambling by residents.	Any	Upheld ban based on superficial (no evidence offered) application of Hudson Test. Because the government could ban gambling it could also ban the advertising for it.
1989	*SUNY v. Fox*	Supreme Court	State University of New York students challenged University's prohibition of for-profit activities on campus.	Commercial promotion of housewares and noncommercial discussion of tips on good homemaking.	Dorm-room product demonstrations that also included noncommercial content.	Affirmed ban by modifying the fourth part of the Hudson Test in saying the restriction of speech need not be the least restrictive, just narrowly defined.
1993	*Discovery Network, Inc. v. City of Cincinnati*	Supreme Court	Publishing company challenged municipal code barring distribution of free advertising magazines in public racks. City argues that ban will help keep city clean.	Discovery Network's ads.	Free advertising magazines in racks. Newspapers distributed similarly were allowed.	Because the ordinance was not content-neutral (banned advertising but not newspapers), it could not qualify as a time, place, or manner restriction so it was rejected.

Year	Case	Court	Description	Topic	Outcome
1993	*Edenfield v. Fane*	Supreme Court	CPA Fane challenged Florida CPA Board's ban on uninvited personal solicitation by CPAs.	Truthful, nondeceptive proposal of a business agreement.	Personal sales	The Court deemed the prohibition unconstitutional based partially on the public's need for information.
1993	*United States v. Edge Broadcasting Co.*	Supreme Court	Federal law prohibits promotion of lotteries in states that do not have lotteries. A North Carolina broadcaster who wanted to accept Virginia lottery advertising challenged this.	On the border between N.C. and Virginia, most of the station's revenue and listeners were from Virginia.	Radio was focus of case but federal law applies to all media.	The Court upheld the law based on the Hudson Test. But it also invoked the Posadas logic by saying that vice products like gambling are not constitutionally protected, and the power to prohibit them includes the lesser power to ban advertising for them.
1995	*Rubin v. Coors Brewing Co.*	Supreme Court	Coors Brewing Co. challenged a federal law preventing brewers from disclosing alcohol content on beer labels.	Alcohol content.	Labeling	The Court unanimously declared the law unconstitutional based on the inconsistency of banning disclosure of alcohol levels on beer while requiring alcohol disclosure on wine.
1995	*Florida Bar v. Went For It*	Supreme Court	A legal referral service challenged a Florida Bar ban on lawyers' direct mail solicitations of accident victims and their families within 30 days of an accident.	Uninvited solicitations of accident victims and their families as clients for lawyers.	Direct mail	Based on the perceived importance of the state's interest in protecting the legal profession and consumer privacy, the Court found the restriction constitutional. The Court also stated it was not required to provide supporting evidence.

(continued)

125

Table 6.3 (continued)

Year	Case	Court Making Final Decision	Issue	Message	Media	Outcome & Significance/ Degree of Protection
1996	*44 Liquormart v. Rhode Island*	Supreme Court	Liquor stores argued that Rhode Island laws preventing advertising of liquor prices (except in stores) were unconstitutional.	Retail liquor prices.	Any	Arguing for the consumer's need for information in a market-based economy, the Court found the laws unconstitutional.
1999	*Greater New Orleans Broadcast Association v. United States*	Supreme Court	FCC rules prevented broadcasters from carrying advertising for private (not state-run or non-Indian) casino gambling.	Privately owned casino gambling.	Radio and television	Based on its application of the Hudson Test, the Court could not justify the advertising restriction.
2001	*Lorillard Tobacco Co. v. Reilly*	Supreme Court	The four biggest U.S. cigarette producers challenged Massachusetts laws restricting outdoor advertising (including visible stadium and store signs) for tobacco products within 1,000 feet of a school or playground. POS ads had to be five feet or higher in stores that allowed children in them.	Tobacco ads.	Outdoor and point-of-sale	Although cigarettes and other tobacco products had to be dealt with differently due to how they're regulated, the Court ruled that the regulations failed the fourth part of the Hudson Test. They were deemed unconstitutional because they were too broad.

Year	Case	Court	Description	Subject	Details
2002	*Thompson v. Western States Medical Center*	Supreme Court	A federal statute prohibiting pharmacies, pharmacists, and doctors from advertising compounded drugs to consumers (FDAMA) was ruled unconstitutional.	Messages promoting compounded drugs.	Any	The Court struck down the ban based on the fourth prong of the Hudson Test that requires a regulation to be narrowly tailored to the interest inherent in the regulation. The Court argued that there were nonspeech methods available to prevent the creation of a mass market for compounded drugs. The Court also introduced a new basis for challenging restrictions on speech: the amount of beneficial speech silenced by the statute.[4]
2004	*Mainstream Marketing Services, Inc. v. Federal Trade Commission*	Supreme Court	The Supreme Court denies certiorari, thereby allowing a ruling to stand by the United States Court of Appeals for the Tenth Circuit upholding the constitutionality of the do-not-call registry. At issue were concerns for consumer privacy and the prevention of potentially harmful or costly telemarketing calls.	Various uninvited commercial messages	Telemarketing, telefaxes.	Based on the application of the Hudson Test, the courts found regulation of unsolicited commercial calls and faxes constitutional, as it protects consumers from the intangible costs associated with unwanted appeals. Noncommercial appeals were specifically excluded from regulation.

(continued)

127

Table 6.3 (continued)

Year	Case	Court Making Final Decision	Issue	Message	Media	Outcome & Significance/ Degree of Protection
2007	Federal Election Commission (FEC) v. Wisconsin Right to Life	Supreme Court	Constitutionality of McCain-Feingold law (the Bipartisan Campaign Reform Act; BCRA) forbidding attacking candidates by name in a general election.	Issue ads by Wisconsin Right to Life mentioning Senator Russ Feingold.	Broadcast	BCRA declared unconstitutional, thereby squashing the 2002 McCain-Feingold statute regulating pre-election broadcast advertising.

[1]Rare insight into the Court's justification for differential treatment of commercial speech is found in a footnote in Virginia Pharmacy that describes it as "more easily verifiable and more durable" than other kinds of speech (Richards, 1997, p. 159).

[2]Teeter and Loving, 2004, p. 853.

[3]The Hudson Test: For commercial speech to come within the First Amendment, (1) it at least must concern lawful activity and not be misleading; (2) it must be determined whether the asserted governmental interest to be served by the restriction on commercial speech is substantial; (3) if both inquires yield positive answers, it must then be decided whether the regulation directly advances the governmental interest asserted, and; (4) whether it is not more extensive than is necessary to serve that interest. Central Hudson Gas & Electric v. Public Service Commission of New York (1980), 447 U.S. 557.

[4]Astrachan et al., 2008, 6.03[4][a], 6–49.

commercial speech under the First Amendment hasn't evolved predictably or always positively. Whereas one decision seems to represent two steps forward (e.g., *Bates v. State Bar of Arizona*, which struck down a ban on price advertising for attorneys and resulted in consumers having greater access to information about legal fees), a subsequent decision looks like two steps backward (e.g., *Florida Bar v. Went For It,* which ruled that a ban on uninvited solicitations of families of accident victims by attorneys was constitutional, thereby limiting attorneys' ability to communicate with consumers). The latter decision was based on the perception that such communication by attorneys is exploitative of consumers' vulnerability.

Second, the ultimate ramifications of a decision can change over time as it is applied to later cases. For example, *Hudson* initially appeared to be a positive step toward defining the limits of the regulation of commercial speech. Advocates of advertising as free speech saw it as shield against capricious restrictions on commercial speech. As the four-part *Hudson* Test was differentially applied, however, it seemed to be anything but. In *Posadas de Puerto Rico v. Tourism Company of Puerto Rico,* the Supreme Court upheld a ban on the advertising of casino gambling to Puerto Rican citizens; and in *SUNY v. Fox*, the Court affirmed a ban on commercial promotions and dorm-room product demonstrations on campus. In both cases, the restrictions appeared capricious and out of sync with *Hudson.*

Third, at no point in its history of treatment by the courts has commercial speech ever been viewed equal with other speech, and at no point in the future is it likely to be viewed as such. Even the Courts' most unequivocal advocates for protection of speech have never advocated dropping the distinction between the two kinds of speech.

Fourth, commercial speech enjoys dramatically more protection now than it did when it was first considered in the 1940s. *Lorillard Tobacco Co. v. Reilly* is a case in point that illustrates the rationale for the Court's decision to ban restrictions that are too broad and sweeping when narrower restrictions might accomplish the same goal. In a 2001 decision, the Supreme Court struck down a state regulation that prohibited outdoor advertising for cigarettes, smokeless tobacco, and cigars located within a 1,000-foot radius of a school or playground. Even though a compelling regulatory goal existed for protecting children from the harm of tobacco usage, the Court made it clear that "the First Amendment will not allow the government to substantially disrupt the flow of lawful commercial information to adult consumers . . ." (Hoefges 2003, 311).

As Hoefges pointed out, *Lorillard* seems to have bolstered protection for commercial speech by getting "legislators to look seriously at more direct, narrow and efficacious means of solving serious social and political problems than banning protected speech" (2003, 311). He cited several lower court decisions in the federal district courts and circuit courts of appeals that relied on *Lorillard* in finding restrictions on commercial speech too broad.

How the Supreme Court will approach future commercial speech cases remains to be seen. Even in the unlikely event that the composition of the Court remains very similar to how it was when *Lorillard* was decided, the justices' approaches to commercial speech can always change. The law reflects the variability of the human beings that evaluate it.

Some reasons for contentious interpretations of commercial speech under the First Amendment are easily identified. To begin with, the authors of the Constitution did not provide the rights later added in the Bill of Rights. The Bill of Rights and the First Amendment were political concessions to overcome the vociferous complaints of the Anti-Federalists, the opponents of the Constitution.

Of necessity, the broad generalizations put forth in the Constitution in the eighteenth century have evolved by interpretation to enable the Constitution of the United States to endure far longer than George Washington expected it to last. Along with many other facets of American life, the significance of advertising and other forms of commercial speech expanded, and interpretations broadening freedom of speech and the press of necessity evolved (Astrachan et al. 2008, 6.02, 6–13). To some, the profit-based purpose and the persuasive content of advertising made it undeserving of First Amendment protection. Moreover, abuses of dishonest sales claims and violations of taste so common in advertising have led critics to want to see it regulated in ways they would not tolerate if applied to political speech (Astrachan et al. 2008, 6.02 [2] [b], 6–13).

On the other hand, the importance of commercial speech to an industrialized, market-based society has only increased since the 1700s. Along with that, Americans have come to expect access to information. The Supreme Court first expressed this "right to receive information" in 1969 and has reiterated it in numerous cases ever since (Astrachan et al. 2008, 6.02[2][b], 6–15–16).

Problematic are at least four substantive issues that result in the unpredictability of commercial speech cases (Hindman 2004, 269). First, there's no one definition of what constitutes commercial speech, and ". . . those subject to regulation argue that the speech in question is not commercial speech, in order to obtain 'full' First Amendment protections. Many cases have grappled with this problem, but drawing a line of demarcation between the two types of speech is neither easy nor objective" (Astrachan et al. 2008, 6.03[3][a], 6–27–29). Furthermore, as Cunningham and Freeman (2003, 7) observed, the Court has more readily identified what is not considered commercial speech than clarifying the distinction between it and other kinds of speech.

Second, the purpose of protecting commercial speech, ostensibly so audiences have access to accurate information on which to base decisions, is
the collectivist rationale, but it isn't always consistently applied. Third, the
Court's assumptions about the abilities of the audience to evaluate the veracity of commercial speech are also not the same in every case. Fourth, most
often the Court has advocated the audience's need for information but has
also promoted less frequently the speaker's right to disseminate information
(Hindman 2004, 269–270).

Hindman saw in these controversies a deeper ambiguity among the Supreme
Court justices about whether to address commercial speech doctrine from a
collectivist or individualist perspective. This balancing of community values
against individual rights is illustrative of the enduring dilemma inherent in
a consumer culture that was originally founded on the individualist-based
principles of classical liberalism. The value placed on providing truthful information to society and the economy that reflects a collectivist rationale can
often conflict with the more individualist-centered concern for a person's right
to expression. Accordingly, "conflict has arisen in part because the majority
of the Court wants to protect commercial speech for its social value—a collectivist rationale—while debate on the issue also includes arguments from,
and language of, an individualistic rationale" (Hindman 2004, 270).

The First Amendment and the Bill of Rights as a whole, like the classical liberal foundations of capitalism, are based on individualist principles.
However, the interpretation and protection of our First Amendment rights
have often revolved around societal or collectivist ideals. The balancing of
these two sometimes contradictory values is a hallmark of modern classical
liberalism that permeates regulatory issues and virtually every social and
economic issue in our culture.

Although it is the nation's most important arbiter of legal limitations on
commercial speech, the Supreme Court itself is an evolving body. Since commercial speech was first addressed by the Supreme Court in 1942 in *Valentine
v. Chrestensen* (a case that examined the legality of distributing handbills
in the street), the U.S. Supreme Court Web site shows there have been six
different chief justices and thirty-three associate justices (not including the
chief justices). The composition of the Court has thus changed throughout
the judicial history of commercial speech.

The Supreme Court is also, by definition, a political body. The justices
(and the chief justice) are appointed by the President and confirmed by the
Senate. Although they serve for life and are not required to seek election or
reelection, the justices' lifetime political leanings and legal careers tend to
win the partisan support that results in an appointment by the President. This
is not to say, however, that every justice holds to an ideological or partisan

view once on the Court. Some justices' records on the Supreme Court appear inconsistent with the early voting patterns that got them nominated in the first place. Although retiring Justice David Souter disputes the notion that justices often surprise the presidents who appoint them, Souter himself surprised his benefactor, President George H.W., Bush by aligning himself with the Court's liberals (Lazarus 2009). In short, Supreme Court justices are political appointees who are politically unpredictable.

Given all this, what now constitutes protected commercial speech? The following summary of the current commercial speech doctrine echoes the substance of the 1980 *Hudson* Test:

> A restriction on commercial speech which does not regulate the content of that speech is constitutional, so long as it serves a significant government interest, is directed only towards regulating the time, place or manner of such speech and implementation of the regulation leaves open alternative channels of communication for the speaker.

A restriction on speech which does seek to regulate the content of that speech is constitutional if:

1. The speech is "commercial" speech, concerns a lawful activity and is not misleading; and
2. A substantial state interest is furthered by the regulation;
3. The regulation directly furthers that interest;
4. The regulation is drawn reasonably narrowly. (Astrachan et al., 2008 6.03[2], 6–19)

If a regulation is content-based, it is subjected to much more careful constitutional scrutiny (Astrachan et al. 2008, 6.03[2], 6–25). Accordingly, the reasons for this are rooted in the risks inherent in silencing truthful speech for government reasons other than consumer protection (6.03[2], 6–25–26).

The Federal Trade Commission

Throughout the long and complicated history of advertising and the First Amendment, most parties agreed on one thing. Advertising for illegal products and untruthful advertising for legal products are not allowed. The former class of advertising is completely banned. The latter class is also not acceptable but is considerably more difficult to define. This is where various regulatory bodies enter the picture.

As shown in Tables 6.1 and 6.2, numerous organizations regulate advertising in one way or another. Of them, however, none has the range of influence or the years of experience in advertising regulation that the Federal Trade Commission does. The Federal Trade Commission Act, on which the FTC is based, has been called "the heart of federal protection of consumers against abusive advertising practices" (Astrachan et al. 2008, 15.03, 15–7, 15–8). The Commission's primary initial charge, however, was not to protect consumers from advertisers. When it was established in 1914, the FTC was created to maintain competition by protecting competitors from each other. Indirectly, of course, this would also serve consumers. It wasn't until 1938 with the passage of the Wheeler-Lea Amendment that the Commission was empowered specifically to engage in consumer protection. (See Table 2.1.) Seemingly, like everything else related to advertising, the FTC is characterized by constant and sometimes dramatic change.

There are three bureaus within the FTC: Consumer Protection, Economics, and Competition. The Bureau of Consumer Protection has the broadest impact on advertising. The Bureau of Economics helps the Commission by evaluating the potential and actual economic consequences of its policies. Using a variety of data, the Bureau may be able to analyze the cost/benefit ratio of a particular policy (Hobbs 2004–2005, 1153). It may also conduct economic studies on behalf of Congress or other agencies when necessary. The Bureau of Competition is responsible for implementing policies that foster competition and for investigating potential antitrust violations. Its jurisdiction over antitrust is shared with the Antitrust Division of the Department of Justice. The Bureaus of Consumer Protection and Competition will be described in greater detail after a discussion of the history of the FTC.

Brief History of the FTC

The present-day power of the FTC is manifested in several ways. Of all the regulatory organizations, it has the broadest jurisdiction over advertising, since it was empowered to regulate deceptive acts and practices injurious to competitors or consumers. The FTC also serves as the model on which many states base their consumer protection agencies. But the Commission's power wasn't always so broad. In fact, its history offers a dramatic illustration of the ups and downs in advertising regulation as we see in the following comment: "The FTC's history is a story of cycles and repetitions. The same thorny issues emerge again and again: troubled relations with Congress and the Courts; shifting interpretations of the Commission's mandate; swings between action and inaction; and conflicts between advisory and adversarial approaches to regulating business" (Murphy and Wilkie 1990, 169 quoting Zuckerman 1990). Table 6.4 offers a snapshot of the FTC's history.

Table 6.4

Brief History of the Federal Trade Commission (FTC)

1914–1940s	Early Years	FTC Act created the Commission during President Woodrow Wilson's Democratic administration. It was initially intended to regulate "methods of competition in commerce." Supreme Court's decision in Raladam in 1931 restricted the FTC's jurisdiction to protecting competitors.
		The 1938 Wheeler-Lea Amendment expanded the Commission's jurisdiction to include consumer protection. The FTC's early years are fraught with problems due to ambiguity of its jurisdiction, inadequate funding, and high personnel turnover. FTC is caught in the roller coaster ride of competing attitudes toward business and government. With the advent of World War I and innovations and abuses in mass production (particularly the meat-packing industry), the FTC's power and funding is curtailed.
1947–1961	Probusiness	The history of consumer culture is sown with the advent of television. The Commission initially gains strength based on the 1938 Wheeler-Lea Amendment. It's reorganized in 1950 and again in 1954 and 1960. With the support of the courts, the FTC gains strength in antitrust and consumer protection. However, relative to the national budget, the FTC's funding decreased significantly.
1962–1977	Proconsumer	President John F. Kennedy's Consumer Message to Congress in 1962 set the stage for an increasingly activist FTC. Ralph Nader, whose book *Unsafe at Any Speed* fueled the automobile safety debate, launched an attack on the Federal Trade Commission. The American Bar Association, under the direction of Miles Kirkpatrick, published a highly critical assessment of the FTC. Congress followed up by demanding more FTC activity. The FTC was reorganized around two principal bureaus: The Bureau of Consumer Protection and the Bureau of Competition. Congress more than tripled the FTC's budget between 1971 and 1979. The FTC introduced the advertising substantiation program, corrective advertising, and began emphasizing trade regulation rules. Congress supported the FTC with more money and new statutes that expanded and toughened the Commission. The FTC targeted some of the most powerful companies in American industry.

1978–1992	Probusiness	By 1978, the Federal Trade Commission had alienated business and Congress. The public was tired of big government, and the FTC had overstepped its ambiguous mandate. Congress passed the 1980 FTC Improvements Act preventing the FTC from using unfairness as a basis for trade rules and giving itself veto power over the Commission, though this was later ruled unconstitutional. The FTC lost 60 percent of its substantive antitrust cases, including its infamous case against the top three cereal makers. Retention of key staff was poor, instigation of new cases was curtailed, and many regional offices were closed. However, Congress ultimately passed the Telephone Disclosure and Dispute Resolution Act of 1992, which was the first of several laws that supported FTC rulemaking by authorizing it to issue rules.
1993–2000	Proconsumer?	The Commission, under the influence of President Clinton, went back to a more moderate role and escalated its consumer protection activity. A number of significant issues arose during Clinton's two terms. A large number of mergers arose, many of which were opposed by the Commission or passed contingent upon FTC's stipulations. It was during this period that media violence, Internet privacy, and R.J. Reynolds's use of Joe Camel in its advertising all became part of the public agenda.
2001–2008	Probusiness?	Building on the activities of the last decade, concerns for both consumers and competitors revolve around the Internet. Contrary to what one might expect based on party affiliation, however, it was during a Republican administration (with a Republican majority in both houses of Congress and a Republican chair of the FTC) that one of the FTC's most popular initiatives was passed. Though not easily enacted, the "do not call" revisions to the Telemarketing Sales Rule were a significant achievement in consumer protection. It was also during Bush's two terms in office that antitrust enforcement in the health care industry and investigation of predatory lending were increased.
2009–	Proconsumer?	With the election of Barack Obama and his appointment of FTC Commissioner Jon Leibowitz along with democratic majorities in both Congressional bodies, there's a democratic majority across the board. This is the first time this has happened since 1980.

Sources: Aaker and Day 1982; Ameringer 2008; Abernethy and Franke 1998; Averitt and Calvani 1989; Baer 1986; Budnitz 1997; Cox, Fellmuth, and Schultz 1969, p. vii; Editors, 1981; Grun 2005; Hermann 1982; Teinowitz 2001; Winerman 2005; Zuckerman 1990.

Though discernable patterns exist in the FTC's history, the last couple of decades seem to indicate a more complex dynamic than the typical seesaw between proconsumer, Democratic leadership and probusiness, Republican leadership. The election of Barack Obama and his appointment of FTC Commissioner Jon Leibowitz to chair the FTC completed the democratic trifecta that occurs when the President, both Congressional bodies, and the FTC chairmanship are all Democratic. This was the first time this happened since 1980.

The varying levels of activity of the Federal Trade Commission over more than the last two decades and the last six presidential administrations might be found in the history of the Commission's budget. As an indicator of Congressional support, the FTC budget may mirror the prevailing attitudes toward regulation. Table 6.5 shows the FTC's budget and the party affiliation of the Presidents, FTC chairs, and the Congressional majority over the last 30 years. (The appropriation was also for all the functions of the FTC and not just the regulation of advertising.)

With regard to FTC antitrust activity, variations in the Commission's level of activism appear to be tied to the performance of the economy and to the political makeup of Congress, for ". . . enforcement is higher during strong economic times and lessens during a weak economy. This supports the idea that government is less likely to hurt business when business is vulnerable. Partisanship in the oversight subcommittee of the Senate was found to influence enforcement levels, with enforcement decreasing during increased Republican strength" (Bjornstrom 2007, 1). Moreover, antitrust offenders are "more likely to offend during economic downturns and to a lesser extent, during Republican administrations" (Bjornstrom 2007, 2 referencing Simpson 1986, 1987).

Astrachan et al. (2008) point out that several events over the last twenty years have had a lasting impact on the regulation of advertising. First, the passage of the little FTC acts by the states since the mid-1980s brought about more cooperation between the Commission and the state attorneys general. Second, Congress revised the Lanham Trademark Act in 1988 thereby broadening the Commission's authority in cases involving false advertising. Third, the FTC expanded the range of "respondents considered liable for violations of the FTC Act beyond advertisers to include other parties such as advertising agencies and attorneys who might have only collateral involvement with the advertisements under examination in a particular case" (Astrachan et al. 2008, 18.01, 18–5). Last, due to the proliferation of telecommunication media and attendant social concerns, the Commission has taken a more activist role in its regulation of advertising. FTC actions in consumer protection in 1995 were up almost 29 percent higher than the year before (Astrachan et al. 2008, 18.01, 18–4—18–6).

Table 6.5

FTC Appropriation History (US$ in millions)

Fiscal Year	% Annual Unemploy.	Presidential Party	Congress Majority[1]	FTC Chair's Party	Amount Authorized	Adj—in 2008 $
1979	5.8	Dem	Dem	Dem	$65	$192
1980	7.1	Dem	Dem	Dem	$66	$172
1981	7.6	Rep	Divided[2]	Dem	$71	$168
1982	9.7	Rep	Divided	Rep	$69	$153
1983	9.6	Rep	Divided	Rep	$67	$144
1984	7.5	Rep	Divided	Rep	$64	$132
1985	7.2	Rep	Divided	Rep	$66	$132
1986	7.0	Rep	Divided	Rep	$63	$123
1987	6.2	Rep	Divided	Rep	$65	$123
1988	5.5	Rep	Dem	Rep	$66	$120
1989	5.3	Rep	Dem	Rep	$66	$114
1990	5.6	Rep	Dem	Rep	$77	$126
1991	6.8	Rep	Dem	Rep	$76	$120
1992	7.5	Rep	Dem	Rep	$83	$127
1993	6.9	Dem	Dem	Rep	$87	$129
1994	6.1	Dem	Dem	Rep	$92	$133
1995	5.6	Dem	Rep	Dem	$99	$139
1996	5.4	Dem	Rep	Dem	$99	$135
1997	4.9	Dem	Rep	Dem	$102	$136
1998	4.5	Dem	Rep	Dem	$107	$141
1999	4.2	Dem	Rep	Dem	$117	$151
2000	4.0	Dem	Rep	Dem	$125	$156

(continued)

Table 6.2 (continued)

Fiscal Year	% Annual Unemploy.	Presidential Party	Congress Majority[1]	FTC Chair's Party	Amount Authorized	Adj—in 2008 $
2001	4.7	Rep	Divided	D/R[3]	$147	$178
2002	5.8	Rep	Divided	Rep	$156	$186
2003	6.0	Rep	Rep	Rep	$177	$207
2004	5.5	Rep	Rep	Rep	$186	$211
2005	5.1	Rep	Rep	Rep	$205	$225
2006	4.6	Rep	Dem	Rep	$211	$225
2007	4.6	Rep	Dem	Rep	$211	$219
2008	5.8	Rep	Dem	Rep	$244	$244
2009	8.5[4]	Dem	Dem	Dem		

[1]The fiscal year and the Congressional terms don't match exactly.
[2]This indicates party majority is not the same in both the House and Senate.
[3]Leadership changed midyear.
[4]Average for January–May 2009.
Sources: http://www.ftc.gov/ftc/oed/fmo/appropriationhistory.htm; CPI Calculator, http://www.bls.gov/; www.senate.gov/pagelayout/history/one_item_and_teasers/partydiv.htm; http://data.bls.gov/PDQ/servlet/SurveyOutputServlet?data_tool=latest_numbers&series_id=LNU04000000&years_option=all_years&periods_option=specific_periods&periods=Annual+Data; Ameringer 2008, 79

Overall, it's difficult to predict the FTC's level of activism in the coming years due to the number and complexity of conflicting factors. On one hand, the dominance of the Democratic Party in the White House and Congress and the FTC chairmanship would seem to augur well for a strong FTC (Wasserman 2009). Incoming FTC chair Leibowitz promised to bring cases against major corporations as well as cases involving: online behavioral targeting, endorsements, and mobile advertising such as texting of spam (Wasserman 2009).

Although 2009 is the first year that Democrats have dominated the Presidency, Congress, and FTC leadership since 1980, the FTC's budget rose significantly during similar Republican domination from 2003 through 2006. Throughout George W. Bush's two terms in office, the Federal Trade Commission along with other government watchdogs have gone to bat for consumers in the areas of telecommunication and digital media, health care, consumer credit, and privacy. On the other hand, the continuing economic crisis might be expected to induce businesses to take more risks while also discouraging regulators for fear of further depressing the economy.

Conventional wisdom suggests that Democratic leadership favors consumers while Republicans support business interests. The shifting emphasis is analogous to the balancing of collectivist values (consumers collectively) against individualist values (individual companies). As consumer culture grows ever more complex, however, the regulatory process becomes more complex as well. Predictions based solely on party politics may be too simplistic.

The Bureau of Consumer Protection

The Bureau of Consumer Protection works to prevent fraud, deception, and unfair business practices in the marketplace that can negatively affect consumers. According to the FTC Web site, it enforces federal laws that protect consumers, empowers consumers with free information to help them exercise their rights and spot fraud and deception, and assists consumers in filing a complaint about fraud or identity theft. There are seven divisions within the Bureau of Consumer Protection:

1. The Division of Advertising Practices
2. The Division of Consumer & Business Education
3. The Division of Marketing Practices
4. The Division of Financial Practices
5. The Division of Enforcement
6. The Division of Privacy & Identity Protection
7. The Division of Planning & Information.

Within the Division of Advertising Practices, myriad regulations governing specific industries (e.g., the funeral industry), advertising media (e.g., the Internet) and promotional practices (e.g., use of the word "free") are enforced. According to the FTC's Web site, The Division of Advertising Practices' enforcement priorities include:

- Combating deceptive advertising of fraudulent cure-all claims for dietary supplements and weight loss products;
- Monitoring and stopping deceptive internet marketing practices that develop in response to public health issues;
- Monitoring and developing effective enforcement strategies for new advertising techniques and media, such as word-of-mouth marketing;
- Monitoring and reporting on the advertising of food to children, including the impact of practices by food companies and the media on childhood obesity;
- Monitoring and reporting on industry practices regarding the marketing of violent movies, music, and electronic games to children;
- Monitoring and reporting on alcohol and tobacco marketing practices.

Note that the ad or campaign in question may have been discontinued well before the FTC's actions against it. Because one of the FTC's principal objectives is to discourage deception and unfairness in the future, an ad need not be in use for the Commission to proceed against it. Advertising messages are notoriously short-lived. So the Commission's actions may be taken against messages that are no longer being aired. Inherent in the FTC's doctrine is the assumption that a violator will continue to offend. However, there are certain exceptions to this assumption (e.g., the ownership and control of the corporate respondent changes; Astrachan et al. 2008, 18.05[1], 18–86, 87).

Principal Areas for Enforcement

Several troublesome areas come under the purview of the FTC with regard to advertising messages. Of these, deception and unfairness are the most problematic for consumers.

Deception. As defined under Chairman Miller during the Reagan administration, the FTC Web site defines deception as follows: "First, there must be a representation, omission or practice that, second, is likely to mislead consumers acting reasonably under the circumstances, and third, the representation, omission, or practice is material."

There are several important elements to this definition. To begin with, almost any aspect of an ad can be the source of deception including the literal, verbal, and visual content of the ad; what was left out of the ad; how the ad was created; and what it directly or indirectly implies. Even an ad that includes a truthful clarification of an inaccurate interpretation of a claim can be found to be deceptive if the net impression is untrue.

Advertisers can also get into trouble for what is not said in an ad. "Deception by omission" occurs when key information is left out of an ad. Teeter and Loving (2004, 810–811) point to the 1984 *Bristol-Myers Bufferin* case, wherein the Commission found the claim that Bufferin was recommended more than any other pain relievers to be deceptive because Bristol-Myers neglected to mention that the claim was true only from 1967 through 1971.

Note that the Commission isn't required to find actual deception. An advertisement need only have the likelihood to deceive to warrant action. The wording was changed in 1984 from "tendency or capacity" to "likelihood" to deceive (Fueroghne 2000, 29). However, protection is restricted to "consumers acting reasonably under the circumstances." This constitutes a shift from its former policy of protecting the most gullible consumer or someone responding to an ad in an atypical way.

Lastly, the deception must be material to the consumer's purchase decision. In other words, had the deception not occurred, the consumer might have chosen a different brand or product (Fueroghne 2000, 33–34).

Unfairness. According to the FTC, "an advertisement or trade practice is unfair if it, first, causes or is likely to cause substantial consumer injury; and, second, which is not reasonably avoidable by consumers themselves; and, third, is not outweighed by countervailing benefits to consumers or competition (Fair 2002, 1).

Unfairness as a basis for FTC action against advertisers and industries has a history of controversy. According to Teeter and Loving (2004), a 1994 amendment to Section Five of the FTC Act requires the Commission to show that the act or practice is actually likely to cause unavoidable and substantial harm to consumers. No longer will the FTC be able to simply assume that an ad will result in significant injury (2004, 806–807).

One defense of potentially deceptive and misleading practices is the substantiation of claims. In the early 1970s, the Commission passed requirements that advertisers must be able to substantiate claims made about their products prior to the dissemination of the claims. The motivation underlying the program was to shift the burden of proof onto the advertiser, thereby reducing the expense formerly incurred by the Commission (Astrachan et al. 2008, 33.05[4], 35–34—35–35). When the country shifted to a conservative majority in the 1980s, the Commission revised the program to allow for substantiation of claims after the claim was disseminated, although advertisers were still required to have a "reasonable" basis for their claims.

Unfairness can be used as grounds for regulating a specific ad and for passing industry-wide rules. Currently the FTC has the authority to pass industry guides and substantive rules, the latter of which are enforceable, though subject to judicial review.

The FTC's industry guides, though not enforceable, are provided to help advertisers avoid making claims or using techniques that are deceptive or unfair. They cover specific industries, like dietary supplements, and promotional practices such as endorsements and testimonials. In general, the legal enforceability of FTC industry guides is in dispute (Astrachan et al. 2008, 32.04[2][d], 32–33). They're intended to provide guidance so offenses can be discouraged before they occur.

Trade Regulation Rules are intended to be legally enforceable, substantive laws. The criteria for valid rule-making are defined by the Commission as

1. A statement as to the prevalence of the practice being regulated
2. A finding that the practice results in substantial consumer injury
3. A finding that the proposed rule would reduce that injury
4. A finding that the rule's benefits would outweigh its costs
5. A finding that consumers are unable to avoid the injury caused by the practice without promulgation of the proposed rule. (Astrachan et al. 2008, 32.02[2], 32–7)

Violation of trade regulation rules can result in stiff fines. Advertisers, ad agencies, and media organizations can be fined $11,000 per violation per day. Advertising practitioners are responsible for knowing all the FTC rules that are likely to apply to them. Depending upon the product, promotional tactics and media involved, practitioners may have to know about a variety of different rules (Astrachan et al. 2008, 32.05[3], 42–43).

Given the FTC's ability to regulate deceptive and misleading claims and enforce violations of trade regulation rules, consumers sometimes question why advertisers in certain product categories (e.g., weight loss) seemingly get away with outlandish claims such as promises of losing thirty pounds or more in one month without diet and exercise. Despite the fact that the FTC has successfully brought a large number of enforcement actions for false or deceptive claims in the weight-loss category, ads with unsubstantiated and misleading claims continue to proliferate as unscrupulous product manufacturers take advantage of consumers' vulnerability (Galloway 2003). The difficulty is that Congress largely divested the FDA of its authority to regulate this industry with the passage of the Dietary Supplements Health and Education Act of 1994 (DSHEA). A product can be banned by the FDA after a supplement is marketed if it is later proven dangerous, but the product is not prescreened from entering the market. Dietary supplements that are not dangerous but are merely ineffective appear to be beyond the purview of the FDA (Galloway 2003).

Common Potentially Deceptive Practices

There are an infinite number of potentially deceptive practices in advertising. The following are some of the more common ones dealt with by the FTC. Some might occur in any medium and for any product whereas others are potentially deceptive techniques used in particular media (e.g., billboards) and with specific types of products (e.g., tobacco). The FTC Web site is the best source of information about deceptive practices by medium or product type.

Testimonials and Endorsements. The FTC passed guidelines for using testimonials and endorsements in 1975 and these, though revised recently, are still operative. The Commission does not distinguish between testimonials and endorsements; the guides apply to both. The guidelines offer common-sense rules pertaining to the type of person making the endorsement as well as to the rules regarding disclosure of remuneration of the endorser. For instance, if an endorser is presented as a typical consumer, he or she should not somehow be affiliated with the advertiser. Moreover, although an endorser can be assumed to be paid for his time, remuneration based on subsequent sales of product has to be disclosed. If an endorser implicitly or explicitly suggests he has used the product, this must actually be the case as long as the advertisement runs (Astrachan et al. 2008, 29.01[1], 29–3—29–5).

Mockups and Demonstrations. Mockups and demonstrations are both legal to a degree. One dated but famous case illustrates when they are not. In the early 1960s, Colgate-Palmolive tried to demonstrate the power of its Rapid Shave shaving cream by showing it capable of softening sandpaper. When real sandpaper proved too difficult to shave, a piece of Plexiglas covered with sand was substituted. After a protracted legal battle, the Supreme Court determined that the substitution in this case constituted a deceptive practice. The Court, however, did not accept the FTC's argument that all mockups were deceptive and therefore illegal (Teeter and Loving 2004, 814–814), only those that deceive or mislead consumers in their expectation of how the product will perform.

For example, without mockups, certain products such as gelatin and ice cream melt under the heat of studio lights. Similarly, blue shirts tend to look white (Giles 2006). In situations where the production aspects of the commercial prevent the product from appearing natural, mockups are allowed.

Comparative Advertising. Drawing explicit comparisons between one brand and another when the competitor is specifically named became relatively common only after the 1970s—for example, Coke versus Pepsi, Burger King versus McDonald's, among others. Although there are no regulations prohibiting comparative advertising in the United States, some advertisers refuse to adopt the approach for fear of confusing consumers or tarnishing the image of the industry, among other reasons. Others see comparative advertising as a means of educating consumers or an inspiration to competitors to improve the quality of their goods. Naturally, comparative advertising is subject to the same legal standards as all advertising and must not be deceptive, unfair, misleading, or unsubstantiated. Any comparative claims that fail to adhere to these standards is likely to run afoul of both self-regulatory organizations and the Federal Trade Commission (Astrachan et al. 2008, 31.01[1], 31–1—31.03[1] 31–9).

For example, Brigham's Ice Cream compared its brand to Häagen Dazs and Ben & Jerry's with the slogan, "Taste the best—at a sensible price." The National Advertising Division (NAD) of the Counsel of Better Business Bureaus found that Brigham's failed to substantiate the claim and asked the company to pull the campaign (Feirstein 2000). The same results occurred when Endust failed to substantiate its claim that it cleaned faster than Pledge, and Texaco failed to substantiate its claim that its gas cleaned motors better than Chevron, resulting in both campaigns being pulled.

However, when Maxwell House compared its coffee to Folgers and claimed Maxwell House was "America's best loved coffee," the NAD ruled that the claim did not require substantiation because the slogan was mere puffery—a boastful opinion. The same ruling was made when Hush Puppies claimed to be "the Earth's most comfortable shoes" in a campaign that pitted the brand against Rockport (Feirstein (2000).

One common source of problems in comparative messages has to do with the use of a competitor's trademark in an ad. If a competing company's trademark is used in such a way as to confuse or deceive consumers, the aggrieved party can sue for trademark infringement under the Lanham Act. "The use of a competitor's mark in truthful comparative advertising is permissible in the absence of customer confusion regardless of whether the use involves a slogan, a photograph, or even an odor" (Astrachan et al. 2008, 31.03[3], 31–31—31–32).

Comparative advertising tends to become more common during lean economic times. Unfortunately, it also tends to become even more aggressive. As a result, advertisers are more likely to complain, which in turn, leads to more lawsuits (Wood 2008, 8).

The use of comparative advertising outside the United States is far more controversial. After a number of years of confusing and contradictory rules among countries in the European Union, a directive was finally adopted in 1997 that standardized policies regarding comparative advertising. The end result is that comparative advertising is legal as long as a relatively complicated list of stipulations is met (Astrachan et al. 2008, 31.04, 31–39—31.05 31–40). However, comparative advertising remains illegal in other parts of the world, particularly in Asian countries such as Thailand (Douglas and Craig 2000). In some countries, it is not illegal but considered poor taste to disparage a competitor.

Puffery. Puffery is as old as advertising itself. It refers to hyperbole in advertising that is presumed to be harmless because no ordinary person could be expected to believe it or make a purchase decision based upon it. According to the FTC's policy statement on deception, "The Commission generally will not pursue cases involving obviously exaggerated or puffing representations, i.e., those that the ordinary consumers do not take seriously" (Fetscherin and Toncar 2009, 147).

Historically, puffery is a holdover from a much earlier time that was characterized by the attitude: "caveat emptor" or let the buyer beware (Preston 1996, 29). The Commission's approach to puffery is based on several assumptions:

1. Sellers are expected to exaggerate the benefits of their goods;
2. Buyers expect sellers to lie;
3. Buyers will not believe everything a seller says about his goods;
4. The average buyer (acting reasonably under the circumstances) will not be influenced by puffery when making a purchase decision.

Due to the hyperbolic nature of puffery, its veracity can't be determined. Consequently, puffery receives full First Amendment protection while objective (and verifiable) claims do not. This creates an obvious paradox: While the FTC's mission is to promote consumer welfare in the marketplace, the Commission is inadvertently discouraging the dissemination of verifiable product information.

Historically, puffery refers to the verbal or written components of ads. Recently, however, the Second U.S. Circuit Court of Appeals' decision in a case involving DirecTV and Time Warner Cable, stipulated that puffery includes visual components of an ad as well (Fetscherin and Toncar 2009; Neumeister 2007). The potential ramifications of the appeals court's decision are significant. The paradox long implicit in the Commission's treatment of puffery could be even more far-reaching.

FTC Legal Remedies

The Federal Trade Commission recognizes five alternative approaches to initiating litigation in deceptive advertising cases. Before taking legal action against an advertiser, the Commission considers alternative remedies available to competitors, consumers, state agencies, self-regulatory bodies, and controls by a federal agency (including the FTC; Astrachan et al. 2008, 17.01, 17–2). When the first four remedies aren't viable and the act doesn't fall under the jurisdiction of any other federal agency, then the FTC steps in. Early on, it may attempt to negotiate a consent agreement wherein the advertiser agrees to stop the offending behavior.

According to the FTC Web site, the vast majority (95 percent) of cases are resolved when an advertiser promises the Commission to stop the offending practice. These consent orders do not constitute admission of guilt by the advertiser (Astrachan et al. 2008, 33.01, 33–1). Such agreements are an appealing way of resolving cases for both the Commission and the advertiser because they can save both parties a lot of expense. Consent orders offer respondents the additional incentive of sparing them negative publicity and concomitant loss of sales. Consequently, most cases against advertisers are resolved through consent agreements.

In cases where the offense puts consumers in serious jeopardy, the Commission may secure an injunction to put an immediate stop to the advertising. Otherwise, if an agreement can't be reached, the FTC will issue an administrative complaint and begin formal proceedings before an administrative law judge. If, after evidence and testimony from both sides are heard, the advertiser is found guilty, the judge may issue a cease-and-desist order. This may be appealed to the full Commission by the advertiser.

In some cases, there is concern that the erroneous impression left by a deceptive or unfair ad will linger long after the advertising has been discontinued. The FTC may then require corrective advertising to be run by the advertiser. The purpose of this is to call attention to the deception and correct it. Corrective advertising was required in 1996 of the Novartis Corporation, makers of Doan's analgesic pills. In all of Doan's advertising and packaging, the advertiser was required to include a statement that Doan's products were no "more effective than other analgesics for back pain relief" (Mazis 2001,

114). This was the first time in almost twenty-five years that the FTC had ordered corrective advertising, which is conducted at the advertiser's expense according to the Commission's specifications regarding how long and in what form (e.g., in which media, on packaging) the message must be run.

In a recent case, Bayer HealthCare Pharmaceuticals was required by the FDA and the attorneys general of twenty-seven states to run corrective advertising for its birth control pill, Yaz, because the regulators concluded that ads overstated the drug's ability to improve women's moods and clear up acne while playing down its potential health risks. Product ads promoted Yaz as a "pill that goes beyond the rest"—a lifestyle drug that goes "beyond birth control." In February 2009, Bayer agreed to spend $20 million on a corrective campaign for the next six years and to submit all Yaz ads for federal screening before they appear (Singer 2009).

In other cases, the Commission may require an advertiser to disseminate additional information through disclosures, direct notification, or consumer education. Disclosures have been required in advertising and on packaging to warn consumers about the health risks of products or to disclaim their efficacy. Direct notification is when the FTC requires an advertiser to contact distributors or purchasers directly, often about the safety or health risks of a product. Consumer education programs may be ordered by the Commission when it feels consumers require more information about their rights, health and safety issues, or other matters relating to the advertised product (Fair 2002, 3–5).

In certain instances, advertisers may be required to pay fines as a means for establishing consumer redress. Until the early 1980s, no court had awarded money damages to a plaintiff under 43(a) section of the Lanham Act. Table 6.6 explains how the Commission brings an action.

The Bureau of Competition

The FTC Act empowers the Commission to regulate unfair methods of competition and unfair practices (Hobbs 2004–2005, 1153). "Unfair methods of competition" gives the FTC jurisdiction over antitrust, whereas "unfair practices" authorizes it to "extend its consumer protection jurisdiction to non-deceptive practices which are nonetheless unfair to consumers" (Hobbs, 2004–2005, p. 1153). Thus, the two mandates correlate with the Bureaus of Competition and Consumer Protection. The Bureau of Competition has particular expertise in cases involving "high dollar volume consumer activities" (Astrachan et al. 2008, 17.03[3], 17–46). It is in this regard that advertisers sometimes run afoul of antitrust regulation.

Advertising may be viewed as an anticompetitive tool that contributes to

Table 6.6

How the FTC Brings an Action

Letters from consumers or businesses, premerger notification filings, Congressional inquiries, or articles on consumer or economic subjects may trigger FTC action. Generally, FTC investigations are nonpublic to protect both the investigation and the companies involved.

If the FTC believes that a person or company has violated the law or that a proposed merger may violate the law, the agency may attempt to obtain voluntary compliance by entering into a consent order with the company. A company that signs a consent order need not admit that it violated the law, but it must agree to stop the disputed practices outlined in an accompanying complaint or undertake certain obligations to resolve the anticompetitive aspects of its proposed merger.

If a consent agreement cannot be reached, the FTC may issue an administrative complaint or seek injunctive relief in the federal courts. The FTC's administrative complaints initiate a formal proceeding that is much like a federal court trial, but it is held before an administrative law judge: Evidence is submitted, testimony is heard, and witnesses are examined and crossexamined. If a law violation is found, a cease and desist order may be issued. Initial decisions by administrative law judges may be appealed to the full Commission.

Final decisions issued by the Commission may be appealed to the U.S. Court of Appeals and, ultimately, to the U.S. Supreme Court. If the Commission's position is upheld, the FTC, in certain circumstances, may then seek consumer redress in court. If the company ever violates the order, the Commission also may seek civil penalties or an injunction.

In some circumstances, the FTC can go directly to court to obtain an injunction, civil penalties, or consumer redress. In the merger enforcement arena, the FTC may seek a preliminary injunction to block a proposed merger pending a full examination of the proposed transaction in an administrative proceeding. The injunction preserves the market's competitive status quo. The FTC seeks federal court injunctions in consumer protection matters typically in cases of ongoing consumer fraud. By going directly to court, the FTC can stop the fraud before too many consumers are injured.

The Commission also can issue Trade Regulation Rules. If the FTC staff finds evidence of unfair or deceptive practices in an entire industry, it can recommend that the Commission begin a rulemaking proceeding. Throughout the rulemaking proceeding, the public has opportunities to attend hearings and file written comments. The Commission considers these comments along with the entire rulemaking record—the hearing testimony, the staff reports, and the Presiding Officer's report—before making a final decision on the proposed rule. An FTC rule may be challenged in any of the U.S. Courts of Appeal. When issued, these rules have the force of law.

Source: Federal Trade Commission, "Facts for Consumers: A Guide to the Federal Trade Commission," March 2004. http://www.ftc.gov/bcp/edu/pubs/consumer/general/gen03.shtm#action.

market domination by one or a few companies. In other situations, advertising is seen as a potentially anticompetitive factor that justifies prevention of corporate mergers. In still other instances, the needs of advertisers are at issue such as when Google sought (and was ultimately granted) approval to acquire DoubleClick, an Internet ad server in 2007 (Schwartz 2008).

Since the Wheeler-Lea Amendment extended the Commission's jurisdiction to include consumer issues, and since the growth of the Commission in the 1960s and 1970s, the FTC's dual missions to protect both consumers and competitors have become increasingly interrelated (Hobbs 2004–2005; Leary 2004–2005). As Hobbs pointed out, the 1972 Pfizer case (which instituted the requirement that an advertiser have a reasonable basis for claims made in consumer advertising) stressed the twin objectives of fairness to competitors and to consumers (2004–2005, 1153–1154). Former FTC Commissioner Leary concluded: "It is increasingly evident that the competition and consumer protection missions of the Federal Trade Commission are more closely related than people have been accustomed to think" (2005–2005, 1147).

One of the best examples of advertising as a competitive issue is found in the FTC's "notorious" cereal case which, "involved an interesting interplay of consumer protection and antitrust issues" (Hobbs 2004–2005, 1154). Initiated as an antitrust case because the top three cereal makers (Kellogg's, General Mills, General Foods) were believed to be maintaining a shared monopoly that led to inflated prices and profits, the case was a smorgasbord of issues over the ten-plus years it was litigated (Editors, *Antitrust Law & Economics Review* 1981).

The defendants were accused of perpetuating its shared monopoly by engaging in intensive product differentiation and brand proliferation through advertising. The cereal makers presumably saturated the marketplace with new products that were successfully advertised through specious differentiation (Hobbs 2004–2005, 1155). In other words, advertising was one of several marketing tools used by the defendants to maintain their joint domination of the cereal market. The case also included several traditional false advertising charges as well (Hobbs 2004–2005, 1155).

The case was eventually dismissed in 1982—a consequence, some would say, of the shift of the prevailing political climate toward the right (Editors, *Antitrust Law & Economics Review* 1981). But the cereal case and others, according to Hobbs (2004–2005, 1155), ultimately showed that not all consumer protection issues relate to deception and not all competition concerns fall under the category of antitrust.

Consequently, advertising falls under regulatory scrutiny for reasons that relate more to competitors than to consumers. Google's 2008 acquisition of DoubleClick was ultimately approved by the FTC, but only after a contentious review. The FTC's concern over advertising was based on fears that the online advertising market would be dominated by Google/DoubleClick and that conflicts of interest would arise if DoubleClick favored Google in its online advertising strategies.

The list of controversies involving advertising and market structure continues to grow as industries reorganize. For example, the restructuring of the newspaper publishing business raises concerns for consumers and competitors alike as the declining number of independent newspapers limits the choices of consumers and advertisers. Similar concerns have been raised regarding the proposed Google/Yahoo partnership. Association of National Advertisers President Bob Liodice says that advertisers are uneasy because "the partnership will likely diminish competition, increase concentration of market power, limit choices, and potentially raise prices for high-quality, affordable" search ads (Havenstein 2008, 12).

Concluding Thoughts about the Future of Regulation

Several trends offer insight into the future of the regulation of commercial speech. First, as has been widely discussed, media are converging at a staggering rate. This phenomenon was aptly described by Ithiel de Sola Pool, a social scientist who led groundbreaking research in technology and its effects on society. He is credited with coining the term "convergence," which he described in this way: "A single physical means—be it wires, cables or airwaves—may carry services that in the past were provided in separate ways. Conversely, a service that was provided in the past by any one medium—be it broadcasting, the press, or telephony—can now be provided in several different physical ways. So the one-to-one relationship that used to exist between a medium and its use is eroding" (de Sola Pool 1983, 23 referenced by Jenkins 2006, 10).

At the same time, corporations are also converging in every possible way—vertically, horizontally and globally. According to Jenkins, "Digitization set the conditions for convergence; corporate conglomerates created its imperative" (Jenkins 2006, 11). It is these two types of convergence that are reshaping consumer culture and the regulation implemented on behalf of both consumers and competitors. When each medium had a single and unique purpose, each was regulated under different "regimes" depending upon its fundamental nature: its degree of centralization, the scarcity of its resources, whether its focus was on news or entertainment, and so forth (de Sola Pool 1983; Jenkins 2006, 10–11). As technology, media, corporate structure, and consumer culture converge, regulatory systems must adapt.

An illustration of this is the FTC's proposed extension of its jurisdiction to include word-of-mouth marketers and social media sites like Facebook. In effect, bloggers and anyone who is compensated for reviewing a product would be held responsible for false statements. There are no legal implications for posting product reviews if no compensation takes place, but consumers who receive remuneration from the advertiser will be treated like an advertiser. Consequently, the consumer can be held to the same standards for deception and unfairness (Bush 2009).

One logical consequence is for the regulatory process to converge. This can be seen in two ways. Within the Federal Trade Commission itself, its dual missions to protect consumers and competitors are increasingly intertwined. According to former Commissioner Thomas B. Leary (2000), the line between consumer protection and competition will fade even more as the world grows smaller. Moreover, this trend is fueled by the indistinct differences between speakers and audiences, and editorial content and user-generated content. Ultimately, regulatory action may be less distinctively directed toward protecting consumers or competitors and more commonly focused on both constituents collectively.

The second area of convergence in regulation is the increasing collaboration between government regulation and self-regulation. The challenge of regulating the Internet (which is both "everywhere and nowhere") makes traditional regulatory regimes impractical. Add to this the inherently international nature of modern media, and the role of self-regulation becomes even more essential. Collaboration among the Children's Food and Beverage Advertising Initiative (established by the Council of Better Business Bureaus at the direction of the FTC), the Institute of Medicine, and Congress is a good example of the convergence of government and industry.

The impetus for both types of convergence is partly financial. At any point in its history, the FTC's budget was a fraction of what was being spent on advertising in the United States. The Commission has a long history of desperately seeking funding from Congress. Even when Congress was being relatively generous, the FTC still operated on very limited funds relative to the industries it polices. This problem has only worsened with the exponential increase in the kinds of advertisers, products, media, media vehicles, and audiences under the Commission's jurisdiction. Self-regulation may be an imperfect solution to regulation but is less expensive.

In contrast to the FTC's early history, the last several decades seem characterized by less-pronounced and exclusive emphasis on either consumers or businesses. If the traditional political seesawing affecting FTC funding and its level of activism has decreased, it might be indicative of a much broader political and cultural convergence that embraces both individualist and collectivist values. Hindman (2004) said that while the First Amendment is based largely on an individualist perspective (consistent with the classical liberal foundation on which it rests), the justices have based protection for commercial speech on social or collectivist values. An analogous conflict is evident in the FTC's history of advertising regulation. If the proconsumer versus probusiness dichotomy that has shaped the FTC's approach to advertising regulation is less prevalent, it may be that individualist and collectivist values are themselves converging much like they have in the Court's treatment of commercial speech.

The issues likely to dominate the regulatory agenda are readily identifiable. The FTC Web site provides a predictable list of concerns, problematic product and service categories, market-structure issues, and especially vulnerable audiences. Some general topics that will recur across audiences and media are identity theft, privacy, viral marketing, multilevel marketing, debt collection, energy and the environment, and access to media and information. Industries that are likely to remain in the spotlight include banking and credit, health care (including diet products and drugs), and media. Mergers and acquisitions and antitrust issues in general can be expected to be on the regulatory agenda in terms of market structure. Children (i.e., nutrition, predatory targeting) and the economically disadvantaged (e.g., predatory lending, Internet-based financial schemes) are two of the consumer groups that will continue to be especially important.

The underlying priorities remain the same in terms of safeguarding free speech—protecting consumers and encouraging market competition. However, the circumstances have changed dramatically and continue to do so. The challenge in regulating commercial speech is in defining it as it constantly evolves. Consumers have shifted from being receivers of content to also being generators of content. Similarly, components of the marketplace (corporations, media channels and vehicles, audiences, etc.) never stop mutating. The quandary in defining commercial speech exhibited by the Supreme Court seems to have spread to other regulatory issues as media converge and definitions of content providers, products, platforms, designated market areas, and regulatory bodies get more complicated. But the nature of the critical issues that represent the focus of advertising regulation remain constant in consumer culture. The conditions are different, but the issues are unchanged.

➤ 7 ◄

Doing the Right Thing When We Don't Know What "Right" Is

Our starting point in the last chapter was that some form of regulation of advertising is necessary to safeguard the needs of consumers, and that regulatory decisions for consumer protection are based on assumptions made about individuals in a consumer culture. This chapter considers the need for ethical decisionmaking, which is equally important in a consumer culture and is also framed within classical liberalism and individualism.

One of the great challenges for students and professionals in advertising is knowing where to draw the line between ethical and unethical behavior. On the surface it may seem a simple task, but most students and professionals in the field wrestle with it at some point in their careers. Some simply avoid the issue by opting to do what is legal, thereby assuming that what is legal is also what is ethical. But most people agree that being ethical means adhering to a higher standard than simply following legal requirements. But what is that standard? What does it mean to be ethical in the advertising profession?

We begin this chapter by examining several major ethical theories and seeing to what extent they help us navigate modern-day dilemmas in advertising. We then consider ethical challenges for the advertising industry. Finally, we consider how our understanding of ethics fits the classical liberal model.

Ethical Models

Deontology

Deontologists hold that certain underlying principles are right or wrong regardless of the circumstances. For that reason, deontology is considered a "rule-based" approach to ethics. To be a moral person, one must not only bring about good results but use the proper means and act with good intentions. The best known deontologist is eighteenth-century German philosopher, Immanuel Kant, who argued that people can develop moral principles through reasoning alone. Following his logic, one could reason that behaviors such as telling a lie are wrong regardless of the outcome, even if the lie was told in order to protect someone's safety. Thus, it is possible to develop infallible, universal laws or categorical imperatives regarding lying and other behaviors. For example, lying is always wrong, killing is always wrong, and so forth. Within the framework of deontology, one must respect all humans and not treat them as a means to an end (Gower 2008).

Deontology is both appealing and comforting because it offers rules that hold across all situations. It gives us confidence that we can always know what is right by following the rules. However, its apparent strength is also its weakness, for it has been criticized for its rigidity and its inability to operate equitably across situations. One such example is advertising to children. Although the use of advergaming and other forms of new technology has focused increased attention on children's advertising, it is an issue with a long history. In the early 1990s, a contentious issue was whether to communicate directly with children or with the parents (Paine 1993). With young children, it made sense to direct the messages to parents for such items as toys, games, and snack food, since parents are the purchasers of the products. However, advertisers knew that they achieved better results by communicating with children, partly because they are less able to exercise critical-thinking skills than adults and also because they want products regardless of whether they are affordable or suitable for them. When children put pressure on parents to buy advertised products, parents are subsequently forced to decide whether or not to give in to the child's wishes, which can strain the relationship if the purchase is not one that they want to make.

A 2008 article in *Best Life* magazine about the marketing of products to children acknowledges the public perception of unethical promotional efforts and encourages parents to fight back. The caption for the article, "Monsters Inc.," says it all: "How to thwart the $17 billion marketing effort to steal your kids' dreams, infiltrate their friendships, plaster their PJs with logos, hijack their imagination, fragment their attention spans, make them obese, and drive a wedge into their relationship with you" (Scott 2008/2009, 128).

Following the deontological perspective, communicating directly with children is potentially exploitative; therefore, it is wrong in any form. Though there is very strong support for placing significant restrictions on children's advertising, most people would agree that some form of advertising may be acceptable within certain limits, particularly for older children and for products that could be beneficial such as healthy food options and exercise. Forming a categorical imperative that maintains that all advertising targeted to children is wrong leaves no room to accommodate any exceptions to the rule.

Even more challenging is an attempt to create a universal law governing children's advertising that can accommodate different standards for different countries. For example, French advertising regulations are more restrictive than American standards, as we learned in Chapter 5, and by law, children in French ads cannot be the principal actors for products they do not personally use or buy (Taylor and Cunningham 2007). For a number of years Michelin used a televised campaign in the United States that could not air in France, the company's home country, in which infants floated on tires in rainy and snowy conditions. The campaign with smiling babies was a favorite of many viewers, but the underlying message played upon parents' fears for their children's safety and the potential guilt that they would feel if their child were injured in an accident. Though the campaign was legal in the United States, it could not air in France because the use of infants to sell tires would violate French law in the belief that "the fragile bond between child and parent is preyed upon in order to sell everything from life insurance to tires" (Taylor and Cunningham 2007, 272). Although American standards place restrictions on children's advertising, it is acceptable to use children as actors in commercials for products they do not use.

Following a deontological perspective, there can be no accommodation for different standards across countries because a universal law must prevail, presumably the French law in this case, which offers greater protection for children. Similarly, comparative advertising (e.g., advertising that touts the superiority of the advertised product over that of a competing brand) is a legal practice in the United States but is illegal in some countries in the world and inappropriate, though legal, in others. The deontological approach would argue that if it is wrong in one country, it must be wrong worldwide.

Moral Relativism

Moral relativism is a perspective that offers a way to achieve some accommodation of cultural differences, for it holds that ethical practices apply standards relative to social, cultural, historical, or personal values. Following this perspective, it is unacceptable for an outsider to judge the moral or ethical acts of another person or group. Moral relativists who take the most extreme position hold that no universal standards exist. There are no absolute rights and wrongs, only different situations.

Because moral relativism accepts cultural differences, it allows us a way out of the rigid absolutism of deontology, which was problematic for issues such as children's advertising, comparative advertising, regulatory differences across cultures, and certain business practices. For example, bribery is not only considered unethical in the United States but illegal; however, it is a way of life in many other countries. Given the unequal power relationships between the United States and most other countries, imposing an American standard upon the world is likely to be perceived as an arrogant act of cultural imperialism. Following moral relativism, it is acceptable for each country to follow its own standard.

Despite some obvious advantages of this system, moral relativists have been harshly criticized because the practices they find acceptable within their own culture often have been condemned by a majority of people worldwide. These include such events and practices as the Holocaust, apartheid in South Africa, genocide, slavery, terrorism, and Nazism. Since these reprehensible acts are not absolutely bad from a relativist perspective, there is no way to condemn them. Thus, what we gained in flexibility from this perspective is lost due to its inability to provide some minimal standards. Choosing between deontology and moral relativism is an unsatisfying option that forces us to conclude that neither can effectively accommodate all ethical dilemmas.

Utilitarianism

A different perspective is utilitarianism, which focuses upon the moral rightness of the results. A simplified explanation is that actions are good if the consequences are good and bad if the consequences are bad. Actions in and of themselves are neither moral nor immoral—it is the results that count. This allows us an alternative to deontology and moral relativism; however, the main challenge is in knowing which consequences take priority over others.

Utilitarianism also maintains that an ethical act produces the greatest possible good for the most people. According to eighteenth-century philosopher Jeremy Bentham, a good or moral act is one "that results in the greatest happiness for the greatest number" (Gower 2008, 5). At face value, utilitarianism may seem to be a workable idea; however, determining the greatest happiness for the greatest number is complex. Gower (2008) uses an example with Beech-Nut apple juice that illustrates the problem. In the 1980s, the Beech-Nut Nutrition Corporation learned that a shipment of apple juice concentrate from a supplier didn't meet the company's standards because some cases of the product contained only flavored sugar water instead of pure juice. Failing to meet standards presented a moral dilemma because Beech-Nut marketed its juice as 100 percent pure. Beech-Nut returned the unused product but struggled to decide what to do about the used concentrate because an examination of the finished product could not reliably determine which cases contained actual juice and which contained sugar water. From a utilitarian perspective, Beech-Nut had to wrestle with the following dilemma: ". . . would destroying all of the apple juice inventory and potentially forcing the company into bankruptcy be the greatest good for the greatest number when there was no suggestion that the product was dangerous or that consumers would even notice it was not 100 percent apple juice? Or would leaving the inventory on the market and remaining financially viable for its shareholders and employees result in the greatest good for the greatest number?" (Gower 2008, 5). Beech-Nut ultimately chose to take its chances with the public and leave the product on the market knowing it was not 100 percent pure, a decision which was acceptable by utilitarian standards but deemed unjust by critics who argued that Beech-Nut sacrificed consumers for the company's long-term economic viability.

A common problem with the advertising of alcohol and other potentially addictive products is balancing the needs of the general public against those of people who are alcohol-dependent. Estimates vary, but approximately 20 percent of drinkers consume 80 percent of the product, according to Miller Brewing Company's expression of gratitude to the "20 percent of beer drinkers who drink 80 percent of the beer" (Jacobson and Mazur 1995, 165). These 20 percent are the heaviest drinkers (e.g., alcoholics and binge drinkers) who literally keep the industry afloat. Following the utilitarian perspective, advertising the product to the general population is acceptable because the majority are neither alcoholics not binge drinkers. However, this ignores the problems that occur when advertising alcohol to a vulnerable group:

> Unfortunately, while beer advertising is aimed at a general audience it reaches especially vulnerable audiences—those who are in the throes of alcohol addiction, heavy drinkers, who have the potential to become alcoholics, and those in recovery programs who are actively committed to overcoming alcohol addiction. The traditional marketing notion of maximizing advertising efficiency by targeting those who are likely to consume relatively more of the product has unique implications when the product is addictive, and when the heaviest users include alcoholics . . . Since there is no indication that alcohol advertising will undergo any further restriction at this time, alcoholics will continue to have to deal with the presence of mass media messages that heavily target them and tap into their vulnerabilities (Wolburg, Hovland, and Hopson 1999, 49–50).

A final ethical dilemma showing the limitations of utilitarianism is the depiction of Native Americans as mascots for sports teams. Choosing an identity for a sports team is a very important marketing decision that has many implications for all forms of promotion including advertising. Some non-Native people regard the use of an Indian mascot as a harmless depiction; however, many Native Americans regard it as a blatant form of racism that promotes harmful stereotypes in a highly visible venue. Since American

Indians comprise only 1 percent of the United States population, some of whom live on reservations and are isolated from non-Natives, they are unable to provide enough interpersonal contact with non-Natives to counter the stereotypical depictions in the media.

The most dominant depictions of American Indians are "a villainous warlike group that lurked in the darkness thirsting for the blood of innocent settlers or the calm, wise, dignified elder sitting on the mesa dispensing his wisdom in poetic aphorisms" (Deloria 2003, 23). Neither depiction is realistic, although the savage sterotype is the better fit for athletic teams that want an identity tied to aggression. Following the utilitarian model, the wishes of the majority (sports fans, most of whom are non-Native people) will almost certainly take precedence over those of the minority (Native Americans), which will provide satisfaction for the greatest number of people. However, applying that rule without taking into account unequal power relationships and differences in group size can lead to an outcome that is arguably unjust.

The different ethical perspectives we have examined so far reflect genuine efforts to find guiding moral principles; yet, absolute rule (deontology) doesn't allow for exceptions to the rule, having no rules (moral relativism) means that anything goes, and attempts at finding a middle ground (utilitarianism) can't effectively overcome problems of privileging those in power when they are the majority. Therefore, the search continues.

Care-Based Theories

The prevailing ethical frameworks approach ethics from a *justice-based* perspective, and they all have their strengths and weaknesses. *Care-based* theories of ethics, which were developed by feminists in the second half of the twentieth century, offer another alternative and provide a counterpoint to several assumptions. Justice-based perspectives assume that people are independent of one another, that moral reasoning is rational—not emotional—and that abstract moral principles can be applied impartially to humans, who are in theory equal and autonomous. In contrast, care-based theorists assume that humans are interdependent and need others for survival (Tronto 1993), that moral reasoning involves the interplay between emotion and reason (Held 1993; Noddings 2003), and that moral solutions must work for people within the context in which they live (Slattery, Garner, Wolburg, and Turner in press). Consequently, finding a workable, ethical solution to problems from a care-based perspective requires recognizing the interdependence among people, finding solutions that emerge from both emotion and reason, and considering the context in which the problem occurs and safeguarding certain interests, if necessary.

Justice-based theories often treat concepts such as power as a zero-sum game, which assumes a finite amount of power among people that makes some winners and others losers. Within that framework, one group can obtain greater power only at the expense of the other because there is only so much power to go around. Care-based theorists are likely look for solutions outside of that framework. They would seek an understanding of how power originates and how both groups can be empowered without privileging one at the expense of the others. Further, they would seek to identify potential vulnerabilities within groups and to understand how the groups relate to each other. Those who are particularly vulnerable would require extra consideration.

Care based-theorists seek solutions to ethical challenges on a case-by-case basis. To do otherwise means applying a blunt instrument across all situations. They recognize that their approach requires stepping out of a comfort zone of "infallible" rules, but because their approach is grounded in human relationships, it is more likely to find solutions based on fairness.

If we rethink the previous examples with children's advertising, lack of disclosure over product quality, advertising of alcohol, and depictions of Native Americans as sports mascots, we can see that justice-based and care-based approaches would follow different paths. Instead of seeking a categorical imperative regarding children's advertising, care-based theorists would look at the situation within a given context and seek an understanding of whether all situations jeopardize the relationship between parents and children or whether it applies to just some situations. They would work toward finding an acceptable solution for all stakeholders (children, parents, advertisers, and media companies that carry advertising), which is likely to be a more labor-intensive process but one that could ultimately provide a better solution than an absolute rule with all its inherent limitations.

Like the children's advertising example that pits parents against children and the alcohol example that pits vulnerable audiences against the majority, Beech-Nut's approach assumes an adversarial relationship between consumers and stockholders, just as the mascot issue assumes an adversarial relationship between non-Native fans and Native people. A care-based approach would not assume a zero-sum game with adversarial roles as a given and would try to find a workable solution for all. This approach would also require extra consideration of any group that might appear to be vulnerable to the outcome. Because the justice-based approach is so ingrained in the culture, we may think that its assumptions are the starting point, when in fact they may not be.

The disadvantage of the care-based approach to ethics is that it is a more recent theory and is still evolving. There are fewer case studies to serve as models, and moral decisions have to be made on a case-by-case basis by investigating the context in which the issue arises. Care-based ethics may be both time-intensive and labor-intensive but can potentially lead to a more satisfying outcome.

What we can conclude from our consideration of justice- and care-based ethical perspectives is that as a culture, our thinking is still evolving for developing a moral framework that works well for all situations. Although most advertisers agree that they should be committed to ethical as well as legal behavior in the marketplace, there is no easy framework in which they can draw the line between ethical and unethical behavior. This will require individuals within the industry to continue to wrestle with the problem of how to promote goods and services to consumers in ways that respect them as individuals without exploiting them in the name of profit.

Ethical Challenges to the Advertising Industry

Inherent Conflicts

Ethics scholar Kim Rotzoll identified several problem areas in advertising that pose inherent ethical conflicts for the advertising industry. Here we consider some of the most problematic ones for the twenty-first century.

1. Advertising Messages Are One-sided and Have the Potential to Deceive

We have already considered the likelihood for deception when advertising messages created in one country target consumers in a country with fewer regulations in place. However, Rotzoll et al. (1996, 187) point out that even domestic advertising has the potential for deception because it represents only the client's point of view—it is "strong on convenience but laced with persuasion" (1996, 187). The inherent conflict of interest for advertisers is that providing all usable information for consumers is counterproductive to selling because it may mean admitting that the product is really no better than the competitor's or is more expensive. It may mean revealing such things as design flaws of the advertised product, potential harm from product use (e.g., the addictiveness of tobacco), and ineffective results (e.g., certain weight-loss products that don't get results). For example, a column in *Consumer Reports* (2009) that shows questionable ads includes one for a Kenmore dishwasher that claims "no other dishwasher cleans better." The phrase "among leading brands" follows in smaller print. The column probes whether *nonleading* brands may clean better or whether other leading brands clean just as well. The point is that the consumer must be on guard against not only what ads actually state but also what they can imply or omit.

In earlier chapters, Preston (1994; 2002) addressed the long-standing but problematic message strategy of puffery and other nonfact claims, such as "Advil works better" or BMW is "the ultimate driving machine." The advantage of such messages for advertisers is that no factual claim is made; therefore, the messages are not regulated and advertisers cannot be held accountable. The messages can be misleading without being deceptive in the legal sense. Preston traces the legality of such claims back to English law in 1602, when a man complained that he was cheated after buying something that didn't live up to the advertised claim. The court ruled that what he thought was a false, deceptive claim was really "an opinion" or "bare assumption," and that he had mistakenly put his trust in a "fact-free" claim (1994, 104). Preston argues that little has changed over time. When Bayer claims to be "the world's best aspirin," the product does not have to go through rigorous comparative testing against other brands of aspirin. The company is merely "puffing," at least in the eyes of the Federal Trade Commission. Consumers who are disappointed by advertising claims such as these find themselves no better off than those governed by seventeenth-century English law.

As a result of advertising's one-sidedness and consumers' reluctance to trust the messages, advertisers have developed different techniques of persuasion. In the late 1800s and early 1900s advertisers did little to conceal persuasive intent, and ads were highly recognizable as such (Bagdikian 1997). But with technological advances, advertising has become more seamless within each medium. Advertisers also began to use "under-the-radar" strategies, which were designed to disguise the ad to such an extent that distrustful consumers "barely know they're being sold" Bond and Kirshenbaum note:

> To cope with all of these new products, new messages, and new media, consumers have developed what we call "marketing radar." That is, they can immediately identify an incoming message as marketing contrived to manipulate them into buying something of questionable value or relevance. Today, nearly half of all college students have taken marketing courses, so they know the enemy and are able to see through the obvious ploys, such as "You will be a better, more popular person if only you would purchase this new peppermint-scented detergent" (1998, 3).

Thus, instead of making advertising more credible, the solution to being the enemy has been to make ads less recognizable. Advertisers already saw many corporations, political candidates, organizations, and others shift a sizable part of their promotional budgets from advertising to public relations, not only because PR can be less expensive but because it is more credible since it is perceived as news. Advertisers have adapted by creating less recognizable promotional messages to avoid the credibility problems of traditional advertising.

2. The Purpose of Advertising Is to Promote the Advertiser's Intent—Good or Bad

Rotzoll et al. (1996, 188) argue that advertising promotes behavior that can be "noble or venal" because it is driven by the advertiser's intent. Their argument is much the same as historian David Potter's in *People of Plenty* (1954)—that advertising doesn't inherently have a conscience. According to Potter, in comparison to other institutions such as the church and the educational system, advertising has no motivation to improve the individual or to provide any social value:

> . . . And, though it [advertising] wields an immense social influence, comparable to the influence of religion and learning, it has no social goals and no social responsibility for what it does with its influence, so long as it refrains from palpable violations of truth and decency. It is this lack of institutional responsibility, this lack of inherent social purpose to balance social power, which, I would argue, is a basic cause for concern about the role of advertising . . . What is basic is that advertising, as such, with all its vast power to influence values and conduct, cannot ever lose sight of the fact that it ultimately regards man as a consumer and defines its own mission as one of stimulating him to consume or to desire to consume (Potter 1954, 177).

Some may argue that since corporate social responsibility (CSR) has become an important part of the marketing function in recent years, advertising has now developed the conscience that Potter (1954) and Rotzoll et al. (1996) found missing. However, others would counter that CSR is at the discretion of the corporation. It is a tool that meets a public relations objective of enhancing the image of a corporation and may not be driven by social goals as much as profit goals.

Even socially constructive campaigns are not without criticism. Many antismoking campaigns have been criticized for their lack of effectiveness among smokers, or worse, for improving the image of the tobacco companies (Wolburg 2006). Similarly, responsible drinking campaigns inherently state that drinking can be a responsible act when, for alcoholics, it is not (Wolburg et al. 1999).

Rotzoll et al. (1996) conclude that because advertising promotes alcohol and tobacco as well as other legal but potentially harmful products, it is inevitable that advertising will continue to be accused of unethical practices by those who disagree with what advertising promotes (e.g., smoking, alcohol consumption, gaming, or mere consumption itself). Rotzoll et al. (1996) also contend that advertising will inevitably be accused of unethical practices by those who disagree with its use as a means of persuasion, especially when products are promoted to vulnerable audiences.

For example, Brenkert (1998b, 1) identified several moral objections to the G. Heileman Brewing Co.'s 1991 campaign for PowerMaster, a brand in the "up-strength malt liquor category" that directed a significant amount of marketing efforts to inner-city blacks, many of whom regarded malt liquor as "the drink of choice." The objections were based on three themes. First, critics claimed that ads drew upon images and themes related to power and boldness, which could only promote satisfaction artificially. Hence, the campaign was said to foster a moral illusion. Second, G. Heileman Brewing Co. was charged with a lack of concern for the harm likely to be caused by the product, since blacks suffer disproportionately from cirrhosis of the liver and other diseases associated with alcohol consumption. Thus, Heileman was attacked for lack of moral sensitivity. Third, the company was accused of taking unfair advantage of inner-city blacks, who were regarded as vulnerable to ads that promised power, self-assertion, and sexual success. For these reasons, the campaign was considered exploitative.

Although Brenkert (1998b) recognized the validity of the charges, he contends that none of the objections justified the criticism leveled at Heileman because the same arguments could be leveled against competitors. Without some mechanism to hold all marketers accountable within a given product category, it is morally unjust to allow one company to market a product and to block another from doing the same. He concluded that "marketers must recognize not only their individual moral responsibilities to those they target, but also a collective responsibility of all marketers for those market segments they jointly target" (1998b, 1). In the end, Heileman decided not to market PowerMaster as a result of criticism of its advertising and marketing strategy from a number of protest groups and from the reversal of support from the Bureau of Alcohol, Tobacco, Firearms and Explosives; however, Brenkert's point is well-taken—that the responsibility goes beyond that of a single brand.

3. The Outcome of Advertising Is Uncertain

Rotzoll et al. (1996) point out that the advertising process is so subjective and the results so difficult to measure that even the professionals within the industry are unable to parse out its effects from other sources of influence. That leaves the outcome of the advertising process open to different interpretations. Some competing sources of influence come from the media itself, such as product placements in television programs, YouTube videos, or films. Nonmediated sources, however, play a significant role, too, including word-of-mouth, cost factors, product quality, competitive factors with parity products, and so forth.

For example, a long-standing concern is the extent to which advertising merely influences the brand choice among those who have decided to use a given product versus an ad's ability to increase the generic demand for the product. In other words, does the advertising of Marlboro cigarettes result in more people smoking cigarettes or does it simply result in more smokers choosing Marlboro over Camel and other competing brands? If the outcome were known, certain actions could be taken to resolve the issue. However, the uncertainty opens the door to speculation and prevents closure.

Similarly, advertising critics complain that advertisers set unattainable standards of beauty for women by the depiction of tall, thin, young models, many of whom have benefitted from plastic surgery and air-brushing of photographs. Questions have been raised concerning the role that advertising plays in fostering that standard. Even though other sources within the media also depict women in a similar fashion, questions remain unanswered concerning the extent to which advertising reflects depictions that already exist or sets the standards that others follow. Because advertising must use symbols and values that are relevant to the culture, the central issue is whether advertising merely reflects the culture or has the power to shape it (Holbrook 1987; Pollay 1986). Even when advertising reflects aspects of the culture that already exist, the mere act of reflection can lead to the shaping of culture because not everything is reflected equally. Values that encourage consumption and indulgence fit better with the goals of most advertising campaigns than self-discipline and frugality. "Hence, while it may be true that advertising reflects cultural values, it does so on a very selective basis, echoing and reinforcing certain attitudes, behaviors, and values far more frequently than others" (Pollay 1986, 33).

Ethnic and racial groups also complain of harmful stereotypes. In the early-to-mid-1900s, people of color were typically shown in roles of servitude towards whites rather than as consumers themselves. African-Americans fought against the stereotypical use of the black mammy who spoke in dialect, such as the early depictions of Aunt Jemima, and Hispanics fought against stereotypical images of lawlessness, such as the Frito Bandito, a gun-toting Mexican bandit who "loves crunchy Fritos corn chips so much he'll stop at nothing to get yours" (Wilson, Gutiérrez, and Chao 2003, 147). Protests resulted in more favorable, less-offensive depictions; however, the extent to which the advertised portrayals lead to prejudice or other negative social factors is very difficult to measure and therefore unknown.

A final example shows our uncertainty regarding advertising's ability to create unhealthy desires for products that consumers can't afford to buy. An article from the satirical newspaper *The Onion* pokes fun at low-income consumers who define themselves by the use of expensive designer brands that are clearly beyond their means. The story opens with the following lines: "Just because I happen to live with my four brothers and sisters in my mom's two-bedroom South Side apartment, work at Taco Bell, and don't have a car, some ignorant types assume that I don't have much money. But, as you can clearly see from my $220 Fubu jacket and $95 Tommy Hilfiger sweatshirt, I could not possibly be poor" (Lucas 2000). The article is brilliantly comical, but beneath the humor we have to wonder how far our fictitious consumer is from reality and to what extent he is a product of advertising. These are questions that go unanswered due to advertising's uncertain outcome.

A Return to the Classical Liberal Model

Given our understanding of ethics, we now return to the assumptions of the classical liberal model—that the "sovereign self-seeking individual" is guided by egoism, intellectualism, quietism, and atomism and acts in a deliberate manner to satisfy self-interest after it has been aroused by a significant promise of reward (Rotzoll et al. 1996, 21). In earlier chapters, we have concluded that these assumptions are quite inadequate; however, the advertising industry continues to hold onto them. Most likely, few professionals in the advertising industry could enumerate the assumptions of classical liberalism; yet, the message strategy and media decisions used in advertising only make sense within the classical liberal model. This view puts a great deal of responsibility on the consumer, who must learn to navigate the marketplace to avoid exploitation.

To compound the burden upon consumers, critics charge that the motivation for ethical conduct within the advertising industry as a whole is the desire to avoid government regulations rather than a recognized need to do the right thing. As a result of federal, state, and local regulations, the industry takes a deontological approach with certain practices, but only those that are regulated (e.g., don't deceive consumers, don't place tobacco ads on television, don't advertise to underage consumers, do carry health warnings on cigarette ads, etc.).

In particular, the efforts at self-regulation are attributed to the need to avoid federal regulation, which can result in stiff penalties or negative media coverage and subsequently can affect public opinion and investor relations. Wayne

Keeley, Director of the Children's Advertising Review Unit of the Council of Better Business Bureaus, maintains that the organization is able to achieve a 95 percent compliance rate among businesses to avoid FTC intervention and its consequences (Taylor et al. 2008). If this assessment is correct, federal regulation can serve as a strong motivation. The difficulty, however, is that government regulation can vary with different political administrations, which leaves much to chance by providing an unstable platform for ongoing ethical standards (Rotzoll et al. 1996).

Aside from legal restrictions, the ethical framework that the advertising industry generally relies upon is utilitarianism. Of the various ethical perspectives, it is the best fit with the classical liberal model and is arguably the easiest standard to meet. Because classical liberalism assumes a self-corrective mechanism, it holds that advertisers pursuing their self-interests will result in the good of the whole, which fits a utilitarian perspective. Rotzoll and his coauthors cite a fitting example in a response by the American Association of Advertising Agencies to a government inquiry about the potential need for limits on the number of commercials in children's programming. "The AAAA's position is that advertising self-regulation provides adequate safeguards against advertising abuses; that advertising does not harm children and that, therefore, there is no need to protect them from it; and that if a program has 'too many' commercials, children will stop watching it. In sum, market forces will serve the interest of children by naturally regulating what is broadcast to them" (Rotzoll et al. 1996, 197 citing Siebert 1988, 2).

Likewise, advertisers can feel a degree of confidence in using one-sided messages and influencing consumers to think or act in accordance with the advertiser's intent despite not knowing the end result of advertising, because they believe consumers will be guided by egoism, intellectualism, quietism, and atomism, the final outcome of which will be the greatest good for the largest number.

There is no final resolution to the question of ethics—only the awareness that the industry's deontological approach to legal issues and its utilitarian approach to the other challenges make it a target for criticism. Perhaps in time, justice-based perspectives will give way to care-based or other perspectives that will set a higher standard for consumer protection. Until then, consumers need to recognize that they are in a power relationship with advertisers, who assume consumers will seek out alternative sources of information and that their needs will be protected so long as they are in the majority.

➤ 8 ◄

Concluding Comments on Advertising and Consumer Culture

The greatest of faults, I should say, is to be conscious of none.
—Thomas Carlyle (1795–1881)

There are an infinite number of criticisms of advertising, more than we can possibly address here in a single book. However, as Thomas Carlyle said, the only *real* fault is being blind to one's faults. And the many controversies in advertising are well-known by advertising practitioners and scholars alike. In fact, the field has a long tradition of scholarship devoted to understanding the historical, economic, and social consequences of advertising. This is not true of all professions, and it speaks well of the collective conscience of the advertising profession.

Self-Reflection Within the Field

In the Preface we indicated that this book provides a philosophical map of advertising seen through the lenses of classical liberalism, institutions, and consumer culture. For insights into both the contributions and misdeeds of advertising, we turned to the field's most preeminent scholars—James Carey, Vincent Norris, David Potter, and Kim Rotzoll. These scholars are in agreement that advertising is a distinctly classical liberal institution. Many of its faults are, in fact, criticisms better directed to the larger classical liberal model that inspired the development of advertising. It is impossible to understand advertising without thoroughly understanding classical liberalism. And to understand classical liberalism, one must confront the conflicting values underlying it. Our ambivalence toward government manipulation of the marketplace, our vacillating feelings toward individualism versus collectivism, and our doubts about the autonomy of man are all implicit in our conflicting feelings about classical liberalism and advertising.

At the same time, many of us would agree that advertising is an institution that must be held accountable. Norris explains that like all institutions, advertising is ubiquitous and influences us in both social and economic ways. Criticism of advertising can be traced to its character as an institution. As a powerful influence upon society, advertising is criticized for not keeping up with social trends (e.g., by reinforcing traditional stereotypes) and for promoting overly provocative images (e.g., by depicting nudity). It is also attacked for disrespecting cultural and national boundaries by preempting indigenous cultures with consumer culture.

The root of this problem can be traced directly to the nature and purpose of institutions. As Johan Stein said, "institutions are intersubjectively shared by a collective of individuals either consciously or unconsciously" (1997, 730). By definition, an institution cannot represent every value or point of view. It will always fail to reflect a sizable portion of the population. And, although advertising (like all institutions) is constantly changing, it may change too quickly, not enough, or in the wrong ways. The fact that the social influence of advertising often ranges well beyond its initial intent further exacerbates the problem. For example, when an ad for a soft drink shows a thin, good-looking young woman drinking a certain beverage, consumers associate the drink with a particular lifestyle and appearance. However, when a young woman is constantly exposed to thin, good-looking models in advertising, she may develop feelings of inferiority if she doesn't resemble the models. Here the advertiser is perpetuating unrealistic standards for women's appearance, albeit unintentionally.

A similar conundrum is associated with advertising's economic function. Advertising makes targeted consumers aware of products and services and teaches consumers about their benefits. Consumers who are convinced of the value of a brand may make a purchase. The problem arises when consumers are continually exposed to the notion that all needs and wants can be satisfied by purchasing something. The impact of a single ad may be negligible. The cumulative result of a lifetime of messages that glorify materialism isn't quite so benign. As Schudson (1984) asserted, needs become ambiguous as individual choices multiply. Our confusion about what we really need is obvious when you consider national debt figures: In 2008, Americans owed 1,000 percent more in unsecured debt than they did in 1969.

These examples illustrate our mixed feelings about advertising and the original classical liberal model. According to the assumptions of classical liberalism, our rational nature is supposed to protect us from making self-destructive assumptions about our appearance or buying things we don't really need. The atomistic character of our society is supposed to keep the marketplace fair and keep our competing self-interests balanced. And since our natural disposition is one of complacence, then we're supposed to require constant incentives to spend. Right?

Clearly, the assumptions underlying classical liberalism are suspect. Our discomfort with modern advertising isn't because it has failed to perform its institutional functions. It's because it has performed them too well. The classical liberal safeguards we've counted upon are no match for the institution of advertising.

Although many of the harshest criticisms of advertising may focus on its social and economic functions, it's the other characteristic of institutions that may ultimately be to blame. Norris said that ubiquity was a prerequisite condition for any institution. But ubiquity may play a much more significant role in how the institution of advertising really performs. As media and advertising technologies developed, advertising became not just ubiquitous but omnipresent, meaning it's gone from being found everywhere to being everywhere at the same time. Even more daunting, it also seems to have become omniscient in that advertisers seem to know so much about us. These qualities contribute a great deal to our discomfort with advertising.

Evolution at Warp Speed

Much like the way technological advances in medicine occur before we have a philosophical framework to deal with them, advertising has evolved into forms and venues faster than we can fully understand them. In part, this is related to the changing definition of advertising. Though defining advertising thirty years ago was relatively easy, it has become so inextricably intertwined within consumer culture as a whole that it's become almost impossible to discern the advertisements from the medium in which they appear. Nontraditional media, social marketing, viral marketing, and other techniques have made it almost impossible to tell the difference between editorial matter and commercial speech. So, while we might agree on some basic definitions, it's clear that the phenomena we're trying to understand are constantly changing.

Another issue within advertising is the difficulty in assigning causality to events, even when they're viewed chronologically. All we can do is understand the confluence of events as they developed over time. The first three chapters of the book offered insights into institutions and their role in society; historical and philosophical ways of thinking about how culture is developed and reinforced over time; and the role of advertising as an institution of consumer culture. Although we offered a chronology of events, it does not allow us to selectively determine the degree of influence of one element or another. Nor does it empower us to predict future developments. Though we don't know the causality, we do know that advertising evolved as our culture and economy have developed, and in the process, citizens have become consumers.

Some of the difficulty in defining and understanding the effects of advertising can be resolved by calling attention to aspects of advertising most people aren't aware of. In Chapter 4, we introduced the principal players involved in advertising in a consumer culture—advertisers, media, and consumers. But over time, the players have become far more complex as well as more intertwined. For example, a consumer posts a positive product review on a blog. The product's marketing director sees the post and offers the blogger a year's worth of the product for posting positive reviews of the product. It's at this point that a consumer evolves into an advertiser in that he's responsible for the veracity of his remarks and for disclosing the fiduciary relationship with the maker of the product. At least this is how the Federal Trade Commission sees it.

The complexity of the corporate environment surrounding consumers is more evident than ever. With rampant vertical and horizontal integration taking place, it's quite possible that two competing brands are owned by the same parent company. And, although we'd like to think of long-standing brands like Budweiser and Good Humor ice cream as being distinctly American, they're not. So while our focus has been on American advertising, consumers, and media, the reality is that we're living in a global economy. There's an inevitable clash when hypercommercialism collides with collectivist-based cultures as advertising spreads consumerist values across borders, as we saw in Chapter 5.

The problems with international law seem insurmountable in comparison to those in the United States. However, as advertising, consumers, and media evolve continuously, so too does regulation, as we saw in Chapter 6. The problem is whether our regulatory system can evolve adequately enough. Given that we began with a culture based on a self-righting marketplace, difficulties with effective regulation are not surprising. In the absence of an all-knowing, all-jurisdictional regulatory body, we've seen collaboration across national boundaries and between the self-regulatory bodies and the government regulators.

Most people would agree that laws provide us with a moral minimum. The really vexing questions surrounding advertising in a consumer culture lie in the gray area of ethical issues, as we saw in Chapter 7. Whichever ethical approach one takes—whether it's balancing rules, focusing on outcomes, emphasizing relative moral standards, or applying case-by-case considerations—we see here the same tensions between individualism and collectivism. Perhaps it's not which ethical approach one adopts, but the fact that one strives to be ethical that matters most. Like medical ethicists, advertising scholars and practitioners continue to grapple with the field's controversies and have established a strong scholarly tradition of self-assessment. As a relatively new profession (compared to medicine) this reflects very positively on the discipline.

In Defense of Advertising

After hearing a first-day description of an Advertising and Society course, a student raised his hand and asked, "Is this class like that Sunday-school class where you learn how to defend your religion?" It was a very good question, but perhaps the bigger question is whether we need to defend advertising.

Is advertising to blame for the excessive spending and borrowing that led us into the worst financial crisis since the Great Depression? Was it advertising that led to our buying houses we couldn't afford and the ensuing epidemic of foreclosures? Is the obesity epidemic among children the fault of advertisers?

Instead of blaming advertising, maybe we should be assigning some responsibility to consumer culture and our anachronistic adherence to classical liberal values on which it was based. Granted, advertising helped create consumer culture, so it shares the blame, but are we really troubled by advertising or by what our culture has become—a material world that is out of control—one that developed too rapidly to be constrained adequately by the legal and ethical restrictions that currently exist.

Perhaps advertising does share the blame, given the difficulty of putting legal and ethical constraints in place fast enough to keep up with changes in the industry. This brings us squarely back to the tension between individualism and collectivism, for we attempt to put legal and ethical restrictions on advertising and other institutions based solely on individualistic thinking. We create acceptable standards that apply to each brand of product, service, cause, political candidate, and so forth, in the belief that addressing the individual players will take care of the whole. Following that thought, as long as each source of advertising plays by the rules, all is well. What is overlooked in the process is the problem that occurs when multiple advertisers promote their product or service.

As we saw in the PowerMaster story (Chapter 7), having a small number of brands of malt liquor promoted to inner-city dwellers may be tolerable, but having multiple brands is problematic. PowerMaster failed to make it into the marketplace, not because it broke any rules that were imposed upon individual producers but because of the collective harm that was anticipated if yet another brand entered the market with a legal but harmful product. Likewise, there is nothing inherently wrong with a fast-food chain offering value meals with supersized portions, but when other advertisers follow suit because value meals resonate with consumers, the culture becomes one of supersized adults and children with a staggering obesity problem. Further, there is nothing inherently wrong with Burger King's promotion of its burgers as a late night snack (in addition to daytime meals); however, when McDonald's advertises its fries with the message, "Cravings have no curfew," and other chains encourage late-night snacking, a fourth meal at midnight can easily become the norm for the target market.

The omnipresent, ubiquitous nature of advertising can't be denied, and the collective impact of multiple campaigns is merely one problem that has largely been ignored within the culture. Furthermore, the ubiquity of advertising creates conditions that our current regulatory system and ethical frameworks can't easily address. Our regulatory system is based on both ad hoc and post hoc approaches, and that makes coping with cumulative effects of several advertisers *before* any damage is done almost impossible.

The first steps in solving these challenges are recognizing the problem and finding creative ways to allow for collectivistic thinking. There's a codependency shared by all institutions in a culture, including advertising. "We do not use institutions, we participate in them" (Norris 1980). The reality is that we shape our institutions as they shape us.

References

Aaker, David A. and George S. Day. 1982. *Consumerism: Search for the Consumer Interest.* New York: The Free Press.

Aaker, David A. and Erich Joachimsthaler. 1999. "The Lure of Global Branding." *Harvard Business Review* (November–December), Reprint #99601.

Abela, Andres V. and Paul W. Farris. 2001. "Advertising and Competition." In *Handbook of Marketing and Society*, ed. Paul N. Bloom and Gregory T. Gundlach, 184–205. Thousand Oaks, CA: Sage.

Abernethy, Avery N. and George Franke. 1998. "FTC Regulatory Activity and the Information Content of Advertising." *Journal of Public Policy and Marketing* 17 (2): 239–256.

Advertising Age. 2008. "Spending in Midst of 3-Year Drop, First Since Depression." 79 (47): 8.

Ameringer, Carl F. 2008. *The Health Care Revolution: From Medical Monopoly to Market Competition.* Berkeley: University of California Press; New York: Milbank Memorial Fund.

An, Soontae and Lori Bergen. 2007. "Advertiser Pressure on Daily Newspapers." *Journal of Advertising* 36 (2): 111–121.

Anderson, Nate. 2009. "FTC Warns of 'Day of Reckoning' for Online Advertisers." ARS Technica (February 12). Available at arstechnica.com/tech-policy/news/2009/02/ftc-warns-of-day-of-reckoning-for-online-advertisers.ars (accessed July 10, 2009).

Anholt, Simon. 2000. *Another One Bites the Grass: Making Sense of International Advertising.* New York: John Wiley and Sons, Inc.

Arnould, Eric J. and Craig J. Thompson. 2005. "Consumer Culture Theory (CCT): Twenty Years of Research." *Journal of Consumer Research* 31(4): 868–882.

Astrachan, James B., Donna Thomas, George Eric Rosden, and Peter Eric Rosden. 2008. *The Law of Advertising.* Newark: Mathew Bender.

Averitt, Neil W. and Terry Calvani. 1986. "The Role of the FTC in American Society." *Oklahoma Law Review* 39: 41.

Bagdikian, Ben H. 1997. *The Media Monopoly*, 5th ed. Boston: Beacon Press.

———. 2000. *The Media Monopoly*, 6th ed. Boston: Beacon Press.

———. 2004. *The New Media Monopoly.* Boston: Beacon Press.

Baer, William J. 1986. "Where to from Here: Reflections on the Recent Saga of the Federal Trade Commission." *Oklahoma Law Review*, 39: 51.

Baker, Russ. 1997. "The Squeeze." *Columbia Journalism Review* (September/October): 30–36.

Baran, Stanley J. and Dennis K. Davis. 1995. *Mass Communication Theory: Foundations, Ferment, and Future.* Belmont, CA: Wadsworth.

REFERENCES

Barboza, David. 2009. "Death Sentences in Chinese Milk Case." *New York Times* Online. (January 22). Available at www.nytimes.com/2009/01/23/world/asia/23milk. html?ref=world (accessed January 25, 2009).

Barrett, Rick. 2008. "Runway to Roadway: Supermodel Revs Up Harley V-Rod Ads." *Milwaukee Journal Sentinel* (October 14): D1.

Barthes, Roland. 1972. *Mythologies*. London: Paladin.

Bates v. State Bar of Arizona, 433 U.S. 350 (1977).

Baudrillard, Jean. 1981. *For a Critique of the Political Economy of the Sign*. St. Louis, MO: Telos Press.

Baumeister, Roy F. 1987. "How the Self Became a Problem: A Psychological Review of Historical Research." *Journal of Personality and Social Psychology* 52 (1): 163–176.

BBC News. 2001. "TV's World Record Breakers." (March 22). Available at http://news.bbc.co.uk/2/hi/entertainment/1219668.stm (accessed Dec. 15, 2008).

Belk, Russell W. 1988. "Possessions and the Extended Self." *Journal of Consumer Research* 15: 139–168.

Bellafante, Gina. 2007. "When Bad Women Generate Good Ratings." *New York Times*, (July 7): A15, 23.

Bennett, W. Lance 1993. "Constructing Publics and Their Opinions." *Political Communication* 10 (2): 101–120.

Bigelow v. Virginia, 421 U.S. 809 (1975).

Bjornstrom, Eileen E. 2007. "The Political Economy of Antitrust Enforcement: Toward a Longitudinal Explanation." Paper presented at the annual meeting of the American Sociological Association (August 11), New York City. Available at www.allacademic.com/meta/p177425_index.html (accessed July 8, 2009).

Blackshaw, Pete. 2009. "Underwriting Your Super Bowl Spot." *Advertising Age* (January 19). Available at http://adage.com/superbowl09/article?article_id=133888 (accessed January 23, 2009).

Board of Trustees of State University of New York v. Fox, 492 U.S. 469 (1989).

Bond, Jonathan and Richard Kirshenbaum. 1998. *Under the Radar: Talking to Today's Cynical Consumer*. New York: John Wiley and Sons.

Boni, Federico. 2002. "Framing Media Masculinities: Men's Lifestyle Magazines and the Biopolitics of the Male Body." *European Journal of Communication* 17: 465–478.

Boorstin, Daniel J. 1974. *The Americans: The Democratic Experience*. New York: Vintage Books.

Bordo, Susan. 1999. *The Male Body: A New Look at Men in Public and in Private*. New York: Farrar, Straus, and Giroux.

Boutlis, Paulie. 2000. "A Theory of Postmodern Advertising." *International Journal of Advertising* 19 (1): 3–23.

Bowles, Samuel. 1998. "Endogenous Preferences: The Cultural Consequences of Markets and Other Economic Institutions." *Journal of Economic Literature* 36 (March): 75–111.

Brenkert, George G. 1998a. "Marketing, the Ethics of Consumption, and Less Developed Countries." In *The Business of Consumption: Environmental Ethics and the Global Economy*, ed. Laura Westra and Patricia Werhane, 91–112. Totowa, NJ: Rowman & Littlefield.

———. 1998b. "Marketing to Inner-City Blacks: PowerMaster and Moral Responsibility." *Business Ethics Quarterly* 8 (1): 1–18.

REFERENCES

Brown, Stephen. 2006. "Recycling Postmodern Marketing." *Marketing Review* 6 (3): 211–30.

Budnitz, Mark E. 1997. "The FTC's Consumer Protection Program during the Miller Years: Lessons for Administrative Agency Structure and Operation." *Catholic University Law Review* 46: 371.

Bush, Michael. 2009. "Bloggers Be Warned: FTC May Monitor What You Say." *Advertising Age* 80 (13): 3, 21.

Carey, James. 1960. "Advertising: An Institutional Approach." In *The Role of Advertising: A Book of Readings,* ed. Charles H. Sandage and Vernon Fryburger, 3–34. Homewood, IL: Richard D. Irwin.

———. 1989. *Communication as Culture.* Boston: Unwin Hyman.

Carr, David. 2002. "Magazine Imitates a Catalog and Has a Charmed Life, So Far." *New York Times* (September 16): C1, C2.

Carter, T. Barton, Marc A. Franklin, and Jay B. Wright. 2005. *The First Amendment and the Fourth Estate: The Law of Mass Media.* New York: Foundation Press.

Casey, Michael. 2009. "Tobacco Firms Accused of Trying to Skew Research." *Milwaukee Journal Sentinel* (January 4): 12A.

Central Hudson Gas & Electric v. Public Service Commission of New York, 447 U.S. 557 (1980).

Cho, Bongjin, Up Kwon, James W. Gentry, Sunkyu Jun, and Fredric Kropp. 1999. "Cultural Values Reflected in Theme and Execution: A Comparative Study of U.S. and Korean Television Commercials." *Journal of Advertising* 28 (Winter): 59–73.

Christians, Clifford, G., Kim B. Rotzoll, and Mark Fackler. 1991. *Media Ethics: Cases and Moral Reasoning,* 3rd ed. New York: Longman Publishing Group.

Clifford, Stephanie. 2009. "Another Los Angeles Times Promotion Draws Fire." *New York Times* (April 11): B2.

Close, Angeline G., R. Zachary Finney, Russell Z. Lacey, and Julie Z. Sneath. 2006. "Engaging the Consumer through Event Marketing: Linking Attendees with the Sponsor, Community, and Brand." *Journal of Advertising Research* 46 (4): 420–433.

Cohen, G.A. 1995. *Self-Ownership, Freedom, and Equality.* Cambridge, England: Cambridge University Press.

Committee on Communications. 2006. "Children, Adolescents, and Advertising." *Pediatrics* 118 (6): 2563–2698.

Computer World. 2008. (September 15): 12.

Consumer Reports. 2009. "Selling it—goofs, glitches, gotchas." (February): 63.

Council of Better Business Bureaus (CBBB) website. Available at www.bbb.org/us/about-children-food-beverage-advertising-initiative/ (accessed July 1, 2009).

Cox, Edward F., Robert C. Fellmuth, and John Schultz. 1969. *The "Nader Report" on the Federal Trade Commission.* Boston: E.P. Dutton.

Croteau, David and William Hoynes. 2006. *The Business of Media: Corporate Media and the Public Interest,* 2nd ed. Thousand Oaks, CA: Pine Forge Press.

Cunningham, Anne and Craig Freeman. 2003. "On the Wings of Nike: A Streamlined Approach to the Commercial Speech Doctrine." *Communications and the Law* (December): 1–32.

Cuprisin, Tim. 2009. " 'Saturday Night Live,' Pepsi Pioneer in Blurring Line Between Shows, Ads." *Milwaukee Journal Sentinel* (February 4): B10.

Davison, W. Phillips. 1983. "The Third-Person Effect in Communication." *Public Opinion Quarterly* 47 (1): 1–15.

REFERENCES

DeFleur, Melvin L. and Sandra J. Ball-Rokeach. 1989. *Theories of Mass Communication.* White Plains, NY: Longman.

de Graaf, John, David Wann, and Thomas H. Naylor. 2001. *Affluenza: The All-Consuming Epidemic.* San Franscisco: Berrett-Kohler.

Deloria, Vine, Jr. 2003. *God Is Red.* Golden, CO: Fulcrum Publishing.

de Mooij, Marieke. 2005. *Global Marketing and Advertising: Understanding Cultural Paradoxes,* 2d ed. Thousand Oaks, CA: Sage Publications.

de Sola Pool, Ithiel. 1983. *Technologies of Freedom.* Berkeley, CA: Belknap Press.

Dickerson, A. Mechele. 2008. "Consumer Over-Indebtedness: A U.S. Perspective." *Texas International Law Journal* 43 (2):135–158.

Discovery Network, Inc. v. City of Cincinnati, 507 U.S. 410 (1993).

Douglas, Susan P. and Samuel Craig. 2000. *International Marketing Research.* New York: John Wiley.

Easton, Nina, Scott Cendrowski, Eugenia Levenson, and Nadira A. Hira. 2008. "Main Street Turns Against Wall Street." *Fortune* (October 13): 96–102. Available at www.proquest.com/ (accessed January 17, 2009).

Edelman, Murray J. 1993. "Contestable Categories and Public Opinion." *Political Communication* 10 (3): 231–242.

Edenfield v. Fane, 507 U.S. 761 (1993).

Editors, 1981. "The FTC's Cereal Fiasco: Congress Won't Let Us Bust 'Em Up.'" *Antitrust Law & Economics Review* 13 (2): 57–63.

Enrico, Dottie. 1990. "Ms., Minus Ads, Makes Debut Today." *Newsday* (July 30): 2.

Entman, Robert M. 1993. "Framing: Toward Clarification of a Fractured Paradigm." *Journal of Communication* 43: 51–58.

Ewen, Stuart. 1976. *Captains of Consciousness: Advertising and the Social Roots of the Consumer Culture.* New York: McGraw Hill.

———. 1996. *PR! A Social History of Spin.* New York: Perseus Books Group.

———.1999. *All Consuming Images: The Politics of Style in Contemporary Culture.* New York: Basic Books.

Fahey, Patrick. 1991. "Advocacy Group Boycotting of Network Television Advertisers and Its Effect on Programming Content." *University of Pennsylvania Law Review* 140: 647–709.

Fair, Leslie. 2002. "Federal Trade Commission Advertising Enforcement." Staff Document of the Division of Advertising Practices of the Federal Trade Commission (September 19): 1.

Farhi, Paul. 2007. "Don Imus Gingerly Steps Back on Air." *Washington Post* Online. Available at www.washingtonpost.com/wpdyn/content/article/2007/12/03/AR2007120300368.html (accessed October 1, 2008).

Featherstone, Mike. 1991. *Consumer Culture and Postmodernism.* London: Sage Publications.

Federal Communications Commission (FCC). 2007. "FCC's Review of the Broadcast Ownership Rules." Available at www.fcc.gov/cgb/consumerfacts/reviewrules.html (accessed September 30, 2008).

Federal Election Commission (FEC) v. Wisconsin Right to Life, 551 U.S. 449 (2007).

Federal Trade Commission. Available at www.ftc.gov (accessed June 30, 2009).

Federal Trade Commission, Bureau of Consumer Protection. Available at www.ftc.gov/bcp/bcpap.shtm (accessed July 3, 2009).

Federal Trade Commission. Bureau of Consumer Protection, General Publications.

REFERENCES

Available at www.ftc.gov/bcp/conline/pubs/general/guidetoftc.htm#bcp (accessed July 10, 2009).

Federal Trade Commission. "Deception." Available at www.ftc.gov/bcp/policystmt/ad-decept.htm (accessed July 6, 2009).

Feirstein, Richard. 2000. "You Need to Know the Rules for Comparative Advertising." *The Business Review* (February 18). Available at http://albany.bizjournals.com/albany/stories/2000/02/21/focus3.html (accessed July 22, 2009).

Fetscherin, Marc and Mark Toncar. 2009. "Visual Puffery in Advertising." *International Journal of Market Research* 51 (2): 147–148.

Fidler, Roger. 1997. *Mediamorphosis: Understanding New Media.* Thousand Oaks, CA: Pine Forge Press.

Finberg, Howard I. 2003. "Enter the Matrix: The FCC's New Rules." *Poynter* Online. Available at www.poynter.org/column.asp?id=56&aid=36005&custom=Convergence+Chaser:+Guide+to+industry (accessed April 25, 2004).

Fine, Jon. 2004. "Mags & Vine." *Advertising Age* 75 (15): 1, 65–66.

Fink, Rychard. 1962. "Introduction." In *Ragged Dick and Mark, the Match Boy*, by Horatio Alger. New York: Collier Books.

Firat, A. Fuat and Clifford J. Shultz II. 1997. "From Segmentation to Fragmentation." *European Journal of Marketing* 31 (3/4): 183–207.

First National Bank of Boston v. Bellotti, 435 U.S. 765 (1978).

Florida Bar v. Went For It, Inc., 515 U.S. 618 (1995).

44 Liquormart, Inc. v. Rhode Island, 517 U.S. 484 (1996).

Foster, Moses. 2008. "The New-Media Age Gives Us Power; It's Time to Create Content that Matters." *Advertising Age* 79 (18): 20.

Fox, Kate. 2008. *Watching the English: The Hidden Rules of English Behavior.* London: Hodder & Stoughton.

Frank, Thomas and Matt Weiland. 1997. *Commodify Your Dissent: The Business of Culture in the New Gilded Age.* New York: Norton.

Free Press. 2009. "Who Owns the Media?" Available at www.freepress.net/ownership/chart.php?chart=main (accessed Jan. 13, 2009).

Friedman, Wayne. 2002. "MasterCard, Universal Eye $100 Mil Deal." *Advertising Age* 73 (48): 1, 56.

Frith, Katherine. 1997. *Undressing the Ad: Reading Culture in Advertising.* New York: Peter Lang.

Frith, Katherine and Michael Frith. 1990. "Western Advertising and Eastern Culture: The Confrontation in Southeast Asia." *Current Issues and Research in Advertising* 12 (1, 2): 63–73.

Frith, Katherine and Barbara Mueller. 2003. *Advertising and Societies: Global Issues.* New York: Peter Lang.

Frutkin, A. J. 2007. "Advanced Placement" *MediaWeek* (April 30) 17 (18): SR4-SR6.

Fueroghne, Dean K. 2000. *Law & Advertising.* Chicago: The Copy Workshop.

Galloway, Chester S. 2003. "The First Amendment and FTC Weight-Loss Advertising Regulation." *Journal of Consumer Affairs* 37 (2): 413–423.

Garofoli, Joe. 2007. "Experts See Firing of Imus as Broadcast Tipping Point/Extraordinary Push by Sponsors, Activist, Network Employees." *San Francisco Chronicle* (April 13): A2.

General Electric. 2008. Fact Sheet. Available at www.ge.com/company/businesses/factsheets/corporate.html (accessed January 14, 2009).

Gerbner, George. 1998. "Cultivation Analysis: An Overview." *Mass Communication and Society* 1 (3/4): 175–194.

Giles, Gilbert. 2006. *White Collar Criminal: The Offender in Business and the Professions.* Piscataway. NJ: Aldine Transaction.

Gitlow v. New York, 268 U.S. 652 (1925).

Goffman, Erving. 1974. *Frame Analysis: An Essay on the Organization of Experience.* New York: Harper and Row.

Golan, Guy and Lior Zaidner. 2008. "Creative Strategies in Viral Advertising: An Application of Taylor's Six-Segment Message Strategy Wheel." *Journal of Computer-Mediated Communication* 13 (4): 959–972.

Goldfarb v. Virginia State Bar, 421 U.S. 773 (1975).

Gower, Carla. 2008. *Legal and Ethical Considerations for Public Relations,* 2nd ed. Long Grove, IL: Waveland Press.

Grant, James. 1994. *Money of the Mind: Borrowing and Lending in America from the Civil War to Michael Milken.* New York: Macmillan.

Greater New Orleans Broadcast Association, Inc. v. United States, 527 U.S. 173 (1999).

Grun, Bernard. 2005. *Timetables of History.* New York: Touchstone.

Guis, M. P. 1996. "Using Panel Data to Determine the Effect of Advertising on Brand-Level Distilled Spirits Sales." *Journal of Studies on Alcohol* 57: 73–76.

Haiken, Elizabeth. 1997. *Venus Envy: A History of Cosmetic Surgery.* Baltimore: Johns Hopkins University Press.

Hall, Edward T. 1959. *The Silent Language.* New York: Doubleday.

Hamilton, Walter H. 1932. "Introduction." In *The Encyclopaedia of the Social Sciences,* ed. Edward R. A. Seligman, 84–89. New York: Macmillan.

Hampp, Andrew. 2007. "Imus Mess Makes Arbiters of Advertisers." *Advertising Age* (Midwest Region Edition), 78 (16): 43.

Harmon, Mark D. 2001. "Affluenza: Television Use and Cultivation of Materialism." *Mass Communication and Society* 4 (4): 405–418.

Havenstein, Heather. 2008. "Big Advertisers Protest Google-Yahoo Search Deal." *Computerworld* 42 (37): 12.

Held, Virginia. 1993. *Feminist Morality: Transforming Culture, Society, and Politics.* Chicago: University of Chicago Press.

Herbst, Moira. 2008. "Bailout Outrage Races Across the Web." *Business Week* Online. (September 25). Available at www.proquest.com/ (accessed Jan. 17, 2009).

Hermann, Robert O. 1982. "The Consumer Movement in Historical Perspective." In *Consumerism: Search for the Consumer Interest,* ed. David A. Aaker and George S. Day, 23–32. New York: The Free Press.

Hiaasen, Carl. 1998. *Team Rodent: How Disney Devours the World.* New York: Ballantine Publishing Group.

Hindman, Elizabeth Blanks. 2004. "The Chickens Have Come Home to Roost: Individualism, Collectivism and Conflict in Commercial Speech Doctrine." *Communication Law and Policy* 9: 237–271.

Hobbs, Caswell O. 2004–2005. "Antitrust and Consumer Protection: Exploring the Common Ground." *Antitrust Law Journal* 72: 1153–1156.

Hoefges, Michael. 2003. "Protecting Tobacco Advertising under the Commercial Speech Doctrine: The Constitutional Impact of Lorillard Tobacco Co." *Communication Law and Policy* 8 (3): 276–311.

Hovland, Roxanne and Gary B. Wilcox. 1989. Advertising in Society: Classic and Contemporary Readings on Advertising's Role in Society. Chicago: NTC Books.

REFERENCES

Hovland, Roxanne, Joyce Wolburg, and Eric Haley. 2007. *Readings in Advertising, Society, and Consumer Culture*. Armonk, NY: M.E. Sharpe.

Hofstede, Geert. 1980. *Culture's Consequences*. Beverly Hills, CA: Sage.

———. 1984. *Culture's Consequences: International Differences in Work-Related Values*. Newbury Park, CA: Sage.

Holbrook, Morris. 1987. "Mirror, Mirror, on the Wall, What's Unfair in the Reflections on Advertising?" *Journal of Marketing* 51 (3): 95–13.

Holt, Douglas B. 2002. "Why Do Brands Cause Trouble? A Dialectical Theory of Consumer Culture and Branding." *Journal of Consumer Research* 29 (1): 70–90.

Iyengar, Shanto. 1987. "Television News and Citizens' Explanations of National Affairs." *American Political Science Review* 81: 815–831.

———. (1991). *Is Anyone Responsible? How Television Frames Political Issues*. Chicago: University of Chicago Press.

Jacobson, Michael F. and Laurie Ann Mazur. 1995. *Marketing Madness: A Survival Guide for a Consumer Society*. Boulder, CO: Westview Press.

Jenkins, Henry. 2006. *Convergence Culture*. New York: NY University Press.

Jhally, Sut. 1990. *The Codes of Advertising: Fetishism and the Political Economy of Meaning in the Consumer Society*. New York: Routledge.

———. 1997. *Advertising and the End of the World*. (video). Northampton, MA: The Media Education Foundation.

Josephson, Susan G. 1996. *From Idolatry to Advertising: Visual Art and Contemporary Culture*. Armonk, NY: M.E. Sharpe.

Kammen, Michael. 1999. *American Culture, American Tastes: Social Change and the 20th Century*. New York: Random House.

Kellner, Douglas. 1989. *Jean Baudrillard: From Marxism to Postmodernism and Beyond*. Stanford, CA: Stanford University Press.

Kim, Jane J. 2008. "Habit-Forming: Borrowers Keep Piling On Debt—As Lenders' Tighter Standards Cut Off Some Avenues, People Tap Credit Cards, Equity Lines." *Wall Street Journal*, April 10, 2008.

Kirkpatrick, David. 2001. "Words from Our Sponsor: A Jeweler Commissions a Novel." *New York Times* Online (September 3). Available at www.nytimes.com (accessed August 5, 2007).

Krugman, Dean M., Leonard N. Reid, S. Watson Dunn, and Arnold M. Barban. 1994. *Advertising: Its Role in Modern Marketing*. Fort Worth, TX: Dryden.

Lane, W. Ronald and J. Thomas Russell. 2001. *Advertising: A Framework*. Upper Saddle River, NJ: Prentice Hall.

Lazarus, Edward. 2009. "Four Myths about the Supreme Court." *Time* Magazine (June 8): 30.

Leach, William. 1993. *Land of Desire: Merchants, Power, and the Rise of a New American Culture*. New York: Vintage Books.

Lears, T.J. Jackson. "American Advertising and the Reconstruction of the Body." In *Fitness in American Culture: Images of Health, Sport and the Body, 1830–1840*, ed. Kathryn Grover. Amherst: University of Massachusetts Press, 1990.

Leary Thomas B. 2000. "Freedom as the Core Value of Antitrust in the New Millennium 7." Before American Bar Association, Section of Antitrust Law, 48th Annual Spring Meeting (Apr. 6), available at www.ftc.gov/speeches/leary/learyantitrust-speech.htm (accessed July 15, 2009).

———. 2004–2005. "Competition Law and Consumer Protections Law: Two Wings of the Same House." *Antitrust Law Journal* 72: 1147–1151.

REFERENCES

Lee, Byunglak and Victor J. Tremblay. 1992. "Advertising and the U.S. Market Demand for Beer." *Applied Economics* 24 (1): 69–76.

Leiss, William. 1976. *The Limits to Satisfaction: An Essay on the Problem of Needs and Commodities.* Toronto: University of Toronto Press.

Leiss, William, Stephen Kline, Sut Jhally, and Jacqueline Botterill. 2005. *Social Communication in Advertising: Consumption in the Mediated Marketplace,* 3rd ed. New York: Routledge.

Lieberman, Trudy. 2000. "You Can't Report What You Don't Pursue." *Columbia Journalism Review* (May/June); 1–9, Available at www.cjr.org/year/00/2/lieberman.asp (accessed July 6, 2001).

Littlejohn, Stephen W. and Karen A. Foss. 2008. *Theories of Human Communication.* Belmont, CA: Thomson Publishing Group.

LNA/MediaWatch Service. 1999. Competitive Media Reporting, Class/Brand$Summary.

Lorillard Tobacco Co. v. Reilly, I533 U.S. 525 (2001).

Lucas, Manny. 2000. "As You Can See From My Name-Brand Clothing, I Am Not Poor." *The Onion* (February 9), Issue 36–04. Available at www.theonion.com/content/node/33490 (accessed January 1, 2009).

Maich, Steve. 2008. "What 'Socialism for the Rich' Looks Like." *Maclean's* 121 (39): 57.

Mainstream Marketing Services, Inc. v. FTC, 358 F3d 1228 (10th Cir 2004), *cert.* denied, 543 U.S. 812 (2004).

Marchand, Roland. 1985. *Advertising the American Dream,* 88–110. Berkeley, CA: University of California Press.

Market Tools Insight Report. 2008. "Nearly 70% of Online Adults Use Social Media, Often Research Products."(August/September). Available at www.marketingcharts.com/direct/nearly-70-of-online-adults-use-social-media-often-research-products-6101/ (accessed Jan.10, 2009).

Mayfield, Antony. 2008. *What Is Social Media?* E-book from iCrossing. Available at www.icrossing.co.uk/fileadmin/uploads/ebooks/What_is_Social_Media_iCrossing_ebook.pdf.

Mazis, Michael B. 2001. "*FTC v. Novartis*: The Return of Corrective Advertising?" *Journal of Public Policy and Marketing* 20 (1): 114–122.

Mazzarella, William. 2003. *Shoveling Smoke: Advertising and Globalization in Contemporary India.* Durham, NC: Duke University Press.

McChesney, Robert W. 2008. *The Political Economy of Media: Enduring Issues, Emerging Dilemmas.* New York: Monthly Review Press.

McChesney, Robert W. and John Nichols. 2002. *Our Media Not Theirs: The Democratic Struggle against Corporate Media.* New York: Seven Stories Press.

McQuail, Dennis. 1994. *Mass Communication Theory.* London: Sage.

———. 2000. *McQuail's Mass Communication Theory.* London: Sage.

McQuail, Dennis, Jay G. Blumler, and J.R. Brown. 1972. "The Television Audiences: A Revised Perspective." In *Sociology of Mass Communications,* ed. Dennis McQuail. Harmondsworth, England: Penguin.

Medoff, James and Andrew Harless. 1996. *The Indebted Society: Anatomy of an Ongoing Disaster.* Boston: Little, Brown and Co.

Merriam-Webster. 1998. *Dictionary and Thesaurus.* Springfield: MA: Merriam-Webster Inc.

Metromedia, Inc. v. City of San Diego, 453 U.S. 490 (1981).

Morrow, Fiona. 2009. "Adbusters Wins Right to Sue Broadcasters over TV Ads." *Globe and Mail* (April 6). Available at www.theglobeandmail.com/servlet/story/RTGAM.20090406.wads0406/EmailBNStory/National/home/.

References

Moses, Lucia. 2008. "Under Pressure." *Mediaweek* 18 (27): 6.

Mueller, Barbara. 2004. *Dynamics of International Advertising: Theoretical and Practical Perspectives.* New York: Peter Lang.

Murphy, Patrick E. and William L. Wilkie. 1990. *Marketing and Advertising Regulation: The Federal Trade Commission in the 1990s.* Notre Dame: University of Notre Dame Press.

Near v. Minnesota, 283 U.S. 697 (1931).

Nelson, Harold L., Dwight L. Teeter, and Don R. Le Duc. 1989. *Law of Mass Communications: Freedom and Control of Print and Broadcast Media.* Westbury, NY: Foundation Press.

Neumeister, L. 2007. "Appeals Court OKs 'Puffery Defense." Available at www.commercialalert.org/news/archive/2007/08/appeals-court-oks-puffery-defense (accessed July 12, 2009).

New York Times. 2009. "Tobacco Regulation, at Last." (June 12). Available at http://nytimes.com/2009/06/12/opinion/12fri1.html?pagewanted=print (accessed June 30, 2009).

New York Times v. Sullivan, 376 U.S. 254 (1964).

Nicholson, Daniel. 1997. "The Diesel Jeans and Workwear Advertising Campaign and the Commodification of Resistance." In *Undressing the Ad: Reading Culture in Advertising,* ed. Katherine Toland Frith, 175–196. New York: Peter Lang.

Noddings, Nel. 2003. *Caring: A Feminine Approach to Ethics and Moral Education.* Berkeley, CA: University of California Press.

Nordberg, Donald. 1997. "Valuelessness and the Plastic Personality: A 30-year retrospective." *Futures: The Journal of Policy, Planning, and Futures Studies* 29 (7): 669–671.

Norris, James D. 1990. *Advertising and the Transformation of American Society, 1865–1920,* 166-167. New York: Greenwood Press.

Norris, Vincent. 1980. "Advertising History—According to the Textbooks." *Journal of Advertising* 9 (3): 3–11.

O'Guinn, Thomas C., Chris T. Allen, and Richard J. Semenik. 2000. *Advertising.* Cincinnati, OH: South-Western College Publishing.

Olper, Leo. 2006. Personal correspondence with Leo Olper, Senior Vice President and Chief Operating Officer, Lapiz Hispanic Marketing, Chicago.

Otnes, Cele and Tina Lowrey. 1993. "Till Debt Do Us Part: The Selection of Meaning of Artifacts in the American Wedding." In *Advances in Consumer Research,* 20, ed. Leigh McAlister and Michael L. Rothschild, 325–329. Provo, UT: Association for Consumer Research.

Otnes, Cele and Linda M. Scott. 1996. "Something Old, Something New: Exploring the Interaction Between Ritual and Advertising." *Journal of Advertising* 25 (1): 33–50.

Paine, Lynn Sharp. 1993. "Children as Consumers: The Ethics of Children's Television Advertising." In *Ethics in Marketing,* ed. N. Craig Smith and John A. Quelch, 672–686. Homewood, IL: Richard D. Irwin.

Pan, Zhongdang and Gerald M. Kosicki. 1993. "Framing Analysis: An Approach to News Discourse." *Political Communication* 10 (1): 55–75.

Parker, Betty and Richard E. Plank. 2000. "A Uses and Gratifications Perspective on the Internet as a New Information Source." *American Business Review* 18 (2): 43–49.

Parmar, Arundhati. 2004. "Drink Politics: Upstart Cola Firms Sound Clarion Call to Global Consumers." *Marketing News* 38 (3): 1.

References

Pérez-Peña, Richard. 2009. "The Popular Newsweekly Becomes a Lonely Category." *New York Times* (Jan. 17): B1, B4.

Phillips, Barbara J. and Edward F. McQuarrie. 2009. "Mona Lisa with a Gucci Purse; How Fashion Images are Consumed." Paper presented at the American Academy of Advertising, Cincinnati, March 28.

Pierce, Emmet. 2009. "Homeownership Goals Created House of Cards: Lender Guidelines Were Obliterated in Buying Frenzy." *San Diego Union-Tribune* (January 5): A1.

Pollay, Richard W. 1986. "The Distorted Mirror: Reflections on the Unintended Consequences of Advertising." *Journal of Marketing* 50 (2): 18–36.

Pompper, Donnalyn and Yih-Farn Choo. 2008. "Advertising in the Age of TiVo: Targeting Teens and Young Adults with Film and Television Product Placements." *Atlantic Journal of Communication* 16 (1): 49–69.

Posadas de Puerto Rico Association v. Tourism Co. of Puerto Rico, 478 U.S. 328 (1986).

Potter, David M. 1954. "The Institution of Abundance." In *People of Plenty*. Chicago: University of Chicago Press.

Preston, Ivan. 1994. *The Tangled Web They Weave: Truth, Falsity and Advertisers.* Madison, WI: The University of Wisconsin Press.

———. 1996. *The Great American Blowup: Puffery in Advertising and Selling.* Madison, WI: University of Wisconsin Press.

———. 2002. "A Problem Ignored: Dilution and Negation of Consumer Information by Antifactual Content." *Journal of Consumer Affairs* 36 (2): 263–283.

Price, Vincent, David Tewksbury, and Elizabeth Powers. 1997. "Switching Trains of Thought: The Impact of News Frames on Readers' Cognitive Responses." *Communication Research* 24 (5): 481–506.

Putnam, Robert D. 2000. *Bowling Alone*. New York: Simon and Schuster.

Reich, Robert B. 1999. "John Maynard Keynes." In *People of the Century: One Hundred Men and Women Who Shaped the Last One Hundred Years*, ed. Time/ CBS News. New York: Simon and Schuster.

Reynolds, Paul D. 1971. *A Primer on Theory Construction*. Needham Heights, MA: Allyn and Bacon.

Richards, Jef I. 1997. "Is 44 Liquormart a Turning Point?" *Journal of Public Policy and Marketing* 16 (1): 156–162.

Richards, Jef I. and John H. Murphy, II. 1996. "Economic Censorship and Free Speech: The Circle of Communication Between Advertisers, Media, and Consumers." *Journal of Current Issues and Research in Advertising* 18 (1): 25–34.

Rogers, Everett. 1986. *Communication Technology: The New Media in Society*. New York: Free Press.

Rotfeld, Herbert. 1992. "Media Standards for Acceptable Advertising and Potentially Desirable 'Chilling Effects' on Advertising Free Speech." In *Proceedings of the 17th Annual Macromarketing Seminar*, ed. T. A. Klein, R.W. Nasson, and L.D. Dahringer, 335–352. Breukelen, The Netherlands: Nijenrode University.

Rotzoll, Kim B., James E. Haefner, and Steven R. Hall. 1996. *Advertising in Contemporary Society: Perspectives toward Understanding*, 3rd ed. Urbana, IL: University of Illinois Press.

Rotzoll, Kim, James E. Haefner, and Charles H. Sandage. 1986. *Advertising in Contemporary Society*. Cincinnati, OH: South-Western Publishing Co.

Rubin v. Coors Brewing Co., 514 U.S. 476 (1995).

Sardone, Susan B. 2008. "Wedding and Honeymoon Statistics." About.com. Available at http://honeymoons.about.com/cs/eurogen1/a/weddingstats.htm (accessed January 10, 2009).

Sarup, Madan. 1993. *An Introductory Guide to Post-Structuralism and Postmodernism.* Athens, GA: University of Georgia Press.

Schiller, Herbert. 1976. *Communication and Cultural Domination.* New York: International Arts and Sciences Press.

Schor, Juliet B. 1998. *The Overspent American: Upscaling, Downshifting, and the New Consumer.* New York: Basic Books.

———. 2004. *Born to Buy: The Commercialized Child and the New Consumer Culture.* New York: Scribner.

Schudson, Michael. 1984. *Advertising, the Uneasy Persuasion: Its Dubious Impact on American Society.* New York: Basic Books.

Schwartz, Matthew. 2008. "Some See Conflicts in Google-DoubleClick Deal." *BtoB* 93 (1): 3.

Scott, Paul. 2008/2009. "Monsters Inc." *Best Life* 128–133, 152.

Severin, Werner J. and James W. Tankard. 1992. *Communication Theories: Origins, Methods, and Uses in the Mass Media.* White Plains, NY: Longman.

Shaw, David. 1999. "Journalism is a Very Different Business—Here's Why; Newspapers Routinely Bite the Hand that Feeds Them (the Advertisers'), and Give Their Customers (the Readers) a Product They Don't Want (Bad or Boring News)." *The Los Angeles Times* (December 20): 3V.

Siebert, Patty. 1988. "AAAA Files Kid-Vid Comments with FCC." *The 4A's Washington Newsletter,* January 2.

Singer, Natasha. 2009. "A Birth Control Pill That Promised Too Much." *New York Times* (February 10). Available at www.nytimes.com/2009/02/11/business/11pill.html (accessed July 22, 2009).

Skidelsky, Robert. 2008a. "Essay: A Thinker for Our Times." *New Statesman* (December 18). Available at www.skidelskyr.com/site/view/new-statesman/ (accessed May 15, 2009).

———. 2008b."The Remedist." *New York Times* (December 14). Available at www.skidelskyr.com/site/view/new-york-times/ (accessed May 15, 2009).

Slattery, Karen, Ana Garner, Joyce Wolburg, and Lynn Turner. In press. "Teaching for Social Justice in the Engaged Classroom: The Intersection of Jesuit and Feminist Moral Philosophies," In *Crossing Borders: Jesuit and Feminist Education for the Twenty-First Century,* eds. Jocelyn M. Boryczka and Elizabeth Petrino.

Sloan, Allan. 2008. "Beltway Medicine Men." *Fortune* 158 (7): 108.

Snow, David A. and Bedford, R. D. 1998. "Ideology, Frame Resonance, and Participant Mobilization." In *International Social Movement Research,* ed. Bert Klandermans, Hanspeter Kriesi, and Sidney Tarrow, 197–217. Greenwich, CT: JAI Press.

———. 1992. "Master Frames and Cycles of Protest." In *Frontiers in Social Movement Theory,* ed. A. D. Morris and C. M. Mueller, 135–155. New Haven, CT: Yale University Press.

Soley, Lawrence C. and Robert L. Craig. 1992. "Advertising Pressures on Newspapers: A Survey." *Journal of Advertising* 21 (4): 1–25.

Stafford, Thomas F. and Marla Royne Stafford. 2001. "Identifying Motivations for the Use of Commercial Web Sites." *Information Resources Management Journal* 14 (1): 22–30.

References

Standard & Poor's Industry Trends. 2006. Available at www.netadvantage.standarda-ndpoors.com.proxy.lib.utk.edu:90/docs/indsur///adv_0807/adv20807.htm#trends (accessed January 10, 2008).

———. 2007. Available at www.netadvantage.standardandpoors.com.proxy.lib. utk.edu:90/docs/indsur///adv_0807/adv20807.htm#trends (accessed August 15, 2007).

Stein, Johan. 1997. "How Institutions Learn: A Socio-Cognitive Perspective." *Journal of Economic Issues* 31 (September): 729–740.

Steinberg, Brian. 2007. "NBC Experiment Doesn't Solve the DVR Dilemma." *Advertising Age* 78 (27):16.

Steinem, Gloria. 1990. "Sex, Lies & Advertising." *Ms.* (July/August): 18–28.

Stelter, Brian. 2008. "YouTube to Offer TV Shows with Ads Strewn Through." *New York Times* (October 11): B2.

Strasser, Susan. 1989. *Satisfaction Guaranteed: The Making of the American Mass Market.* New York: Pantheon Books.

SUNY v. Fox, 492 U.S. 469 (1989).

Tan, Alexis. 1985. *Mass Communication Theories and Research*, 2nd ed. New York: Macmillan Publishing Company.

Taylor, Ronald E. and Anne Cunningham. 2007. "Protecting the Children: A Comparative Analysis of French and American Advertising Self-Regulation." In *Readings in Advertising, Society, and Consumer Culture*, ed. Roxanne Hovland, Joyce Wolburg, and Eric Haley, 265–273. Armonk, NY: M.E. Sharpe.

Taylor, Ronald E., Keith R. Fentonmiller, R. Michael Hoefges, Carol J. Pardun, and Wayne J. Keeley. 2008. "Solving the Childhood Obesity Epidemic: The Role of Advertising Regulations and Self-Regulation." Panel presentation at the national conference of the Association for Educators in Journalism and Mass Communication, Chicago, August.

Teeter, Dwight L. and Bill Loving. 2004. *Law of Mass Communications: Freedom and Control of Print and Broadcast Media.* New York: Foundation Press.

Teinowitz, Ira. 2001. "Muris to Lead FTC in Return Engagement: Regulatory Philosophy May Signal Shift from Pitofsky Era." *Advertising Age* 72 (1) (March 5): 1.

Thompson v. Western States Medical Center, 535 U.S. 357 (2002).

TNS Media Intelligence. 2007. "2007 US Advertising Expenditures Wrap-up: Spend Up Just 0.2%." Available at www.marketingcharts.com/television/tns-issues-2007-us-advertising-expenditures-wrap-up-spend-up-just-02-3952/.

Tronto, Joan. 1993. *Moral Boundaries: A Political Argument for an Ethic of Care.* New York: Routledge.

Tschoegl, Adrian E. 2007. "McDonald's—Much Maligned, But an Engine of Economic Development." *Global Economy Journal* 7 (4): 1–16.

Tuchman, Gail. 1978. *Making News: A Study in the Construction of Reality.* New York: Free Press.

Twitchell, James. 1996. *Adcult USA: The Triumph of Advertising in American Culture.* New York: Columbia University Press.

United States v. Edge Broadcasting Co., 509 U.S. 418, 113 S.Ct.2696 (1993).

Valentine v. Chrestensen, 316 U.S. 52 (1942).

Vanderbilt, Tom. 1997. "The Advertised Life." In *Commodify Your Dissent: The Business of Culture in the New Gilded Age*, ed. Thomas Frank, Matt Weiland, and Tom Frank, 127–142. New York: Norton.

REFERENCES

Veblen, Thorstein. 1932. *The Theory of the Leisure Class: An Economic Study of Institutions.* New York: Modern Library.

Venger, Olesya and Joyce Wolburg. 2008. " 'Selling Sin' in a Hostile Environment: A Comparison of Ukrainian and American Tobacco Advertising Strategies in Magazines." *Journal of Current Issues and Research in Advertising* 30 (2): 49–65.

Virginia State Board of Pharmacy v. Virginia Citizens Consumer Council, Inc., 425 U.S. 748 (1976).

Vranica, Suzanne. 2007. "A New Force in Advertising—Protest by Email." *Wall Street Journal* (March 22): B1.

Wang, Jimmy. 2009. "Now Hip-Hop, Too, Is Made in China." *New York Times* (January 24): C6.

Wasserman, Todd. 2009. "New FTC Asserts Itself." *Brandweek* 50 (April 27): 17.

Watson, James L. 1997. *Golden Arches East: McDonald's in East Asia.* Stanford, CA: Stanford University Press.

Williams, Raymond. 1980. "Advertising, the Magic System." In *Problems in Materialism and Culture: Selected Essays,* 170-195. London: Verso.

Wilson II, Clint C., Félix Gutiérrez, and Lena M. Chao. 2003. *Racism, Sexism, and the Media: The Rise of Class Communication in Multicultural America,* 3rd ed. Thousand Oaks, CA: Sage Publications.

Winerman, Mark. 2005. "The FTC at Ninety: History through the Headlines." *Antitrust Law Journal* 72: 871–897.

Winsted Hosiery Co. v. Federal Trade Commission, 272 F. 957 (2nd Cir. 1921), 802.

Wolburg, Joyce M. 2001. "Preserving the Moment, Commodifying Time, and Improving Upon the Past: Depictions of Time in U.S. Magazine Advertising." *Journal of Communication* 51 (4): 696–719.

———. 2003. "Double-Cola and Antitrust Issues: Staying Alive in the Soft Drink Wars." *Journal of Consumer Affairs* 37 (2): 340–363.

———. 2006. "College Students' Responses to Anti-Smoking Messages: Denial, Defiance, and Other Boomerang Effects." *Journal of Consumer Affairs* 40 (2): 293–323.

Wolburg, Joyce M., Roxanne Hovland, and Ronald E. Hopson. 1999. "Cognitive Restructuring as a Relapse Prevention Strategy: Teaching Alcoholics to Talk Back to Beer Ads." *Alcoholism Treatment Quarterly* 17 (4): 29–52.

Wood, Douglas J. 2008. "Legal Issues to Watch in 2009." *Advertising Age,* December 15, p. 8.

Wood, Douglas J. and Bob Liodice. 2006. "Top Legal Issues for 2007." *Advertising Age,* Midwest region edition, 77 (55): 8.

World Advertising Research Center. 2009. "Ad Guru Geier Tells Obama How to Rescue US Economy" (January 26). Available at www.warc.com/New/PrintNewsItem.asp?NID=24592 (accessed January 30, 2009).

World Bank. 2008. Global Monitoring Report 2008. Available at http://web.worldbank.org/WBSITE/EXTERNAL/EXTDEC/EXTGLOBALMONITOR/EXTGLOMONREP2008/0,,menuPK:4738069~pagePK:64168427~piPK:64168435~theSitePK:4738057,00.html (accessed Dec. 31, 2008).

Wright, Tom. 2007. "Altria Seeks Indonesian Smokers." *Wall Street Journal,* Eastern edition (July 2): B3.

Yao, Deborah. 2009. "Expect to See More Advertising Literally Pop Up on TV Screen." *Milwaukee Journal Sentinel* (August 3): D3.

REFERENCES

Yoong, Sean. 2007. "Malay Government May Ban Ads on Kids' TV." *Marketing News* 41 (6): 32.

YouTube. 2008. "Whopper Virgins—The Making of the Campaign." Available at www.youtube.com/watch?v=RSiPFRMwTcY&

YouTube. 2009. JCPenney's "Stay Out of the Dog House This Holiday." Available at www.youtube.com/watch?v=SecVCh9dg4I (accessed February 14, 2009).

YouTube. 2009. "Pepsi MacGruber Ad." Available at www.youtube.com/watch?v= avjOMd170MA

Zuckerman, Mary Ellen. 1990. "The Federal Trade Commission in Historical Perspective: The First Fifty Years." In *Marketing and Advertising Regulation: The Federal Trade Commission in the 1990s,* ed. Patrick Murphy and William L. Wilkie, 169–202. Notre Dame, IN: University of Notre Dame Press.

Index

Roxanne Hovland is Professor of Advertising in the School of Advertising and Public Relations in the College of Communication at the University of Tennessee, Knoxville. She conducts research on gender issues in advertising and advertising regulation. She's also interested in a variety of economic and social matters involving advertising and consumer culture. Her work appears in the journals *Sex Roles, Journal of Interactive Advertising, Journalism Quarterly, Alcoholism Treatment Quarterly, Journal of Macromarketing,* and *Communications and the Law.* She coauthored (with Gary Wilcox) *Advertising in Society,* which was named one of the most influential books in advertising by readers of the *Journal of Advertising.* She also coedited *Readings in Advertising, Society, and Consumer Culture* with Joyce Wolburg and Eric Haley. She received a Master's degree in advertising and a Ph.D. in communications from the University of Illinois and earned a B.S. from the University of Florida.

Joyce M. Wolburg is Associate Dean for Graduate Studies and Research and Chair of the Department of Advertising and Public Relations in the Diederich College of Communication at Marquette University in Milwaukee, Wisconsin. Her research interests include international advertising, smoking-cessation campaign strategies, the ritual meaning of binge drinking among college students, and social/legal/ethical issues in advertising. Her work has appeared in various journals including *Journal of Advertising, Journal of Consumer Affairs, Journal of Advertising Research, Journal of Current Research and Issues in Advertising,* and *Journal of Consumer Marketing.* She is a coeditor with Roxanne Hovland and Eric Haley of *Readings in Advertising, Society, and Consumer Culture,* and she received her Ph.D. and M.S. degree in communication at the University of Tennessee, Knoxville.